Patrick Adair, Andrew Stewart

A True Narrative of the Rise and Progress of the Presbyterian Church in Ireland, 1623-1670

Patrick Adair, Andrew Stewart

A True Narrative of the Rise and Progress of the Presbyterian Church in Ireland, 1623-1670

ISBN/EAN: 9783337324919

Printed in Europe, USA, Canada, Australia, Japan

Cover: Foto ©Lupo / pixelio.de

More available books at **www.hansebooks.com**

A TRUE NARRATIVE

OF

THE RISE AND PROGRESS

OF THE

Presbyterian Church in Ireland

(1623—1670)

BY THE REV. PATRICK ADAIR

MINISTER OF BELFAST

ALSO

THE HISTORY OF THE CHURCH IN IRELAND SINCE THE SCOTS
WERE NATURALIZED, BY THE REV. ANDREW STEWART
MINISTER OF DONAGHADEE

WITH AN INTRODUCTION AND NOTES

BY W. D. KILLEN, D.D.

BELFAST: C. AITCHISON
LONDON: HAMILTON, ADAMS, & CO.
EDINBURGH: A. ELLIOT
1866

CONTENTS.

INTRODUCTION ix

CHAPTER I.

Mr. Robert Blair removes from Glasgow College to Bangor—State of the Country—Mr. Blair's Ordination—His Labours and Danger 1

CHAPTER II.

Glendinning and the Antrim Meeting—Colwort, Welsh, and Dunbar—Echlin's Opposition—Primate Ussher—Livingston and Stewart—Opposition from Separatists and Conformists - 16

CHAPTER III.

False Excitement at Larne—Deposition of Blair and Others—Their Difficulties and Restoration—Second Deposition—Proposed Removal to New England—Return from Sea—Dangers of the Ministers—Escape to Scotland—Death of Cunningham—Mr. Blair proposes to go to France - 32

CHAPTER IV.

Continued Sufferings—Tumult in Edinburgh, and Overthrow of Prelacy in Scotland—The Black Oath—Coalition between Papists and Prelatists—Abounding Wickedness—Ussher's Prediction—Strafford's Proceedings 52

CHAPTER V.

Horrors of the Irish Rebellion of 1641—Preservation of Dublin Castle by Owen O'Connolly—Proceedings of the Lords Justices 69

CHAPTER VI.

The Scotch Army in Ulster—The first Presbytery meets—Sessions Erected, and Ministers Appointed—Discipline of the Presbytery   88

CHAPTER VII.

The Covenant administered in Ulster—Taken at Carrickfergus, Comber, Newtonards, Bangor, Broadisland, Islandmagee, Antrim, Ballymena, Coleraine, Dunluce, Derry, Raphoe, Letterkenny, Ramelton, and Enniskillen   -   -   -   -   102

CHAPTER VIII.

Cases of Discipline—The Mock Presbytery of Route—Ministers Settled at Ballymena, Antrim, Cairncastle, and elsewhere—The Presbytery and the Commissioners of Parliament—Ministers settled at Ray, Letterkenny, and other places—Dr. Colville of Galgorm—Defeat of the Scotch Army at Benburb   119

CHAPTER IX.

Ministers settled at Ballymoney and Billy—Privy Censures—Colonel Monck and Sir Charles Coote—The Engagement—Monck surprises Carrickfergus—Sir Robert Adair   -   -   135

CHAPTER X.

The Representation—Renewal of the Covenant—Colonel Monck and the Presbytery—Sir Alexander Stewart besieges Derry—Ker and O'Quin Suspended and Restored   -   -   -   -   153

CHAPTER XI.

Scheming of the Lord of Ards—His Disputes with the Presbytery—Arrival of Cromwell in Ireland—Sir James Montgomery of Greyabbey—Death of Owen O'Connolly—Ministers Praying for Charles II. are apprehended—Conference between them and Colonel Venables—Their Hardships   -   -   -   -   167

CONTENTS.

CHAPTER XII.

Continued Trials of the Ministers—Their Discussion at Antrim with Taylor and Weeks—Conference at Belfast with Commissioners of the Revenue—Messrs. Ferguson and Adair go to Dublin and confer with Fleetwood and Others—Mr. Adair's Papers Seized and Recovered—Ministers and People refuse the Engagement tendered by the Commissioners of the Revenue—Ministers enjoy greater Liberty—A Proposal to Transplant the Scottish Settlers to Tipperary miscarries . - - - 182

CHAPTER XIII.

The Resolutioners and Protestors—The Church recovers her Liberty—The Act of Bangor—Supervision of Candidates for the Ministry—The Meetings of Down, Antrim, and Route, with Lagan—Expansion of the Church—Ministerial Maintenance—Character of Sir John Clotworthy - - - - - - 204

CHAPTER XIV.

Henry Cromwell succeeds Fleetwood in Ireland—Ministers to receive each £100 per annum—Synod at Ballymena—Dangers of the Ministers—Death of Oliver Cromwell—Proceedings of Monck—Presbyterians anxious for the King's Restoration—Meeting of the Convention in Dublin—Patrick Adair called there—Arrangements respecting Ministers—Political Manœuvering - 222

CHAPTER XV.

Restoration of Charles II.—Mr. Adair's Experience in Dublin—Synod at Ballymena—Address to the King—Episcopacy re-established—Bramhall, Jeremy Taylor, and Leslie—A Party of Horse sent to disperse a Synod at Ballymena—Deputation of Ministers to Dublin—Jeremy Taylor's Visitation—Thirty-six Churches declared Vacant—Hardships of Ministers · 238

CHAPTER XVI.

Proceedings of the Irish Parliament—Burning of the Solemn League and Covenant—Perplexity of the Ministers— Great Field Meet-

ings—Michael Bruce—Defections from the Good Cause—Three Ministers sent to Dublin—Their Petition to the Duke of Ormond—Conduct of the Ministers - - - - - - - 253

CHAPTER XVII.

Blood's Plot—Ministers ordered to be Apprehended—Troubles of Mr. Boyd—Hardships of the Imprisoned Ministers—Disarming of the Northern Presbyterians—Execution of Lecky—Some Indulgence granted—Messrs. M'Cormick and Crookshanks—Bishop Leslie a Persecutor—His Death - - - - 270

CHAPTER XVIII.

Presbyterians begin to build Preaching Houses—Oppressions and Avarice of the Episcopal Clergy—Lord Robarts—Meeting of Ministers—Collection for Distressed Ministers in Holland—Bishop Leslie and Bishop Boyle persecute—Application to the Lord Lieutenant—Deaths of Ministers—Ministers Ordained—Strange Catastrophe in a Dublin Theatre - - - - 288

History of the Church of Ireland, by the Rev. Andrew Stewart, of Donaghadee · · · · · · · · · 305

GENERAL INDEX - · · · · · · · 323

INTRODUCTION.

HE work now presented to the public was written towards the close of the seventeenth century. Its author intended to bring down the Narrative to the beginning of the reign of William III.; for, in the original title-page, he announces a division into four parts—the first extending from 1622 to 1642; the second from 1642 to 1661; the third from 1661 to the death of Charles II., in 1685; and the fourth from 1685 to "this present year"—obviously alluding to a period of deliverance, when the history would reach a pleasing termination. Mr. Adair died in 1694; and either death, or the increasing infirmities of age, prevented him from completing his undertaking. The manuscript ends, somewhat abruptly, about the close of the year 1670—or rather before the middle of the reign of Charles II.

This Narrative was evidently designed by its author for the press; but the imperfect state in which it was left by him, prevented its immediate publication. Many ministers and others, who survived him, were aware of its existence:

a

in 1697, the Synod of Ulster voted a small sum to the Rev. William Adair, of Ballyeaston, for his trouble in transcribing "his father's Collections, containing a history of the church from 1621 to 1670;"* and, in 1713, his successor in the ministry, the Rev. Dr. James Kirkpatrick, of Belfast, bears emphatic testimony to the value of the compilation. He states that he had been permitted to peruse it, and that he had availed himself largely of the information it supplies in the preparation of his *Presbyterian Loyalty*. "The history itself," says he, "contains a curious collection of some very surprising affairs, and perhaps may be exposed to public view in due time."† This idea is now, for the first time, realised; as the disputes which commenced in the North of Ireland soon after the appearance of *Presbyterian Loyalty*, between the Subscribers and the Non-Subscribers—and which continued so long to distract the Presbyterian community—completely occupied the attention of those who might otherwise have taken an interest in the publication. For many years during the last century the possessor of the manuscript was unknown; and those who were anxious to consult it, sought for it in vain. In 1764, an advertisement appeared once

---

* The following is the Minute adopted by the Synod held at Antrim, June 2nd, 1697:—"Mr. William Adair has copied out his father's Collections, containing a History of this church from the year 1621 to the year 1670: his care and diligence approven and kindly taken: for defraying what expenses he has been at to an amanuensis, allow him 40 shillings out of the R. D.: and, moreover, appoint Messrs. Archibald Hamilton, and Alexander Hutcheson, to revise the said Collections, and give their judgment of them at the next Synod at Dromore." Extracted from the MS. Minutes by Rev. R. Park, clerk of Assembly.—Some of the short notes in the margin of the M.S. were probably made by this Revision Committee.

† *Presbyterian Loyalty*, p. 167.

and again in the *Belfast News-Letter*, offering a reward for its discovery—but apparently without any result. At length, about the year 1810, the late Dr. Stephenson, of this town, father of the present eminent physician of the same name, found it among the papers of his friend the late W. Trail Kennedy, Esq. of Annadale. In 1825, it was for a short period in the possession of the late Rev. Dr. Reid, author of the *History of the Presbyterian Church in Ireland*, who, with his own hand, made a copy of the greater part of it.

The manuscript recovered by Dr. Stephenson is at present the property of the Rev. W. Bruce, of Belfast, who very kindly permitted me to have the use of it for some time. It is contained in a bound volume, about eight inches long and six inches broad; and, including a few blank spaces— left for the insertion of documents which were never transferred to them—extends to 319 pages. Though the ink in many places is much faded, the manuscript is still legible; several transcribers have obviously been employed in its preparation, and some portions of it can be read much more easily than others. By far the larger portion of it is written in very excellent round-hand—in all likelihood the penmanship of an amanuensis employed by the Rev. W. Adair, of Ballyeaston. The title-page betrays the tremulous hand of age, and is probably the autograph of the author. I have compared the copy made by Dr. Reid with the ancient volume, page for page, and can vouch for its accuracy. Dr. Reid has modernized the spelling; improved the punctuation; removed some very obvious clerical errors; occasionally omitted a superfluous phrase; and, in a few cases, substituted an intelligible word for another long since obsolete. When anything has been added by way of explanation it has been enclosed in brackets; and, in every case, the exact meaning of the writer has been carefully preserved. From Dr. Reid's copy—as likely to be much better understood by the reader—the greater part of the present text has been printed. In the original manuscript there are very few resting-places; and, for convenience, the Narrative has been now divided into chapters, with their contents prefixed.

Dr. Reid in his History has noticed most of the events recorded in this volume; but not a few incidents, as yet quite unknown to the public, are here detailed; so that all who desire to be acquainted with the early struggles of Presbyterianism in Ireland will peruse this Narrative with peculiar interest. As an account of important political, as well as ecclesiastical, transactions, it is entitled to special confidence. Its author lived throughout the whole period of which he treats; he was himself an actor in many of the scenes which he describes; and he was respected by all his brethren for his probity, piety, and discretion. He was not free either from the prejudices of his party or the superstitions of his age; but he possessed a sound and vigorous judgment; he was a devout observer of the ways of Providence; and, because of the consistency and self-denial with which he adhered to his principles in trying times, his memory deserves to be cherished by all right-hearted Presbyterians. His style, though homely, is generally neither feeble nor obscure. He was accustomed to speak in the

Scottish dialect; and, when he does not use his vernacular tongue, he may be expected to clothe his thoughts in language somewhat different from that of a native English writer.

Mr. Adair was a Scotchman of highly respectable parentage. From boyhood he took an interest in ecclesiastical affairs; and, on the 23rd of July, 1637—when the famous Janet Geddes threw the stool at the head of the Dean of Edinburgh as he was proceeding to introduce the Service Book, and when the promoters of the Liturgy were balked by a mob of women—Patrick Adair was in the Scottish metropolis, and a witness of the uproar. When licensed, he came over to Ireland as a preacher; and, on the 7th of May, 1646, he was ordained to the pastoral charge of the parish of Cairncastle, near Larne, in the County of Antrim. In 1674 he was removed from Cairncastle to Belfast—where he officiated about twenty years. For nearly half a century he was a minister of the Presbyterian Church in Ireland; and, during that eventful period, he was deputed by his brethren to act as their spokesman and representative on many critical occasions. In 1652, at a public discussion in the town of Antrim with two leaders of the Sectaries, he conducted the argument very much to the satisfaction of his friends; he had various conferences with Fleetwood and others who ruled in Ireland during the Commonwealth; he was one of the ministers ejected at the Restoration; and, a few years before his death, he had the honour of an interview with King William III. With another of his brethren, he was sent over on that occasion to London by the Presbyterians of Ulster, to congratulate the Prince on his arrival in England.

The Rev. Dr. James Kirkpatrick, the author of *Presbyterian Loyalty*, was the son of a Presbyterian minister well acquainted with the writer of this Narrative, and was himself removed from Templepatrick to the congregation over which Mr. Adair presided in Belfast about twelve years after that gentleman's decease. He is, therefore, competent to bear testimony to the character of his distinguished predecessor. His attestation is remarkable. " Mr. Adair," says he, " was a man of great natural parts and wisdom, eminent piety and exemplary holiness, great ministerial gravity and authority, endowed with savoury and most edifying gifts for his sacred function, wherein he was laborious, painful, and faithful; was a constant, curious, and accurate observer of all public occurrences; and, with all these rare qualities, he had not only the blood and descent, but the spirit and just decorum of a gentleman."*

A considerable number of the Scottish licentiates who settled in Ireland early in the seventeenth century, received ordination from the bishops of Ulster after a Presbyterian fashion. When, for example, Mr. Livingston of Killinchy was ordained, those parts of the established ritual to which he objected were omitted, and old Bishop Knox of Raphoe, coming in among the neighbouring Presbyterian ministers as one of themselves, joined with them in the imposition of hands. When Mr. Blair, Mr. Hamilton, and others were ordained, the same course was adopted. These facts are

---

* *Presbyterian Loyalty*, p. 166.

recorded by Episcopal, as well as by Presbyterian writers. They are described with much minuteness by Dr. Leland, a Fellow of Trinity College, Dublin, and an accurate investigator, whose *History of Ireland* appeared in 1773. "On the plantation made in the reign of James," says he, "the new colonists had been supplied with teachers principally from Scotland. They formed their churches on the Presbyterian model, and *many refused to accept Episcopal ordination. To quiet such scruples, the bishops, by the approbation of Ussher, their learned metropolitan,* consented to ordain them to the ministry, without adhering strictly to the established form, and to admit some of their brethren of the Scottish Presbytery to a participation of their office. Thus the Scottish teachers enjoyed churches and tithes without using the liturgy."* Dr. Peter Heylin—a bitter high-churchman, who flourished at the very time when these Scottish ministers were in Ulster, and who, from his position as chaplain to Charles I., had the best means of information respecting all the ecclesiastical movements throughout the three kingdoms —uses even stronger language than Leland when speaking of the Church of Ireland in the early part of the seventeenth century. "The adventurers of the Scottish nation," says he, "*brought with them hither* such a stock of Puritanism, such a contempt of bishops, such a neglect of the public liturgy, and other divine offices of this church, that there was nothing less to be found amongst them than the government and forms of worship established in the Church of England." He adds, as he goes on to denounce the Puritans who settled

---

* *History of Ireland*, II. 481.

in Ireland about this period,—" Not contented with the articles of the Church of England, they were resolved to frame a Confession of their own ; the drawing up whereof was referred to Dr. James Ussher . . . . by whom the book was so contrived that all the Sabbatarian and Calvinian rigours were declared therein to be the doctrines of that church . . . . and finally such a silence concerning the consecration of archbishops and bishops (expressly justified and avowed in the English book), as if they were not a distinct order from the common Presbyters. All which, *being Ussher's own private opinions*, were dispersed in several places of the articles for the Church of Ireland, approved of in the Convocation of the year 1615, and finally confirmed by the Lord Deputy Chichester in the name of King James."*

But, where bigotry bears sway, everything is seen through a discoloured medium ; and the best authenticated facts will be disputed. Though the account usually given of the manner in which Blair, Livingston, and others, were ordained, has passed current for more than two centuries, a late writer, noted for the intensity of his theological prejudices, has thought proper to call it in question. The objector is no less a personage than the author of the *History of the Church of Ireland*, the Right Rev. Dr. Mant, Bishop of Down, Connor, and Dromore. " It might," says he, " be reasonably questioned how far these narratives are worthy of credit."†

---

* *History of the Presbyterians*, Book XI., p. 388. Heylin was born in 1600, and died in 1662. Through the influence of Laud he was made Chaplain-in-Ordinary to Charles I. in 1629.

† *History of the Church of Ireland*, I. 453. London, 1840.

"The mind of the reader, if it does not repudiate the account at once, and altogether, will probably fluctuate between doubts."* And what is the only evidence he is able to produce in support of his scepticism ? It appears that a Royal Visitation Book of Down and Connor, which reports the admission of Blair and Livingston to the ministry, "*takes no notice* of any deviation from the regular form of ordination as prescribed by law."† Every one must see that such an objection is quite frivolous. If the law was not strictly observed, we could scarcely expect its transgressors to report the infraction. Had the Visitation Book declared that Blair and Livingston were ordained *in all respects* according to the Episcopal ritual, there would be validity in the demurrer; but the record contains no such allegation. "The form of ordination in the Book of Common Prayer, and no other," argues Bishop Mant, "is prescribed by the Act of Uniformity, 2nd year of Elizabeth, chapter II."‡ The Right Reverend Prelate himself supplies a ready reply to this reasoning; for he informs us that, several years before the appearance of the Scottish ministers in Ulster, "*by the intervention of the executive authority*, although not repealed, the Act of Uniformity ceased to be enforced, and the violation of it was connived at."§ The argument from the Act of Uniformity

---

* *History of the Church of Ireland*, I. 453.

† *Ibid*, I. 453.

‡ The form of ordination in the Book of Common Prayer is *not* mentioned in the Irish Act of Uniformity ; neither is the necessity of Episcopal ordination there prescribed. Hence, Echlin and Knox may have felt themselves at liberty to act as they did.

§ *History of the Church of Ireland*, I. 338.

thus goes for nothing. And what is the testimony which Bishop Mant has arraigned as unworthy of credit? It is that of Blair and Livingston—two of the gentlemen ordained—backed by a long array of other evidence. Blair and Livingston have left behind them separate narratives, in which each minutely describes the manner of his own ordination; and no writer before Bishop Mant has dared to challenge their veracity. Both were able, learned, and holy men; both were signally honoured by the great Head of the Church in turning many to righteousness; both suffered most severely for the cause to which they were devoted; both wrote their depositions, the one in Scotland and the other in Holland, shortly before they died, and at a time when they could have had no personal interest in concocting fabrications; and yet, if we are to listen to the insinuations of Dr. Mant, both may *reasonably be suspected of wilful falsehood!* Patrick Adair, their contemporary, in the following Narrative, endorses their representations.* Andrew Stewart, another of their brethren, in a History now for the first time published, virtually does the same;† and even Peter Heylin avers that they scorned to submit to the ritual of the Church of England. It would be easy to furnish additional proof—but it is surely unnecessary. The man who deems Blair and Livingston unworthy of credit, must be left to his unbelief.

The late Diocesan of Down, Connor, and Dromore severely condemns the Scottish preachers for taking office in the Irish Church, when they did non-approve of its Liturgy and Constitution. Had they gained admission by

---

* See p. 10 of this volume. † See p. 318 of this volume.

equivocation or fraud, there would be some pith in the criticism; but, when their case is fairly stated, even a microscopic censor may find it difficult to point out anything like transgression. They acted throughout with the utmost frankness; they fully proclaimed their principles; and, instead of being denounced as disingenuous, some may be disposed to think that they rather erred on the side of excessive scrupulosity. The bishops, as well as the executive government, had long openly concurred in the non-observance of the Act of Uniformity—the Irish Church was still in a very unsettled condition—and the Scottish preachers, shut out from the ministry at home, felt at liberty to avail themselves of the laxity of its regulations. They were required to enter into no unholy compromise; they were invited and encouraged to occupy a field of labour "white to the harvest," and why not embrace such a precious opportunity? The King of the Church graciously signified his approval of their conduct, by pouring down a rich blessing on their ministrations. Bishop Mant, indeed, contemplates with wonderful complacency their subsequent expulsion from their livings; but a writer of a more catholic spirit would have stigmatized the policy which deprived the country of the services of such eminent evangelists. Those who admitted them to the ministry on Presbyterian principles, were bound, in honour, to tolerate their neglect of the Book of Common Prayer; and the Executive Government, which connived at their settlement, should also have thrown over them the shield of its protection. But, they were not long enclosed in the Episcopal net, when a mean attempt was made to coerce them to conformity. The conduct of the bishops was as inconsistent and ungenerous as it was unjust and oppressive. Blair and his brethren exhibited a stern integrity which casts a darker shade of infamy over the memory of their persecutors; and the patience with which they submitted to poverty and sufferings, rather than defile the sanctuary of conscience, challenges our highest admiration.

Dr. Mant's work was published several years after the appearance of Dr. Reid's *History of the Presbyterian Church in Ireland;* and though the bishop quite ignored the labours of his learned predecessor, it is notorious that he quietly appropriated some of his materials.* Nor is this the gravest charge which may be preferred against the Right Rev. author. Though exculpatory evidence of a satisfactory character was before him, he doggedly reiterated slanders most injurious to Irish Presbyterianism. A single instance of such unfairness—suggested by the following Narrative—may here be adduced. Mr. Adair has shown † that the conspiracy, known as "Blood's Plot," which created a great sensation early in the reign of Charles II., was concocted chiefly by the old Cromwellians, in Dublin and elsewhere. The Presbyterians of Ulster, as a body, were altogether opposed to the movement. Dr. Reid, in his History, has published the evidence supplied by Adair; and every reader of ordinary candour must admit that he has completely vindicated the reputation of his co-religionists. But, Bishop Mant took no notice of the defence; and, as if such a thing had never even been

---
* See *Dublin Christian Examiner* for October and December, 1840.
† See *Narrative*, Chap. xvii., page 271, &c.

attempted, cooly repeated the original calumny! According to him the conspiracy was hatched "between the fanatics of England and Scotland and *the rigid Scotch Presbyterians in the Irish Counties of the North*.* Comment on such a statement is unnecessary. The historian fills a noble office; and he is deserving of all honour if he faithfully registers events and wisely reviews them; but he forfeits all title to respect if he basely panders to his prejudices, and becomes either a special pleader or a false witness.

The late Bishop of Down, Connor, and Dromore, is not the only Episcopal writer who has recently challenged the veracity of the fathers of Irish Presbyterianism. Dr. Elrington, late Regius Professor of Divinity in the University of Dublin, has also stepped forward as their accuser. "It is stated confidently," says he "that when Bishop Echlin, of Down, suspended two remarkable Puritans, Blair and Livingston, Blair appealed to the Primate, who immediately desired the bishop to relax his erroneous censure. The whole narrative is *suspicious in the extreme*." † The fact here disputed does not rest on the unsupported authority of Blair. It is attested, still more circumstantially, by the other minister involved in the sentence of suspension. "We," says Livingston, referring to Blair and himself, "with Mr. Dunbar, Mr. Welsh, Mr. Hamilton, and Mr. Colwort, went to Tredaff [Drogheda], to 'Dr. Ussher, called Primate of Armagh, not only a learned, but a godly man, although a bishop. Thither came also Sir Andrew Stewart, afterwards Lord Castlestewart,

---

* *History of the Church of Ireland*, I. 637.
† *Life of Archbishop Ussher*, p. 146. Dublin, 1848.

to deal for us.* The Primate, *very cheerfully*, dealt for us with the bishop, *so as we were at that time restored.*† Patrick Adair, who had often conversed with ministers and others acquainted with the whole transaction, here bears the same testimony.‡ And what is the counter-evidence produced by Dr. Elrington? None whatever! With all the books and manuscripts in the library of Trinity College, Dublin, at his command, he has not been able to furnish even one scrap of contradiction. He can only say, " That Archbishop Ussher should countenance what was too flagrant a breach of discipline for Bishop Echlin to pass over, *is not within the limits of credibility.*"§ By the same species of reasoning, Dr. Elrington could have disproved the occurrence of the Revolution, or the existence of Napoleon Buonaparte.

On another point, the Professor of Theology in Trinity College, Dublin, has impugned the truthfulness of Blair. Ussher is represented by that minister as listening patiently to his objections to the Anglican Service Book, and as admitting the validity of his arguments. " In March, 1627," says Blair, " my noble patron [Lord Claneboy], having had a great esteem of Primate Ussher, would have me to accompany him to a meeting of the nobility and gentry of Ulster

---

* Sir Andrew Stewart was probably induced to take a deeper interest in this affair in consequence of his relationship to Josias Welsh. That minister's mother was first cousin to Lord Castlestewart.—See *Life of John Welsh*, by the Rev. James Young, p. 71, note. Edinburgh, 1866.

† *Livingston's Life, Wodrow Society, Select Biographies,* I. 145.

‡ Adair was well acquainted with both Blair and Livingston. Kirkpatrick says, " Mr. Adair was a great intimate, and in some respects, a disciple of the famous Mr. John Livingston."—*Presbyterian Loyalty*, 165.

§ *Life of Archbishop Ussher*, p. 147.

with the Primate. Accordingly, I went [to Dublin], and had a kind invitation to be at his table while I was in town. But, having once met with the English Liturgy there, I left my excuse with my patron—that I expected another thing than formal liturgies in the family of so learned and pious a man. The Primate excused himself, by reason of the great confluence that was there; and had the good nature to entreat me to come to Tredaff, where his ordinary residence was, and where he would be more at leisure to be better acquainted with me. I complied with the Primate's invitation, and found him very affable, and ready to impart his mind. He desired to know what was my judgment concerning the nature of justifying and saving faith. . . . From this he passed on to try my mind concerning ceremonies, wherein we were not so far from agreeing as I feared; for, when I had freely opened my grievances, he admitted that all these things ought to have been removed; but the constitution and laws of the place and time would not permit that to be done."*

According to Dr. Elrington, the account here given by the minister of Bangor " contains many circumstances notoriously false."† And how does this writer attempt to sustain so very grave an indictment? He appeals to the evidence of the Archbishop's chaplain. "Dr. Bernard," says he, " giving a detail of the arrangements of the house at Drogheda, states, that morning and evening prayers, according to the Liturgy, were read every day, and that the

---

* Blair's *Life*, p. 64. Ed. Edinburgh, 1754.
† *Life of Archbishop Ussher*, p. 148.

Archbishop never failed to attend, except prevented by illness."* Blair speaks of what occurred in 1627, whereas Bernard refers to what was customary after the adoption of the Irish canons in 1634—so that his statement is very little to the purpose. On such evidence no upright judge would convict any one of falsehood. Even supposing that the routine of the house at Drogheda, as described by Bernard, had been observed ever since Ussher's advancement to the Primacy,† it would not follow that Blair has uttered an untruth; as, under the circumstances, the humble-minded Archbishop might, out of deference to his guest, have made a temporary change in his domestic arrangements. Though he was bound in public to adhere to the Liturgy, he could have free prayer in his own dwelling: and why should Blair be set down as a liar because he intimates that Ussher once availed himself of a privilege to which he was undoubtedly entitled? The most objectionable sections of the Prayer Book—such as the Athanasian Creed, with its eternal condemnation of all who do not hold every jot and tittle of its nearly incomprehensible distinctions, the Burial Service, the Service for Confirmation, and the Bap-

---

* *Life of Archbishop Ussher*, p. 148-9.

† Bernard was not competent to speak of the arrangements of Ussher's household at the period of Blair's visit to him at Drogheda. About the time of the meeting in Dublin in spring, 1627, he received an appointment, which led to his separation *for several years* from the Archbishop. "Now," says he, "a preferment too early for those years, for his [Ussher's] sake conferred upon me, was no temptation to me, in that it took me too soon from him; but *not many years after* it pleased God I was called to him again."—*Life and Death of Dr. James Ussher*, by Nicholas Bernard, D.D., p. 93. Dublin, 1656. He returned to Drogheda in 1634.—See *Epistle Dedicatory to his Farewell Sermons*. London, 1651.

tismal Service—were not rehearsed at household worship; and though a portion of the Liturgy may have been repeated daily in the Primate's presence, it does not follow that he was not ready to acknowledge the defects of many parts of the volume. The fact that he prepared a new Confession of Faith for the Church of Ireland supplies clear proof that he was not thoroughly satisfied even with the Thirty-Nine Articles.

It so happens, however, that the Rev. Dr. Bernard, the gentleman brought forward to convict Blair of falsehood, is himself rather a slippery witness. His conscience certainly possessed marvellous elasticity, for, after having long been a minister of the Episcopal Church, in which he attained the dignity of a Dean, he passed over into the service of Oliver Cromwell, in whose household he acted as Almoner or Chaplain; and, at the Restoration, he once more changed with the times, and rather signalised himself by his zeal for Conformity. It is also noteworthy that his testimony as to the arrangements of Ussher's household varied with his position. In 1661, when he had returned to Episcopacy, he makes the deposition reported by Dr. Elrington; but, in 1658, when the fear of Oliver, his master, was still before him, he delivers very different evidence. "Ussher," says he, "had prayers constantly in his family four times a day—at six in the morning and eight at night *they were such wherein the gifts of those who were his chaplains were exercised;* but, before dinner and supper, in the chapel was the forenamed [Liturgy] also observed. Indeed, he was not so rigid *as to tie all men, in private, to an absolute necessary use of it*, or in the public, that a sermon was not to be heard unless that [Liturgy] did precede."* The witness here obviously sustains the account of Blair, and makes it probable that the minister of Bangor himself, in the use of free prayer, acted as chaplain to Ussher during his visit to him at Drogheda.

Those who carefully peruse the following Narrative may well be amazed at the ignorance of Irish Presbyterian affairs displayed by some of the most eminent of our Episcopal writers. Bishop Heber, in his *Life of Jeremy Taylor*, has occasion to notice the state of this country about the middle of the seventeenth century; and the flippancy with which he makes the most absurd and ridiculous averments reveals the incautious haste with which he must have prepared that piece of biography. He gravely informs us, for example, that, in the rebellion of 1641, the Protestant Episcopal clergy of Ireland " had *all* been swept away from that ill-starred kingdom." "Their places," he adds, "had been supplied by the most zealous adherents of the Commonwealth and the covenant."† It appears, however, from Adair, that the overflowing flood had not created such universal desolation; for a goodly number of these High Church clergy were still forthcoming to forswear Episcopacy and proclaim themselves Covenanters. Bishop Heber's account of what happened in Ireland at the Restoration is no less extraordinary. " Fortunately," says he, " for good taste and rational piety, the friends of both were triumphant; and, more happily still for the national honour and prosperity,

---

* See *Dr. Reid's Seven Letters to Dr. Elrington*, p. 65. Glasgow, 1849.
† *Life of the Right Rev. Jeremy Taylor, D.D.*, I., 164. London, 1824.

the restoration of both was effected *without any of those severities towards Dissenters* which, in England and Scotland, disgrace the annals of Charles the Second."* Had Heber diligently studied the history of the period, he would have discovered that Irish Presbyterians were the very first thrown into the furnace of persecution. In the following Narrative, some of the severities they endured are graphically described by one of the sufferers. Presbyterian ministers were ejected from their livings; forbidden to assemble in Synods or in Presbyteries; obliged to meet their people for worship at dead of night; exposed to ruinous fines, if they ventured to celebrate the Lord's Supper; hunted by a brutal soldiery; thrown into prison; or forced to make their escape from the country. In one day Bishop Jeremy Taylor himself drove no less than thirty-six of them from their pulpits.

The Presbyterian pastors of Down and Antrim in the time of Charles I. were men of singular gifts and zeal; and the account given by Adair of their labours is most interesting and edifying. The great and godly Ussher honoured them as true heralds of the cross, and was most desirous to make their services available for the benefit of the North of Ireland. But the gentle Primate was not fit to contend with such strong-willed and unscrupulous partisans as Laud and Wentworth. Under the pressure of their tyranny, he could only shed tears and give way. It was not strange he was so unwilling to molest these ministers merely because they could not conscientiously adopt the Service Book. In weight of character and pastoral accomplishments, Blair, Welsh,

---

* *Life of the Right Rev. Jeremy Taylor, D.D.*, I., 165.

Hamilton, Livingston, and others, were immensely superior to the Episcopal clergy around them; and, in scholarship, some even of the bishops who oppressed them, were greatly their inferiors. Blair, who was a gentleman by descent, had been six years a Professor in the College of Glasgow before he came to Ireland; Welsh, the grandson of John Knox, and the great grandson of Lord Ochiltree, had also been a Professor in the same university;* Hamilton, the nephew of Lord Claneboy, was a man of learning; and few at the present day possess the literary acquirements of Livingston, the great grandson of Alexander, fifth Lord Livingston. When in Holland he held fellowship with giants in literature, such as Voet and Leusden. Before his death, he had a copy of the Old Testament, translated out of the original Hebrew into Latin, ready for the press. He was acquainted not only with Greek, Latin, Hebrew, Chaldee, and Syriac, but also with several of the modern Continental languages, including French, Italian, German, Spanish, and Dutch.† Even a scholar, like Jeremy Taylor or Reginald Heber, might not care to stand a competitive examination on the tongues with such a rival. And yet the Lord Bishop of Calcutta speaks of the Presbyterian ministers of Ulster in the seventeenth century as if they were almost beneath contempt. Referring to the Dioceses of Down, Connor, and Dromore at the time of the Restoration, he thus expresses himself:—

"It was in this part of Ireland more than any other that the clearance of the Episcopalian clergy had been most

---

* *Life of John Welsh*, by Young, p. 413.
† *Life of Livingston. Wodrow Society. Select Biographies*, I., 195-6.

effectual, and that their places had been supplied by the sturdiest champions of the covenant, taken, for the most part, from the west of Scotland—disciples of Cameron, Renwick, and Peden—and professing, in the wildest and most gloomy sense, the austere principles of their party. Such men as these, *more prejudiced in proportion as they were worse educated than the other adherents of Calvin*, were neither to be impressed by the zeal with which the new Prelate (Jeremy Taylor) discharged the duties of his station nor softened by the tenderness and charity expressed in his deportment towards themselves."*

The recklessness of these representations must be obvious to every one even superficially acquainted with Presbyterian Church History; for Peden was unknown in Ireland at the period here mentioned; Renwick was yet unborn; and Cameron did not commence his career as a preacher until long afterwards. The assertion that the disciples of Cameron, Renwick, and Peden, were now creating confusion in the North of Ireland, involves an anachronism which betrays its absurdity. We have various means of ascertaining the real character of the ministers expelled from the Irish Establishment by Jeremy Taylor. Mr. Adair was one of these men; and every discerning reader of this Narrative may see that he was neither ignorant, hot-headed, nor impracticable. He was a sedate, sensible, and earnest pastor, who scorned to be a time-server, and who preferred the safe-keeping of a good conscience to a comfortable temporal provision. Jeremy Taylor, could, no doubt, soar higher on the wings of

---

* *Life of Jeremy Taylor*, I., 166-7.

fancy, and clothe his ideas in more gorgeous, or more graceful, diction; but his theology was thoroughly unsound; his piety was rather monkish than evangelical;* and there are not wanting evidences that Mr. Adair had studied more profoundly the mystery of godliness, and was better qualified to minister to minds diseased. And, even on lower grounds, the pastor of Cairncastle may bear a not unfavourable comparison with the Bishop of Down, Connor, and Dromore. Mr. Adair was a scion of one of the most respectable families in the West of Scotland—Jeremy Taylor was the son of a Cambridge barber. Mr. Adair was married to the daughter of Sir Robert Adair, of Ballymena—one of the very worthiest and most influential of the landed proprietors of the country; Jeremy Taylor, with all his learning and rhetorical ability, might never have been permitted to wear a mitre, had he not been pleased to marry an illegitimate daughter† of Charles I. Michael Bruce, of Killinchy, another of these sufferers for Nonconformity, was one of the most awakening preachers of his age. His intrepidity, his zeal, his exalted holiness, and his majestic eloquence, have earned for him imperishable renown. At the Restoration there was no bishop in Ireland who could point to so high a lineage. The best blood of Scotland flowed in his veins; for his lineal ancestor, John de Bruce, was uncle to Bruce of Bannockburn. His great grand-father, Robert Bruce, had laid aside the em-

---

* Bishop Rust, his friend and successor in the See of Dromore, in a funeral sermon, not inappropriately describes his character when he declares that "he had piety enough *for a cloister.*"

† She is said "both in countenance and disposition to have displayed a striking resemblance to her unfortunate father."—*Heber's Life of Jeremy Taylor*, I. 56.

broidered scarlet dress of the courtier, to enter the ministry of the Presbyterian Church; and was one of that noble host of confessors who contended side by side with Andrew Melville in the struggle for ecclesiastical freedom. He was the most influential Privy Councillor in the kingdom when James VI. went to Denmark for his bride; and when the royal pair appeared among their subjects, this same Robert Bruce was selected, at the coronation, to place the crown on the head of the first Protestant Queen of Scotland. And there were others of these ministers, of whom Bishop Heber speaks so disparagingly, who would have been entitled to respect in any church in Christendom. Thomas Hall, the pastor of Larne, was a man of singular excellence; and a work on the Shorter Catechism, which he has left behind him, may still be studied with advantage. Thomas Peebles, of Dundonald, is described by Adair as "learned and faithful, eminent in the languages and history;" and Thomas Gowan, of Antrim, taught there philosophy for many years, and published two valuable Latin Treatises on Logic.

Heber certainly did not mean to be ironical when speaking of "the tenderness and charity" exhibited in the deportment of Jeremy Taylor toward the Presbyterian ministers of Down and Antrim; and yet, in this sense only, have his words any point or significance. Every one acquainted with the facts is well aware that the tender mercies of the bishop were cruel. Had Jeremy Taylor been removed from this world before he reached the Episcopal throne, he would have left behind him a far more savoury reputation; for the author of the *Liberty of Prophesying* no sooner became a Lord Spiritual, than he seemed to be another man. As if oblivious of all the principles propounded in that celebrated treatise, he took the lead in the race of intolerance. He occupies the unenviable position of the first persecutor of the Irish Presbyterian ministers after the Restoration. Such was his zeal to put them down, that he stretched his power beyond its proper bounds, and anticipated the progress of legislation. In the spring of 1661, he declared their pulpits vacant, simply because they were not episcopally ordained; though the Act of Parliament authorizing such severity was not passed until four years afterwards.* Finding them by no means so pliant as others who had taken the Solemn League and Covenant, he completely lost his temper; and even Heber is constrained to acknowledge that his very first sermon before the two Houses of Parliament in Ireland, displays "traces of disappointment and irritation."† Nothing, indeed, can be more shameful or insulting than the strain in which he there attacks the unhappy Nonconformists. "We have seen," says he, in the *Epistle Dedicatory*, " *the vilest part of mankind*—men that have done things so horrid, worse than which the sun never saw—*pretend* tender consciences against ecclesiastical laws."‡ These words obviously refer to the death of Charles I.; but he was aware that the Presbyterians had no share in that transaction; and the Chaplain of the Cavaliers knew well that

---

* See *Mant*, I. 646. Presbyterian Ordination was recognized by law in the Church of England, in the reign of Elizabeth.
† *Life of Taylor*, I. 168.
‡ See this *Epistle Dedicatory* in Taylor's Works, VI. 336. London, 1812. When Taylor came to Ireland, shortly before Cromwell's death, Oliver gave him "a pass and a protection for himself and his family, under his sign manual and privy signet." —*Rawdon Papers*, 189.

his own party contained as vile men as England could produce.

It is very painful to be obliged to speak thus of Jeremy Taylor; but the truth must be told; and the blundering of his Right Reverend biographer cannot be permitted to pass unnoticed. Heber states that, "though Bishop Taylor was a nominal member of the Irish Privy Council, there is no reason whatever to suppose that he took a part in the measures of any administration."* Letters written at the time by individuals connected with the Government warrant a very different inference. Thus, Lord Orrery, in a communication addressed to the Duke of Ormond, bearing date April 16th, 1662, expressly declares that *the bishops* complained of "indulgences" granted, among others, to the "*Nonconformists of the North*," which, says he, "*made us call them to advise* what was fit to be done." He adds, "If the laws be not put in execution, *the Church will be dissatisfied*."† There can be no doubt that Jeremy Taylor was at least one of the bishops here described as consulted on this occasion, and as stimulating the Executive to severity. His sermon to the two Houses of Parliament, and his treatment of the Presbyterian ministers of Down and Antrim, abundantly prove that he was no sleeping partner in the business of persecution.

It is due to the memory of the fathers of the Presbyterian Church in Ireland to publish this Narrative of their labours and sufferings; and the present generation may derive much

---

* *Life of Taylor*, I. 50.
† See this letter quoted in *Mant*, I. 637.

advantage from its perusal. The history of Irish Presbyterianism presents strange vicissitudes. In the times of Blair and Livingston it began to take root in the land; but its growth was suddenly arrested by the suspension of its ministers, and the imposition of the Black Oath: it revived in the days of the covenant, but it was permitted to prosper only for a few years: it was sternly discountenanced by Cromwell, and yet, towards the close of the Protectorate, it recovered its position and extended its influence: at the Restoration it was well-nigh crushed to death, and during all the times of Charles II. and his brother James, it was obliged to maintain a continued struggle for existence: it revived once more in the reign of William III., and in the reign of Queen Anne it was again threatened with extinction: on the accession of the House of Hanover to the throne, it was rescued almost from the grave; but, for the seventy-five years following, it was so oppressed by poverty that many of its ministers and people left their native shores, and hastened away to the American wilderness: at the commencement of this century its pastors had a most miserable subsistence, and most of its houses of worship were little better than mere ruins; and yet, at this moment, its adherents are the bone and sinew of the inhabitants of Ulster, and constitute the one-half of the church-going Protestant population of Ireland.

The period included in this Narrative was distinguished by the occurrence of the first great religious Revival in the Presbyterian Church of Ireland. It is here described with much simplicity; and those who have witnessed the visitation of 1859, may observe a marked resemblance between these two extraordinary awakenings. Manifestations of folly, such as those recorded by Adair, were common to both. When the Heavenly Husbandman sows good seed, the enemy will be always ready to sow tares; but no wise man will, on that account, deny the excellence of the divine plantation. There are none so blind as those who believe that a year of grace is nothing but a year of delusion. The excitement of 1859 has now completely passed away, but its blessed fruits remain, and shall endure throughout eternity.

This Narrative clearly shows wherein consists the true excellence of the Christian ministry. The founders of the Presbyterian Church in Ireland were devotedly attached to its worship, polity, and discipline; but they had higher and better recommendations. They were eminently holy men; they were able preachers; they were wise to win souls; they were instant in season and out of season. The people greatly valued their ministry, for they fully proclaimed the gospel, and commended themselves to every man's conscience. The right form of church government is Heaven's own ordinance; but it is only when in the hands of men animated by the Spirit of the living God that it can be properly appreciated. Such was Presbyterianism in the days here described. Its ministers were true witnesses for Christ; they taught His doctrine; they exhibited His temper; they walked in His ways. Their Divine Master gloriously set his seal to their commission. Multitudes were added to the Lord. And so it will be always. No religious community can flourish without a converted and earnest ministry. Happy is the church furnished with many such pastors as Patrick Adair.

BELFAST, *May 8th*, 1866.

A True Narrative,* &c.

CHAPTER I.

MR. ROBERT BLAIR REMOVES FROM GLASGOW COLLEGE TO BANGOR—STATE OF THE COUNTRY—MR. BLAIR'S ORDINATION—HIS LABOURS AND DANGER.

N the year 1622 comes to Bangor that famous minister of Christ, Mr. Robert Blair, who was the first and greatest instrument for preaching of the Gospel in the North of Ireland.† He had been six years Regent in the College of Glasgow, in which time he employed himself in

---

* The following is the full title-page, apparently in Mr. Patrick Adair's own handwriting:—"A True Narrative of the Rise and Progress of the Presbyterian Government in the North of Ireland, and of the various troubles and afflictions which ministers and people adhering to that way did meet with from the adversaries thereof, and of their constant adherence thereunto notwithstanding. Divided into four parts: The first, which is mainly introductory, from the year 1622 to the year 1642; the second, from the year 1642 to the year 1661; the third, from the year 1661 to the death of King Charles II.; the fourth, from the entrance of King James II. upon his Government unto this present year. Faithfully collected from the records of the Presbytery. Whereunto is annexed—An exact account of the manner of their exercise of that government, in all the parts thereof, for the information of such as desire to be informed." Zech. iv., 6. "Not by might nor by power, but by my Spirit, saith the Lord of Hosts." Psalms viii., 2. "Out of the mouth of babes and sucklings hast thou ordained strength because of thine enemies, that thou mightest still the enemy and the avenger." In the days of Blair the year commenced on the 25th of March; and, according to the old reckoning, he was probably invited by Lord Claneboy to Bangor in 1622; but he actually arrived there early in 1623, and not in 1622, as stated by Adair. Dean Gibson died on the 23rd June, 1623.

† Mr. Blair was certainly the most able and influential of the Scottish ministers, who now settled in Ireland, but he was not the first in point of time. Edward Brice settled in Broadisland, or Ballycarry, in 1613.

A

that office, not only by diligent teaching of philosophy to the scholars, but training them also in the exercises of piety. Many of them became seriously exercised in conscience; many singular instances whereof are mentioned in a Narrative left by himself concerning that part of his life. He becomes by degrees to be eminent, even when he was a Regent, both for learning and piety; and, among other effects of his piety, it was his custom, in the times of vacancy* from his work in the college, to spend that time in visiting the most eminent ministers and Christians in divers parts of the land, and spend some time with them in conference and prayer, for his edification, being then a young man. One vacancy he would go to the North of Scotland — a hundred and forty miles from Glasgow— where he conversed with famous Mr. Robert Bruce† and Mr. David Dickson,‡ both at that time confined upon their non-conformity—besides many others, ministers and eminent Christians, as he acknowledged, to his great edification. Another time he travelled towards the South, where, among others, he visits one Mr. Oswell,§ an ancient minister of Christ. This Mr. Oswell much encouraged him, then a young man, to steadfastness against the growing corruptions of those times—bishops growing to a height in Scotland, and the Articles of Perth Assembly‖ then being concluded and urged upon faithful ministers; and told him a passage that,

---

* *i.e.*, vacation.

† Some account has been given of this eminent minister in the Introduction. He died in 1631; aged 77. His contemporaries describe him as "tall and dignified, a venerable and heroic man, his countenance majestic, and his appearance in the pulpit grave, and expressive of much authority."

‡ Mr. Dickson was minister of Irvine, and afterwards Professor of Divinity in the University of Edinburgh.

§ or Oswald.

‖ These Articles sanctioned kneeling at the communion, the observance of holidays, episcopal confirmation, private baptism, and the private dispensation of the Lord's Supper.

when himself was a young man, he had occasion to visit and converse with Mr. Greenham, that singularly pious and faithful minister of Drayton, in England. While he was at his house he perceived numbers of good people, one after another, repairing to Mr. Greenham from other places—besides his own people—for conference, and satisfying them in their doubts and exercise of conscience, in which Mr. Greenham was singularly gifted. Mr. Oswell, in discourse with Mr. Greenham making his observation of the people's so frequent repairing to him for such ends, and men of his sort being under a cloud, Mr. Greenham answered that there ought in this to be observed the singular goodness and power of God to his suffering servants; that, whereas the Bishops had taken church power out of their hands, and erected a kind of worldly jurisdiction over people instead of Christ—the Lord was, in the consciences of the godly, everywhere erecting a throne for Himself, and uniting them to the ministers, with the undervaluing of the usurped power of the prelates. This passage Mr. Blair related to a minister of Ireland many years after, and bid him tell it his brethren for their encouragement under men's oppressions. Indeed, the continued experience of the suffering church of Christ in these nations hath proved these many years that Christ hath always kept up a throne for Himself in the hearts of the godly in these lands, opposite to that usurped power of prelates—yea, in the hearts of the multitude of common people in this North of Ireland, though few persons of quality in this country joined with these ministers.

Mr. Blair becomes weary in so long trafficking with Aristotle and conversing with philosophical notions, and resolves to accept a call to the ministry. But, though divers parishes earnestly called him, Archbishop Law, perceiving he was not for conformity, and otherwise knowing his abilities, did obstruct any settlements in his diocese. In the meantime there was in Glasgow a minister from the French Church—Monsieur Basnage—sent over for a collection for relief of Rochelle, then in great straits. This minister conversed equally with the Episcopal party and the Nonconformists, in order to the errand he came for, till he had gathered what was offered. At last he spoke to Mr. Blair in private, telling him that, though he had carried himself indifferently towards both parties in the Church of Scotland, lest he should have marred the work he came for, yet now, having done his business, he freely declared to Mr. Blair, whom he liked and whom not. He also told Mr. Blair what good he heard of him, and that he perceived the Bishop's party had a pique at him, and before a year went about he would find the effect of their displeasure; and, withal, not to be discouraged; for, if he should be troubled by them, he entreated him to come to France, where, first, he should have a place in the college for teaching philosophy, till he had learned the French tongue; and then have a ministerial charge; and he would be the more welcome in France that he suffered by them in Scotland.

Shortly after, Mr. Blair fell into some difficulties in Glasgow. The Bishop had a jealous eye over him, and a pique at him upon account not only of his nonconformity, but that he, in a public meeting of the members of the college and ministers of the town, had contradicted the Bishop asserting all things in Perth Assembly were carried orderly. Mr. Blair, having gone there on purpose, in time of vacancy, to see the manner, did testify openly that the Archbishop of St. Andrew's publicly declared in his disputes, that, though there were none there to conclude the Articles but the Bishop and King's Commissioner, they should be concluded.* This provoked the Bishop to bitter words against Mr. Blair. And, withal, at that time famous Mr. Boyd, of Trochrigge, with some ministers, reproving the Bishop for having put some young godly students from the communion-table because they would not kneel, did occasion the removal of that shining light Mr. Boyd from being Principal of the College. In his stead was sent from court, by the Bishop's procurement, Mr. Cameron, who, at that time, was much noticed for his learning and abilities. His design was to bring masters and students in Glasgow to conformity, wherein he did much traffict† with Mr. Blair; but Mr. Blair having now fully studied those controversies, and being fixed, Cameron could get no ground upon him, whereupon he resolved to have him removed from the college; and for that end laboured to render him obnoxious as not well affected to monarchical government. But that failed him,—Mr. Blair's notes upon Aristotle's Ethics and Politics being revised, and by himself explained to satisfaction of all the members of the college. He engaged Mr. Blair to disputation anent some Arminian tenets which he sustained in his theses, labouring to affront him, but

---

* *i.e.*, adopted. The Archbishop of St. Andrews mentioned in the text as acting so dictatorially in the Perth Assembly in 1618 was the famous John Spotswood, the author of a History of the Church of Scotland. The Bishop of Glasgow, of whom Blair complains, was James Law. Livingston, in his Characteristics, tells a singular story respecting these two gentlemen. Mr. John Davidson, minister of Prestonpans, being Moderator of the Provincial Synod of Lothian, wherein Mr. John Spotswood, minister at Calder, and Mr. James Law, minister at Kirkliston, were arraigned for playing at foot-ball on the Lord's Day—insisted that they should be deposed for such conduct; but it was carried that they should be simply rebuked. On this occasion Mr. Davidson thus addressed the Synod:—" And now, brethren, let me tell you what reward you shall get for your lenity—these two men shall trample on your necks, and the necks of the ministry of Scotland." "Thereafter," says Livingston, "Mr. Spotswood was first Bishop of Glasgow, and after of St. Andrews, and Mr. Law became Bishop of Glasgow, and both did much mischief." Livingston himself was one of a number of students excluded by Law from the communion-table at Glasgow for refusing to kneel.

† *i.e.*, deal or discourse.

gained nothing; the Lord helping his servant to defend the truth with prudence and sobriety, as well as with learning. But when Mr. Blair perceived he could not live peaceably in that place, nor with safety; neither was there access for his entering into the ministry in Scotland, the Bishops putting out many eminent worthy ancient ministers for their nonconformity, and barring the door against young men Nonconformists, therefore he much inclined to go to France in compliance with that motion which was made to him by the French Minister. Yet, in the meantime, there comes an invitation to him from the Lord Claneboy, patron of the parish of Bangor, in Ireland. This at first he received with a kind of indignation, having a great antipathy against going to Ireland. But thereafter he dealt with God by prayer to direct him according to what was His will, and, at the close of his prayer, he found himself as sensibly rebuked as if one standing by had audibly said—" Thou fool art taking the disposal of thyself, not submitting to me. Thou must either preach the Gospel in Ireland or nowhere at all."

Being thus rebuked, he found himself bound in spirit to set his face towards Ireland; and yet, for all this, was not persuaded to settle there, loathing that country, and hankering still after France. Yet, the Sovereign Lord thrust him over into Ireland wholly against his inclination. So, coming over, and landing at Glenarm, he goes towards Carrickfergus; and, having come within a mile of the town, upon the top of the hill Bangor in these parts appeared to him; at sight of which the Lord did unexpectedly fill his heart with such a sweet peace and extraordinary joy that he could scarcely contain himself, but was forced to lie down upon the grass to rejoice in the Lord, who was the same in Ireland that he was in Scotland.

The next day, coming towards Bangor, it was suggested to him that there being an old man in that place who was a

Conformist, [and who] might [have] labour[ed] to obstruct his
entry, that old man was now sick, and would not rise again.
This suggestion at first he rebuked, not knowing whence it
came ; but, when he came to Bangor, he found it true, being
the first thing was told him uninquired ; yet, though he saw
the Lord thus clearing his entry, he gave not over to plead
that God might obstruct it, and for that end was very plain
with the Lord Claneboy, shewing him what accusations had
been against him in Glasgow as disaffected to the civil
government—though he had fully cleared himself—and that
he could not submit to Episcopal government, nor any part
of the Liturgy—to see if these things would cause him relinquish his invitation : but that lord, having had information of the dispute in Glasgow by a minister who was
present, was satisfied as to that; and, for his nonconformity,
he said he was confident to procure his entry without conformity. However, thereafter he was much satisfied he had
been thus free; especially when troubles came some years
after, neither patron nor bishop could say he had broken
with them. He preached, upon invitation of the patron and
sick incumbent; and after three Sabbaths some ancient men
of the congregation came to him, in name of the rest,
entreating him not to leave them, and gave him all the
encouragement they could, which call he laid much weight
upon for his farther clearing. Besides, the dying man did
much encourage him to undertake the charge, professing his
great repentance that ever he was a Dean, speaking more
peremptorily and terribly against that way than (as Mr. Blair's
own Narrative of his life says, from which all these passages
are taken)* ever he durst do, either before that or since ;
and charged Mr. Blair, in Christ's name, and as he would

---

* Many other statements in this part of the narrative are taken from Blair's Life ;
but Adair mentions various incidents not to be found there. He may have received
additional information from Blair himself.

expect a blessing on his ministry, to be steadfast in that good way he had begun in; and, reaching out both his arms, drew Mr. Blair's head into his bosom, and, laying his hands on his head, blessed him. The room being dark, some of the people standing by, hearing his discourse, and comparing it with former ways, could not believe it was he who spoke, but rather an angel from Heaven. Mr. Blair refuted that conceit, and the man died a few days after.

But, before we go farther, it is fit to declare what was at that time the case of this North of Ireland. 'Tis said the most part of considerable lands in Ireland were possessed in ancient times by the English. But the civil wars in England between the houses of York and Lancaster did draw from Ulster the able men of the English nation to assist their own faction in England. Thereupon the Irish in Ulster killed and expelled the remnant of the English out of that province, and molested all the rest of Ireland; Ulster being in their conceit like the thumb in the hand which is able to grip and hold against the four fingers — Leinster, Munster, Connaught, and Meath.

The civil wars ending in the beginning of the reign of King Henry VII., the suppressing of the Irish rebels was not much laboured by the English party (partly through division at home, and partly through wars with France and Scotland) till the reign of Queen Elizabeth, who did much to finish that rebellion, which yet was not fully extinguished —the Scots with Islanders sometimes joining with the Irish, and sometimes acting by themselves against the English— till King James' coming to the Crown of England. The wars lasting so long, the whole country upon the matter did lie waste, the English possessing only some few towns and castles, and making use of small parcels of near adjacent lands; and the Irish staying in woods, bogs, and such fast places. But, in the reign of King James, that distressed land began again to be planted both by English and Scots, the Irish remaining not only obdurate in their idolatry, but also in idleness and rudeness. In this time the parts of Scotland nearest to Ireland sent over abundance of people and cattle, which planted the country of Ulster next the sea; and albeit, among these, Divine Providence sent over some worthy persons for birth, education, and parts; yet the most part were such as either poverty or scandalous lives, or, at best, seeking better accommodation, did set forward that way. The wolf and wood kern* were greatest enemies to the first planters, but the long-rested land did yield to the labourer such plentiful increase that many followed these first essayers. Little care was taken by any to plant religion. As were the people, so, for the most part, were the preachers. The case of the people throughout all the country was most lamentable, being drowned in ignorance, security, and sensuality, which was Mr. Blair's great discouragement to settle in these parts.

However, there were some few godly men in the country before him. There was in the next parish—Holywood—a very godly man, Mr. Robert Cunningham, with whom he became intimately acquainted, to both their comfort and edification. They often visited one another, and spent many hours—yea, days—in prayer. Mr. Cunningham became singular and eminent in holiness and usefulness in the ministry, in a greater degree by Mr. Blair's coming to Ireland.

There was also in the County of Antrim Mr. John Ridge, of the town of Antrim. There had also been in Carrick-

---

* *i.e.*, the robber issuing from the woods. "The *kerns* were light troops, armed with swords and javelins, and generally so irregular that kern and robber were sometimes synonymous."—*Gordon's History of Ireland*, I., 237.

fergus a gracious and able man, Mr. Hubbard, under the
protection of the old Lord Chichester, who had been
Deputy of Ireland, and carried great favour to godly men.
Mr. Cartwright had been his tutor in his younger years;
but he was dead before Mr. Blair came. My Lord Claneboy
procured Mr. Blair's admission to the ministry, having
before, at his desire, informed the Bishop* of his settled
principles against conformity; and besides, Mr. Blair, fearing
he had not been plain enough with the Bishop, declared the
same to himself at their first meeting—notwithstanding the
Bishop declared himself most willing he should be planted
there, saying he heard good of him, and would impose no
conditions upon him, himself was old, and could teach him
ceremonies, and Mr. Blair could teach him substance, only
he must ordain him, otherwise neither of them could answer
the law nor brook the land. Mr. Blair told him that was
contrary to his principles—to which he replied wittily and
submissively—whatever you account of Episcopacy, yet I
know you account a Presbyter to have divine warrant—will
you not receive ordination from Mr. Cunningham and the
adjacent brethren, and let me come in among them in no
other relation than a Presbyter? This Mr. Blair could not
refuse, and so the matter was carried. Being entered into
the ministry, he was four times in public preaching every
week, with variety of matter and method in all these ; and
one day or two every week instructing in the grounds of
religion, and examining and pressing to family worship in
divers quarters of the parish, which he continued the whole
time of his ministry there. 'Tis worthy observation that
one Saturday, at night late, having all the day sat at his study,
and his candle going out, he called for another from the

---

* Echlin, Bishop of Down and Connor.

mistress of the house, which she at first refused, telling him it was fit he should go to rest; at last, through his importunity, she was forced to go to the room under his chamber for a candle—when the room below was taking fire through the bricks in his room; whereupon, she calling to him, he suddenly raised the bricks, and got the fire quenched—which was the more observable that the house wherein he was, being situate below the rest of the town, and there blowing a strong north wind all that night, which would have carried the flame to the rest of the town, there would have been no possibility to preserve it.

The custom was, in the first year of his ministry, not to pitch on a book or chapter to go through, but to make choice of such passages of Scripture as held forth fundamental and most material points of religion, and close this course with one sermon of heaven's glory and another of hell's torments. Sometimes, in choosing his text and meditation, he was much difficulted and deserted—but thereafter in delivery was singularly assisted—yea, sometimes in the beginning of his sermon much straitened, and thereafter much enlarged.

In the second year of his ministry a plentiful harvest was almost wholly spoiled with excessive rains after it was cut down, so that the corn, especially in that parish, being later than in places about, was seemingly past hopes of recovery; upon which he kept a public fast; and God ordered that the day thereafter there blew so mighty and strong a wind for twenty-and-four hours together, that it recovered the corn beyond expectation, both that which was growing in the fields on the stooks and that which was smoking in the stacks. Some neighbouring ministers joined in the same duty, and found the same effects: but, which was better, the people began to relish the duty of prayer much more than formerly, both in private and in their families, insomuch that one who was a godly man took up this opinion, that, in all cases and difficulties, there needed no other means but prayer; and, being a man skilful in horses, told Mr. Blair, who had sent for him to a sick horse, he needed no other means but to go to his chamber and pray; but Mr. Blair, not without some difficulty, got him convinced that it was a tempting of God to neglect other means.

Mr. Blair and Mr. Cunningham resolved to celebrate the Lord's Supper four times a year in each of their parishes, where proficients in both parishes did all these eight times communicate together, and these communions became so edifying, and were so blessed, that multitudes of professors from all places of both counties ordinarily resorted to them, and some from Tyrone—there was such a spirit of zeal and power of God poured forth at that time.

About that time Mr. James Hamilton, a learned and godly young man, being a daily hearer of Mr. Robert Blair, shewed much tenderness and ability. He being then chamberlain* to the Lord Claneboy his uncle, Mr. Blair, and Mr. Cunningham, put him to private essays of his gifts; and, being satisfied therewith, Mr. Blair invited him to preach publicly at Bangor in his uncle's hearing, he knowing nothing till he saw him in the pulpit (they fearing my lord would be loath to part with so faithful a servant). But, when my lord heard him in public, he put great respect upon him the same day; and shortly after entered him unto a charge at Ballywalter, where he was painful, successful, and constant, notwithstanding he had many temptations to follow promotion; but was graciously preserved from these baits, and made a successful instrument in the work of Christ in these parts.

Mr. Blair had for a time elders and deacons for the exer-

---

* *i.e.*, agent or factor, living in his own house.

cise of discipline, who, for the time they were permitted, were very useful in the congregation; scandalous persons having been convinced, and publicly professing their repentance before the congregation; till a proud young man, the son and heir of a rich man, falling into scandal, proved obstinate, and appealed from the session to the Bishop—whereby the order of that discipline was broken. But God struck that young man a little after that he died, and a brother better than he succeeded him. It was observed that, after the Bishop's official had wrung the discipline out of their hands, compounding with the rich for money, and sending the poorer sort to public penance (as they call it), there was no blessing nor edification to the people seen to follow that work; yet, in parishes where were godly ministers, the Lord's husbandry always prospered.

About this time, the devil stirred up a man in Mr Blair's parish to stab him. One day, Mr. Blair spending a day in family humiliation, there came two men to his gate, knocking. He (having before ordered that none that day should open the gate but himself) comes to it, and the pretended errand was to advertise Mr. Blair that one of them had a child to baptize. Mr. Blair, having spoken a little to him in order to that duty (as his use was), dismissed him. But the other, being the other's landlord, and their chief constable in the parish, desired to speak with Mr. Blair in private. Mr. Blair looking on him, apprehended his eyes to be like the eyes of a cat in the night, and that he had some mischief in his heart. However, keeping his eyes upon him, and at some distance from him, he took him into the church which was near his house. Presently the man fell a-trembling, which so increased that he could not speak, and was like to throw him out of the seat he was on.* Mr. Blair laid his

---

* This man was evidently under the influence of a species of *delirium tremens*. Mr. Blair was not aware that he was suffering from disease brought on by drunkenness.

arm about him, and asked what troubled him. After a little while's silence, and the trembling ceasing, he told Mr. Blair how the devil had for a long time appeared to him, first at Glasgow, where he bought a horse from him, he receiving sixpence in earnest, and that, off-hand, he offered him a great purse full of silver and gold if he would be his, making no mention of the horse. The man said he blessed himself, and so the buyer, with the silver and gold, which was poured out on the table, instantly evanished. Some days thereafter he had appeared to him at his own house, naming him, and said, " You are mine, for I did earl you with a sixpence, which you have." Then he asked his name; he answered " Nihil Domus," which likely the man said wrong for "*Nihil Damus*," i.e., "We give nothing."* Thus, the man being molested with many apparitions, comes over to Ireland, thinking to shun them; but he also oft appeared to him in Ireland, and now of late he oft commanded him to kill and slay, or he would kill him. Mr. Blair asked him, Whom? He answered, any that comes in his way, but the better were the better service; and the man said often his whinger had been drawn and kept under his cloak, to obey Satan's command, but still somewhat held his hand that he could not strike. When he had told these things to Mr. Blair, he fell again a-trembling, and became speechless, and looking at Mr. Blair in a lamentable manner, designed Mr. Blair to be the person he aimed at, and then fell a-crying and lamenting. Mr. Blair shewed him the horribleness of his ignorance and drunkenness. He made many promises of reformation, which were not well kept; for, within a fortnight after, hav-

---

* It would appear that these two Latin words—*Nihil Damus*—that is, *we give nothing*—were supposed to be among the names by which the devil reveals himself. Whether the designation "old nick" is a contraction for "old nihil," or whether it is derived from *Nick*, an evil spirit of the waters, in the Northern mythology, I cannot undertake to decide.

ing sat long at drink, and going home late, the devil again appeared to him, and challenged him for opening to Mr. Blair what had been in secret between them, and pulled the cap off his head, and tore the band from his neck, saying to him,—"On Hallow Night I shall have thy soul and body in despite of the ministers, and all that will do for thee." Whereupon being terrified and driven to his bed, he sent for Mr. Blair presently, and told him what now had passed, and entreated Mr. Blair for Christ's sake to be with him that night. Mr. Blair, having instructed him and prayed with him, parted, and promised to be with him that night, provided he would fly unto Christ for a refuge, and not to him, who was but a weak sinful creature. Mr. Blair had resolved to spend the day before that night in family humiliation, but had forgot till near night; upon which he was much troubled, and went to his chamber to prayer. Being in some doubt what to do, he durst not break his promise, yet he thought he was unprepared for such a pitched battle with Satan. However he went, and calling the people of the village together, to the man's house, he spent the night in prayer, expounding the doctrine of Christ's temptations with singing psalms; and, after that, other texts till the next morning, with prayer and singing psalms. In the morning, the man took great courage to himself, and thereafter became more reformed, though he remained still ignorant. A while after, he fell sick, and seemed very penitent, and upon Mr. Blair's asking him, he declared he had never appeared to him after that night.

CHAPTER II.

GLENDINNING AND THE ANTRIM MEETING—COLWORT, WELSH, AND DUNBAR—ECHLIN'S OPPOSITION—PRIMATE USSHER—LIVINGSTON AND STEWART—OPPOSITION FROM SEPARATISTS AND CONFORMISTS.

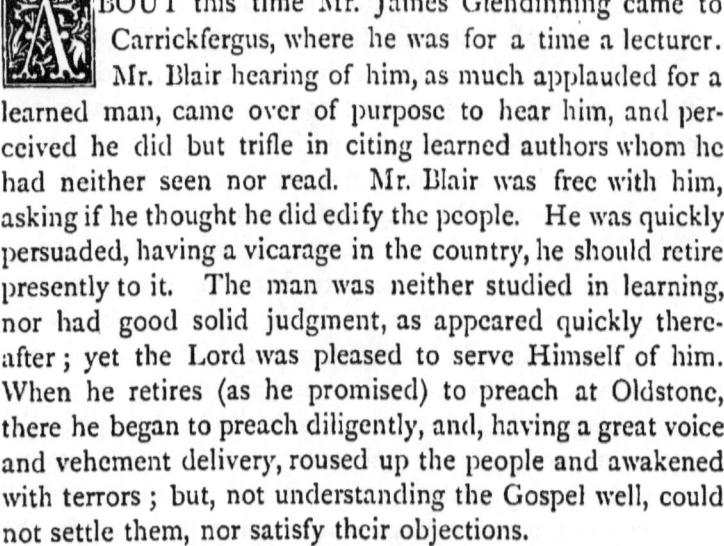ABOUT this time Mr. James Glendinning came to Carrickfergus, where he was for a time a lecturer. Mr. Blair hearing of him, as much applauded for a learned man, came over of purpose to hear him, and perceived he did but trifle in citing learned authors whom he had neither seen nor read. Mr. Blair was free with him, asking if he thought he did edify the people. He was quickly persuaded, having a vicarage in the country, he should retire presently to it. The man was neither studied in learning, nor had good solid judgment, as appeared quickly thereafter; yet the Lord was pleased to serve Himself of him. When he retires (as he promised) to preach at Oldstone, there he began to preach diligently, and, having a great voice and vehement delivery, roused up the people and awakened with terrors; but, not understanding the Gospel well, could not settle them, nor satisfy their objections.

There was at Antrim Mr. John Ridge, a judicious and gracious minister, who, perceiving many people on both sides of the Six-mile Water awakened out of their security, and willing to take pains for their salvation, made an overture that a monthly lecture might be set up at Antrim, and invited to bear burden therein, Mr. Cunningham and Mr. Hamilton with Mr. Blair; who were all glad at the motion, and complied at the first, and came prepared to preach. In the summer day four did preach, and when the day was shorter, three. This monthly meeting, thus beginning, continued many years, and was a great help to spread religion through the whole country. Sir Hugh Clotworthy was very hospitable to the ministers that came there to preach. His worthy son, now Lord Viscount Massareene, together with his mother and lady, being both of them very religious and virtuous women, did greatly countenance this work.

Mr. Glendinning, who at the first was very glad of this confluence, when his emptiness began to appear, did begin to be emulous and envious; yet the brethren cherished him, and the people carried a respect towards him; yea they were bountiful to him, till he was smitten with erroneous conceits. He watched much and fasted wonderfully; and began publicly to affirm that he or she who, after having slept a little in bed, then turned from one side to another, could not be an honest Christian.* This rigorous paradox the hearers did bear with, in respect of the rigorous course he took with himself. But he began to vent other conceits, privately condescending on a day that would be the day of judgment; and that whoever would join with him in a ridiculous way of roaring out some prayer, laying their faces on the earth, would be undoubtedly converted and saved. Some judicious gentlemen to whom he imparted his folly, loving him dearly because at first he had been instrumental of their good, resolved not to let him come before the public with these conceits in his head; and presently posted away to Mr. Blair, requesting him with all expedition to repair to them. The day being then at the shortest and the journey considerable, Mr. Blair made such haste to obey their desire that he stayed not so much as to break his fast. When he came at nightfalling to the place where he [Glendinning] was, in a godly family (his own house being lately

---

* He probably imagined that the individual who lay awake in bed was unduly indulging himself.

accidentally burned), with many good people with him, he
found him so fixed in erroneous conceits that he laboured to
persuade Mr. Blair to join with him. He had long fasted, and
at supper they thought Mr. Blair could have persuaded him
to eat,—having usually before hearkened to his counsel. To
induce him, Mr. Blair told him he was yet fasting for his sake,
and if he would not eat with him he would fast with him;
but this prevailed not; so the rest eat their supper upon
Mr. Blair's entreaty, till he discoursed with Mr. Glendinning;
and, after supper, they being alone, only his wife sitting by,
he asked Mr. Blair if he would believe he was in the right if
his foot could not burn in the fire. Mr. Blair answered, if
he offered to do so, he would be further confirmed that he
was a deluded man; but before Mr Blair had spoken the
words, his foot was in the midst of the fire, he holding the
lintel [of the fire-place] with both his hands; but Mr. Blair
pulled so hard that both were thrown into the midst of the
floor. The gentlemen, upon this noise, coming in, some
of them were angry that Mr. Blair should have pulled
his foot, thinking the heat of the fire might have helped to
burn away his folly. There, in presence of them all, he
agreed with Mr. Blair that, if before the morrow Mr. Blair
were not of his mind, he was contented to be forsaken as a
deluded man. Mr. Blair accepted the condition, and so they
agreed. But Mr. Blair must lie in bed with him; and being
laid, he presently fell asleep; but Mr. Blair, though having
fasted all day, yet remembering the condition was short,
continued fasting and praying. There was not one hour past,
when his wife, who lay in another room, came in muttering
that the matter was revealed to her, and that the day of
judgment was presently coming. He being hereby awakened,
triumphantly did leap out of his bed, saying, "You will be
next." Mr. Blair, who had not so much as warmed in the

bed, being somewhat astonished, did rise also, and got courage to encounter these deluded enthusiasts, and set them to open their revelations, not doubting to find absurdities and contradictions therein; they in the meantime being so confident as to desire him to write to carnal friends lest they should be surprised with the coming of that day. Mr. Blair took pen and paper pretending to write their informations, enquiring first of him and then of his wife; but immediately found their contradictions. Whereupon, throwing away the paper, said, "Will you not see your folly." He inviting Mr. Blair to pray, did himself begin. Mr. Blair stood to see his new way (formerly mentioned), whereby he supposed to convert Mr. Blair. When he had seen and heard the absurdities thereof in their idle roaring repetitions, he requiring him in the Lord's name to be silent, kneeled down and prayed with humble confidence, hoping to be heard. That gentleman lying in the next room being surprised through fear, and lying sweating in his bed, supposing the woman muttering had been the apparition of a spirit, when he heard Mr. Blair's voice in prayer, did arise and join with Mr. Blair; besides, his roaring before Mr. Blair began, had awakened some who lay at a distance, and so all jointly continued a space in prayer. When Mr. Blair had ended, Mr. Glendinning took him apart, and confessed that he saw now he was deluded, and entreated Mr. Blair to see how the matter might be covered and concealed. Mr. Blair called the gentlemen to hear his confession. They being very glad, he warned them that matter was not yet at an end, as the event proved; for he, falling from evil to evil, did at last run away to visit the Seven Churches of Asia. However, they thanked God for what was done; and Mr. Blair, calling for bread and drink, refreshed himself, went to bed to rest, and so did all the family.

It is observable from this discourse what a deep design Satan had herein against the work of God in the County of Antrim; for he, knowing this man was very instrumental in rousing up many out of their security, thought, by deluding him, to shake, if not to crush, that blessed work. But the wisdom, power, and goodness of God so ordered that, except his own wife (of whom few had any good opinion before) there was neither man nor woman stumbled at his fall, but on the contrary were thereby guarded against delusion, magnifying the Word of God and the Holy Scriptures, and learned to work out the work of their salvation in fear and trembling, and not doting on the bodily exercise of watching and fasting, whereby that man thought to cry up himself.*

And now, having lost this one man, the Lord was pleased to give to the church in these parts three able and gracious men, first, Mr. Henry Colwort, who came over with Mr. Hubbard, formerly mentioned, and was entertained by the godly and worthy Lady Duntreath, of Broadisland, as an helper to an old worthy minister there, Mr. Edward Brice. But, Mr. Glendinning departing, he was brought to Old Stone, where he laboured diligently, and did bear burthen at the monthly meetings, being a man of a fervent spirit and vehement delivery in preaching. This variety of gifts glorifieth the Giver; for his next neighbour, Mr. Ridge, as he was in his carriage, so [was he] in his doctrine, grave, calm, sweet, and orderly, pressing weighty important points to good purpose.

The Lord was also pleased to bring over from Scotland Mr. Josias Welsh, the son of Mr. John Welsh, that famous man of God, who, both in Scotland and France, was rarely

---

* The absurdities here recorded may well remind us of some of the scenes connected with the awakening of 1859. In times of such excitement we may always reckon upon exhibitions of folly and extravagance. But the work of God may still be known by its proper evidences.

instrumental for converting and confirming the souls of the people of God. A great measure of that spirit which wrought in and by the father, rested also on the son. Mr. Blair, meeting with him in Scotland, and perceiving of how weak a body, and of how zealous a spirit he was, exhorted him to haste over to Ireland, where he would find work enough, and, he hoped, success; and so it came to pass; for he, being settled at Templepatrick, became a blessing to that people; and, being under great exercise of spirit, spoke vehemently to convince the secure, and sweetly to comfort the cast down.

Also, the Lord brought over to Larne, that ancient servant of Jesus Christ, Mr. George Dunbar, who had been deposed from the ministry of Ayr by the High Commission Court in Scotland, and by the Council was banished to Ireland. So careful was the Lord of this plantation of his in the North of Ireland, that, whoever wanted, those in that place might not want. The Lord greatly blessed his ministry. All these three now mentioned, as they laboured diligently within their own charges, so were they still ready to preach at the monthly meetings when they were invited thereunto—so mightily grew the word of God, and his gracious work prospered in the hands of his faithful servants, the power of man being restrained from opposing the work of God.

About that time Mr. Blair perceived Echlin, Bishop of Down, privily to lay snares, being not willing openly to appear—the people generally approving and commending the labours and success of His servants. And first, he wrote to Mr. Blair to be ready to preach at Bishop Ussher's triennial visitation; the [Primate] himself being then in England, but in his room were two Bishops and a Doctor, his substitutes and delegates. If any ask how Mr. Blair could countenance these prelatical assemblies, the ensuing discourse will declare; but it may rather be wondered how these prelatical meetings did countenance such as Mr. Blair, knowing his judgment and practice to be opposite to them in their way; and it should be also considered that the ministers of Ireland at that time were not under an expressly sworn Covenant against them, as afterwards ministers were when the Covenant was engaged into.

Before the appointed day came, Bishop Echlin sent Mr. Blair advertisement that another was to supply the place, so he might lay aside thoughts of it—the message by word thus contradicting his writing, that he might leave Mr. Blair in an uncertainty, and so pick a quarrel at his pleasure. Mr. Blair had meditated on 2 Cor., iv. 1. [and preached notwithstanding]. Besides other points he specially insisted to show that Christ our Lord had substituted no Lord Bishops in his church, but presbyters and ministers both to teach and govern the same; and proved this, first, from the Holy Scriptures; secondly, from the testimony of purer antiquity; thirdly, from famous divines who had been seeking reformation these 1300 years; and lastly, from the modern divines both over seas and in England—closing all his proofs with the consent of the learned Doctor Ussher, thereby to stop their mouths; and finally, he closed with an exhortation that, seeing the truth was proven clearly and undeniably, they would use moderately what power, custom, and human laws did put in their hands; and so they did indeed, neither questioning him nor any other. Only the Bishop of Dromore, one of the delegates, being brother-in-law to Primate Ussher,* spoke to Mr. Blair privately, desiring him also to be moderate over them, as they had not questioned him, and so bade him farewell.

This snare being broken, the crafty Bishop fell a-weaving another more dangerous, for he knowing that one of the

---

* This was Theophilus Buckworth, married to Ussher's sister Sarah. See Ussher's Life, by Elrington, Appendix, i. ix. Bishop Buckworth died in 1652.

judges—the Lord Chief Baron—who came yearly to that circuit court, was a violent urger of English Conformity, did write to Mr. Blair to make ready a sermon against the next assizes. This was the more dangerous, because the Judges were to communicate that day, being Easter Day. Mr. Blair comes, prepared by prayer and meditation, committing the matter to the Lord, who has all hearts and mouths in his own hand. The Scotch gentlemen there present waiting on the Judges told one of them, whom they counted truly religious, that they wondered how they could communicate on the Lord's Day, being taken up with civil affairs the whole Saturday. He answered, he wished it were otherwise; and said further, if any one were prepared to preach that day, he would hear him. They answered him (Mr. Blair not knowing of the matter) that the preacher appointed for the Lord's Day would preach on the Saturday also; whereupon some were sent to Mr. Blair upon that effect. He wondered at the unexpected motion; but durst not refuse, there being three or four hours for meditation before the hour appointed for the sermon. Upon the Lord's Day he resolved not to take notice of their communicating, neither was it expected from him; so, when he ended, he went to his chamber, and they to their work, which was ended in the eighth part of an hour.* After the afternoon sermon, made by the curate of the place, one of the Judges sent for Mr. Blair, and desired private conference with him in his chamber. He told him he was well satisfied with Saturday's sermon, and more with that which he delivered on the Lord's Day; for there, said he, you opened a point which I never heard before—viz. the covenant of redemption made with the Mediator, as Head

---

* The Lord's Supper was dispensed to the Judges by the curate, after Mr. Blair had preached and left the church. Adair here refers to the brevity of the Episcopal Communion Service.

of the Church elect. He entreated him to go through the heads of the sermon; then, both opening their books, did consider all the points and proofs, turning to all the places cited. He was so well satisfied that he protested, if his calling did not tie him to Dublin, he would gladly have come to the North, and settled under such a minister. In the end he told Mr. Blair he would be sent for to supper, warning him that his colleague was violent for English Conformity. He entreated him that if he asked any captious questions at him, he would answer them very circumspectly. He was sent for and used very cordially and kindly, without any captious questions. Thus the Lord brought off his servant with credit and safety, notwithstanding of the Bishop's snares, and with this advantage, that Judge Major* who had discoursed with him sent for the Bishop to his chamber, and in the presence of some persons of honour, charged him to lay aside evil will against Mr. Blair, and to have a care that no harm nor interruption should come to his ministry; and, if any came, he would impute the same to him, and hereof did take the Master of Ards present to witness.

When Primate Ussher came back to Ireland, the Lord Claneboy did take Mr. Blair along with him to a meeting of nobility and gentlemen where the Bishop was to be, in order to be acquainted with him. The Bishop received him kindly, and desired him to be at his table while he was in town. The next day, coming to dinner, Mr. Blair met with the English Liturgy in his family; but he came not again, leaving his excuse with his Patron, that he expected another thing in the family of so pious and learned a man. But the Bishop excused the matter by reason of the great confluence which was there, and invited him to come to Tredaff [Drogheda], where his ordinary residence was, where he would be more

---

* Or Maior. The other judge was Sir Richard Bolton. See *Reid's History of the Presbyterian Church in Ireland*, I. 125, note.

at leisure to be better acquainted. Mr. Blair obeyed the desire, and found him very affable and communicative in conference. He desired to know of Mr. Blair what his mind was of the nature of justification and saving faith. He told him his mind was that he held the accepting and receiving of Jesus Christ as he is offered in the Gospel to be saving faith—with which he was well satisfied, confirming the same in a large discourse, clearing the matter by the similitude of a marriage wherein it's not the sending and receiving gifts which make the marriage, but the accepting of the person. He spoke also about ceremonies, and desired Mr. Blair's mind therein, saying that he was afraid their unsatisfiedness therein might endanger their ministry, and, said he, "it would break my heart if that successful ministry in the North were interrupted. They think to cause me to stretch forth my hand against you, but all the world shall never make me to do so." When he had drawn forth Mr. Blair's mind thereanent, he said, "I perceive you'll never be satisfied therein, for still you enquire what ought to be done. I confess all these things you except against might—yea, ought to be removed—but that cannot be done." He replied he had read all the arguments used by Mr. Sprint in a treatise called "Cassander Anglicanus, or a Necessity of Conformity in case of Deprivation," and I had, said he, seen all these fully answered in a treatise called "Cassander Scoticanus, or a Necessity of Nonconformity in hope of Exaltation." Their conference being ended, the Bishop dismissed Mr. Blair very kindly, though he gave him no high titles at all; and he proved thereafter very friendly when trouble came on the ministers of the North, as will appear hereafter.*

After all the former helpers the Lord gave, Mr. John

---

* Several matters here mentioned are not to be found in the Life of Blair; and we have thus evidence that Adair did not derive all his information from that work. In Baxter's Life by Sylvester (I. 13), Sprint is named as a writer against the Nonconformists; but I have not seen his work.

Livingston was sent over. He was a man of a gracious melting spirit, and was desired much by godly men about Torphichen, where he had preached as an helper to another, yet was still opposed by the Bishops; but old Bishop Knox of Raphoe refused no honest man, having heard him preach. By this chink he and sundry others got entrance; and, he being settled at Killinchy, in County of Down, the Lord was pleased greatly to bless his ministry, both within his own charge and without, where he got a call; but he continued not long, the troubles coming on.

Likewise Mr. Andrew Stewart, a well-studied gentleman, and fervent in spirit, was settled at Dunegore, and prospered well in the work of the Lord; but his ministry was of short continuance, dying in the midst of the troubles that then came. All this time the Lord was pleased to protect the ministry, by raising up friends to the ministers, and giving them favour in the sight of all the people about them—yea, the Bishop of Down himself used to glory of the ministry in his dioceses. Yet they wanted not difficulties enough. Some of the inferior clergy provoked Mr. Blair to dispute, by letters, about wherein the difference lay between them: but a modest answer—how unsafe it was to do so—did gratify them. After that there was sent a Dean to reside at Carrickfergus, to encounter the brethren and bear them down. But some of them waited on him; and, putting some civilities upon him, they invited him to concur with them at the monthly meeting at Antrim. They did not expect he would yield to the motion; yet, by their visit and invitation, they gained so much that he proved not unfriendly.

As for the Papists, they became very bold through the land by occasion of the intended match between Prince Charles and the Infanta of Spain, so that in every shire they set up their old convents, and even in the city of Dublin itself; and so the rebellion some years thereafter followed.

The Irish priests generally were ignorant dolts, living in whoredom and drunkenness—yea, one that came from Rome with pardons, and had got a deal of money thereby, when he was brought to my Lord Claneboy, in whose land he was taken, scarce understood Latin. Yet, two Irish friars, who had been trained up in the University of Salamanca, in Spain, gave the ministers a defiance, provoking them to dispute. The particular heads were condescended upon, and time and place appointed, [but] at the appointed day, Mr. Blair coming to assist Mr. Josias Welsh against these two friars—for all their bragging—they appeared not.

They had also an assault from the Separatists. Some of that faction in England, hearing that there was a people zealous for the Lord in the North of Ireland, came to Antrim, where their monthly meetings were, and there set up their dwellings, thinking to fish in these waters. They thought that zealous people would seek after them, and did not call on any—but therein they were frustrated of their expectation; for, seeing they came not to the public worship, none there did own them, or take any notice of them, till the minister of the place sent some judicious Christians to confer with them about cases of conscience. They made the report to the minister concerning these persons, that they thought they did not understand these purposes, nor could they at all discourse concerning the points by them propounded—only they fell a jangling against the Church of Ireland. The next time Mr. Blair came to Antrim, the minister desiring him to go with him, that they might confer with these people, they found them rude and somewhat uncivil—they could not well tell what they held, for they concealed themselves. Yet, in the end, they began to try whom they could seduce, and with one of great tenderness they prevailed not to communicate with the congregation. But immediately thereafter the Lord smote him with distraction, from which he no sooner recovered but he abhorred these seducers—so careful was the Lord to preserve his people within these bounds from all sorts of seducement.

The blessed work of conversion was now spread beyond the bounds of Down and Antrim to the skirts of the neighbouring counties—whence many came to monthly meetings and the Sacrament of the Lord's Supper: and the throngs were so great that sometimes they were forced to preach without the church, as well as within, and that without forethought of it. But God did remarkably, with more than ordinary assistance, help his servants, and the people did so hang on them for preaching as to be never enough satisfied. Some of the ministers were jealous and afraid of the people's applause, and too great eyeing them, especially about the Six-mile Water and Antrim, insomuch that Mr. Blair said before many—" Our tide hath run so high that there will be an ebb. No doubt our restraint is near, and troubles are hastening."

Another assault Satan made at that time by an English Conformist, called Mr. Freeman, a strong opinator, who, falling upon Arminian books, drank in their opinions, and began boldly to propagate the same. This man having a strong body, able to watch and fast, made himself very plausible by a seeming strictness of life and austerity, and thereby did insinuate himself into the affections of people, inviting them to conference and singing psalms. Being thus much followed, he vented his opinions, not only by preaching, but by spreading papers, one of which had this inscription—"Of the three generations of Noble Christians." Many copies of this were spread among the people, some whereof came to the hands of their worthy ministers. Mr. Blair, being asked his judgment of it, said all the three generations might be ranked among ignoble heathens, and that there was nothing of christianity therein but the product of self-flattering nature—no expression holding forth any thing of Christ or of His grace or sanctifying spirit. Yet this man went on drawing disciples after him, having his person and practice in admiration.

The Patron, a gracious gentleman, Mr. Rowley, invited him to one of these monthly meetings at Antrim. He, undertaking the journey with the Patron, gave it out confidently that he would confute and silence all the ministers. They, at their meeting, hearing of his boasting, engaged Mr. Blair to encounter him, lest the people among whom he lived should be ensnared by him to the great prejudice of the Gospel. So they met at the Castle of Antrim, where the Patron and he had waited for a disputation. Mr. Freeman would choose both the matter and manner of the procedure. The matter was the doctrine of reprobation, and he to impugn. They told him that another method was better, but withal gave way to his. The first argument he brought, was easily answered and retorted back upon himself; the second had the same issue. But he, keeping still his ground and humour, told them he was coming on with the strength of his arguments. But the Lord did smite him with such confusion that he spoke nonsense, so that the scribe could set down nothing of it. All the hearers were sensible of this, and some fell a laughing. The Patron, turning to Mr. Blair, said, "You know what he would be at, set it in order and give an answer unto it;" to whom Mr. Blair replied, How could he know, seeing he knew not himself; but, said Mr. Blair, "seeing it is late, and you all see him in confusion, let him recollect his thoughts, and we shall meet in this place next morning." Mr. Blair came to the place appointed, where he did not find him; and so, going to his chamber, he found him with his Patron, writing out arguments from an Arminian author, Grevinchovius.* Mr. Blair, snatching the book out of his hand, said to him, "Now I perceive your subdolous dealing," and so he began to catechise him, asking him if he believed all events came to pass according to the determinate counsel of God? to which he answered by a flat denial, bringing a number of his arguments. "Then," said Mr. Blair, "how know you not that it is written, 'He hath determined the times before appointed and the bounds of their habitation,' but you say you would take a course of your own, and would not seek the Lord, behold, then, you do violence to and contradict the Scriptures." His answer was that what he had cited of Scripture was no where written in the Bible. Mr. Blair, perceiving his gross and bold ignorance, desired the Patron to cast up Acts xvii. 26, 27. This being done, he could say nothing but that he thought there had been no such thing in the Scripture. "Then," said Mr. Rowley, "we need no more disputation. I see evidently his erroneousness and ignorance of the Scriptures." "Mr. Freeman." said he, "I have followed you too long, here I renounce you, I will have no more to do with you."

So Mr. Blair and he were left alone to confer together, where he told him that when he saw some of his papers, he perceived he was ill grounded in religion, and, by what now had appeared, very ignorant of the Scriptures. He thanked Mr. Blair that when others did laugh at him yesternight, he did not so, but spoke to him meekly and gravely. But Mr. Blair dealt plainly with him, and told him that perceiving him to be of a melancholy temper, though he had carried hitherto jokingly, yet, when he should lay matters to heart he might

---

* Grevinchovius was a noted Dutch Arminian divine, who flourished in the early part of the seventeenth century. He was obliged to leave Holland after the Synod of Dort, in 1618.

be in danger of distraction, for, if he still carried jokingly, he might be in hazard to turn loose and openly profane. He offered no answer, but showed by his smiles a waving of Mr. Blair's warning; but the event followed sadly, for he being deserted of the people who formerly admired him, turned very solitary, and at last fell into mischievous practices.

CHAPTER III.

FALSE EXCITEMENT AT LARNE—DEPOSITION OF BLAIR AND OTHERS—THEIR DIFFICULTIES AND RESTORATION—SECOND DEPOSITION—PROPOSED REMOVAL TO NEW ENGLAND—RETURN FROM SEA—DANGERS OF THE MINISTERS—ESCAPE TO SCOTLAND—DEATH OF CUNNINGHAM—MR. BLAIR PROPOSES TO GO TO FRANCE.

THE Gospel was flourishing by the ministry of His servants before mentioned—no public opposition being made thereunto. All Satan's devices proving abortive, he was at last let loose to devise a pernicious device. There being many converts in all these congregations, the Destroyer did set himself mainly against the people about Lough Larne—by this stratagem playing the ape upon some ignorant persons, and did counterfeit the work of the Lord in the midst of the public worship. These persons fell a mourning, and some of them were affected with pangs like convulsions;* and daily the number of them increased. At first both pastors and people pitying them had charitable thoughts, thinking it probable it was the work of the Lord; but thereafter, in conference, they could find nothing to confirm these charitable thoughts. They could neither perceive any sense of their sinfulness nor any panting after a Saviour. So the minister of the place did write to some of the brethren to come thither, and with him to examine the matter. They, coming and conferring with these persons, found it to be mere delusion and cheat of Satan to slander and disgrace the work of the Lord. And the very next day one of Mr. Blair's charge, in the midst of public worship, being a

---

* These manifestations strongly resemble much that was witnessed in 1859. We here see that the early Presbyterian ministers judged very correctly respecting them.

dull and ignorant person, made a noise, stretching her body incontinent. Mr. Blair rebuked that lying spirit which disturbed the worship of God, charging the same, in the name and authority of Jesus Christ, not to disturb the congregation; and, through God's mercy, they met with no more of that work. All this was so notoriously known that Primate Ussher got word of it; and the next time Mr. Blair saw him, said he had reason to bless the Lord, who had assisted him so confidently to conjure, as he worded it, that lying spirit. Yet for all this, a matter of accusation was brought against the ministers, as if they had taught the necessity of a new birth by bodily pangs and throes.*

The cause of these accusations was Mr. Henry Leslie, who, being a violent and vain-glorious man† envying the credit and respect these ministers had of all good people, entertained correspondence with one Mr. John Maxwell, minister at Edinburgh, who was gaping for a Bishopric;‡ and they so dressed the matter between them that the said Maxwell carried a letter from Leslie to the Court, containing the calumnies and accusations formerly mentioned. The timorous Bishop of Down, getting some notice of this, thought it time to bestir himself, and presently suspended four of the ministers, Mr. Dunbar, Mr. Blair, Mr. Welsh, and Mr. Livingston—whereupon Mr. Blair presently had recourse to Primate Ussher, speaking somewhat of an appeal which he never intended to make use of. But he presently wrote to Bishop Echlin to relax that erroneous suspension—which was instantly done. So, for a season, they went on in

---

* The same absurd accusation was preferred against some parties interested in the Revival of 1859.
† Leslie was now Dean of Down. In 1635 he succeeded Echlin as Bishop of Down and Connor, and after the Restoration was promoted to the Bishopric of Meath.
‡ In 1633 he was made Bishop of Ross, in Scotland. He was afterwards Bishop of Killala.

C

their ministry, till a letter came from Court, the substance whereof was that accusation formerly mentioned, requiring the examination of the truth thereof, and to censure accordingly. The Bishop, knowing presently the falsehood of the accusation, and concealing the contents of his majesty's letter which was just and fair, took another way. He cited the four ministers he had suspended, and urged them to a subscription. They, in defence, answered that there was neither law nor canon then in the kingdom requiring the same. Notwithstanding, he, out of his cruelty, proceeded to the sentence of deposition, May, 1632. Primate Ussher, being acquainted with this, was very sorry, but said he could not help it; yet desired them to make their address to the two Lord Chief Justices, who then, under his majesty, governed the kingdom. Mr. Blair, repairing to them, received for answer that there was no redress to be had but from the king himself, to whom that misinformation had come; and so Mr. Blair, by the earnest persuasion of his brethren, was soon persuaded to undertake a journey to England. This and some more toil which befel him was revealed to him before it came to pass, together with the event (as follows) which he disclosed to none but Mr. Cunningham. This journey of Mr. Blair to England was much censured in the judgments of some wise men, who seemed to know the times best, it being (they thought) altogether needless to complain at Court of what Bishops had done to such as he, they having such power and interest at Court, and none durst appear for those that were disaffected to Episcopal government. Though he had letters to the Scotch noblemen who were at Court, and was well acquainted with the secretary of Scotland* (his eldest son having been his best beloved scholar at Glasgow), yet he did forecast all the difficulties mentioned; and, notwithstanding,

---

* William Alexander, first Earl of Stirling.

resolved to bestow pains and charges to seek redress, committing the event to Him who is a King over kings, and hath all hearts in His hand. He had but one argument:—The king is the ordinance of God as a refuge under God for the oppressed. They had used all other means, and ought not to neglect the highest. If their desire were granted—viz. that the truth of the information against them might be tried, they had gained their point; and, if refused, they had endeavoured their utmost duty, satisfying their own consciences, and refuting those who say ordinarily they leave and forsake their ministry.

So he set forth on the journey in company with some merchants; and was, though not used to such long journeys, more than ordinarily helped in strength of body even beyond these merchants who used to travel that way—which they ascribed to his errand; and there were many prayers for him at that time, especially by many praying people concerned in his journey, both in his own parish and in the other three, and likewise by other congregations who yet enjoyed their own pastors. Toward the entry upon his journey a sudden fit of the gravel seized on him when he was riding, threatening the stopping his journey. But while he was riding, and lying on the crutch of the saddle, his heart cried earnestly to God that he would be pleased to spare him till he was better accommodated for it; which was no sooner spoken than granted. Shortly after his coming to Court, which then lay at Greenwich, the king's progress being begun, he was promised by the Earl of Stirling, that, if the petition was sent to him by the king, he should have a speedy despatch according to his mind, without expense either of time or money. He promised the more liberally because he never expected it would be sent to him. But Mr. Blair, thinking that the whole difficulty lay therein, bended up all the earnestness he could in prayer and dexterity of endeavours, to have it carried so. And so it was carried. He therein was overjoyed, so that he did leap for joy. But when the fearful man failed in performing his promise, fearing Bishop Laud more than God, he was much dejected in Greenwich Park. Thereat he fell to the ground praying fervently, though briefly, almost in the same words—submitting all his enjoyments, yea, his life itself, for the liberty of enjoying gospel ordinances; and, after the third time, his great heaviness was removed, his prayer taken off his hand, and, as he conceived, granted; though then he saw no probable means how to attain the same. But the means he thought would undo the business (to wit the Secretary of England) was the Lord's means to do the same. But he was put to great pains and charges in following the king's progress to the New Forest, beside Bewly; where he lay in the fields all night, not without danger of his life—the Lord making an Irish gentleman, who was driven to the same necessity with him, his guard in the night when robbers did beset them. This time and place the Lord made choice of to bear through his petition, when no bishops were with the king. Yea, his majesty, perusing the draught penned by the Secretary, in answer to his petition, did, with his own hand, insert a clause which he durst not petition for—viz. that if the information made to him proved false, the informer should be punished. Upon this he assured all men as he had occasion, that there was not a more just prince on earth, he being rightly informed.[*] The Secretary's servants told Mr. Blair that their master had been put to more pains in this, than in any particular of that kind; and that his majesty had taken more

---

[*] This was not the only occasion on which Blair was in the royal presence. After the death of the Rev. Alexander Henderson, he was selected by the unhappy monarch as his chaplain. He was more acceptable to Charles than any other Presbyterian minister of the age.

inspection thereof than ordinary; for, he being far from the Court, a-hunting, had no Bishop with him. The letter was directed to Strafford; so he went home, and was overjoyed with great joy, especially considering he had brought a favourable letter from the king. The politicians, who had blamed his going before, were silent, and thought there was somewhat in it which they understood not. But godly people were saddened for this, that he to whom the letter was directed, was not yet come to Ireland, and came not for almost a twelvemonth; and yet this was rather an advantage, for the letter, though it did not take off the sentence, yet did weaken the same, so that they went on teaching their people—only *propter formam*, they went not up to the pulpit, but stood by the precentor. At last, the Lord Deputy coming over, Mr. Blair went to Dublin, and delivered his majesty's letter, which he utterly slighted, telling him he had his majesty's mind in his bosom. He reviled the Church of Scotland, and menaced Mr. Blair, desiring him to come to his right wits, and then he should be regarded. Mr. Blair perceiving his rage (which he thereafter excused to be affected only, and not real, to draw forth the pride of a Puritan) came no more to him, but went to Primate Ussher; and when he heard how that lofty man had answered the king's letter, his eyes watered for sorrow. Mr. Blair returning found his friends celebrating the Lord's Supper, who were exceedingly grieved that the king's letter had no other effect. Yet the hard usage Mr. Blair met with had some good effect; for after some space that wise and gracious man, Sir Andrew Stewart, making a visit to the Lord Deputy, and commending his other actings, convinced him that he had not done well in using so roughly a minister of the gospel, bringing to him his majesty's letter; and further enquired if that man's carriage had provoked him. The Lord Deputy confessed that the man's carriage had been very modest, humble and courteous—but now, says he, let us help it the best way we can; and so, according to the advice of the said Sir Andrew, he wrote to the Bishop of Down that he would grant them a time—viz. six months. This came when all their hopes were gone, in May, 1634. The first who told Mr. Blair of it, and who had heard of it at Antrim, was thought by him to be drunk—when the man was fasting, he used so great diligence to come to him. After that Mr. Blair, for three nights, slept none at all—the first night was spent in admiration; the second in praises to God, with such of his charge as used solemnly to pray with him; the third, the letter being now delivered and they formally free to act in their public ministry, he could not rest, remembering the next day was the ordinary day of his lecture at Bangor, and he was then distant from it fourteen miles—so he arose and stole away from the rest; but, ere he could reach Bangor, there was there assembled a great congregation, not only of his own flock, but out of neighbouring congregations, being all overjoyed. Mr. Josias Welsh told him that his wife, in his absence at London, told him, let none who call on the name of the Lord doubt but all of you who are now silenced shall preach in your own pulpits, but it will be but a short time. He said he was offended then at her peremptory words; but knowing her otherwise to be most modest, he now perceived she knew more of the mind of God than they did. Before she sickened, she was forewarned her end was come, and sickened the next day.

These six months, granted to them, were well improved; and the people made more progress in the ways of God than ever before. The four silenced ministers, preaching together at a monthly meeting, did cause such joy as could hardly be expressed. And, when their time was well near expired, that excellent gentleman who before was instrumental, had procured a new prorogation for other six months, the warrant whereof was come to Mr. Blair's hands. But that violent man, Bishop Bramhall, of Derry, with all importunity extorting from Mr. Blair a dispute about kneeling in receiving the Lord's Supper—wherein he succumbed in the judgment of the conformed clergy, denying the Papists were idolaters in adoring the host in the mass—procured from the Lord Deputy the recalling of his second letter; and so all hopes of longer liberty were cut off. They closed with solemn celebrating the Lord's Supper, and delivered up their people to the great Bishop of Souls from whom they had received their charge; and, being convened the third time, received the sentence of deposition; at which time Mr. Blair cited the Bishop* to appear before the tribunal of Jesus Christ to make answer for that wicked deed; to which he replied, "I appeal from justice to mercy." But Mr. Blair said his appellation was like to be rejected, seeing he acted against the light of his conscience. Shortly thereafter he sickened; and when his physician, Doctor Maxwell, came to him, and enquired what ailed him, he was long silent (as also he had been silent for many days before he took bed), and at last, with great difficulty, he uttered these words, "It's my conscience, man;" to which the Doctor replied—"I have no cure for that." This report the Doctor made to the old Lord of Ards, who forbad him to repeat that to any other. But his daughter-in-law, the Lady Ards, replied—"No man shall get that report suppressed, for I shall bear witness of it to the glory of God, who hath smitten that man for suppressing Christ's witnesses."† After this deposition Bishop Bramhall

---

* Echlin, Bishop of Down and Connor.
† The deposition of the ministers took place in November, 1634, and Echlin died on the 17th of July, 1635. The conversation which took place between Blair and the Bishop at their last interview is preserved in a manuscript, published by Dr. Reid.—*History Presbyterian Church in Ireland*, I. 175.

did hunt out his pursuivants to apprehend them,* yet they preached ordinarily in their own houses and in other friend's houses.

A little before this deposition—in February, 1634—the ministers and Christians, having no hope to be freed from the Prelate's tyranny, appointed Mr. Livingston, together with William Wallace,† to go to New England, to try the condition of the country, and agree for a place to settle in: for which end they were to go to London and take opportunity of shipping there with the first ship in the spring, and return by the first convenience. But Providence crossed their design—first, by keeping them fourteen days and more at Groomsport for wind, made their going to London too late, so that the first ships were gone before they reached it; and then, embarking in another, storms and contrary winds beat them back. And Mr. Wallace took so ill with the sea that physicians advised him not to go forward; and it having been so ordered by the ministers in Ireland that Mr. Livingston should not go alone, they returned a little before the four deposed ministers (whereof Mr. Livingston was one) got their liberty. Shortly after, in June, the Lord called home worthy Mr. Welsh. Mr. Blair and Mr. Livingston, hearing of his dangerous sickness the Sabbath before, came to Templepatrick in the night-time. Among many gracious edifying expressions he had also some wrestling. One time when he said "Oh, for hypocrisy," Mr. Blair said to the great company of Christians there present, "See how Satan nibbles at his heel when he is going over the threshold to heaven." A little after, Mr. Livingston being at prayer at his bed-side, and the word "Joy" coming out of his mouth, he took hold

---

* The Bishops at this time were authorised by Government to throw men into prison.

† William Wallace is described by Livingston, in his Life, as "a good man and a learned Humanist." At one time he taught a Latin School at Stirling, and under him Livingston received an excellent classical education.

of his hand, and desiring him to cease a little, clapping both his hands, cried—"Joy, joy, joy, for evermore," and then desired him to go on in prayer, and then, within a little expired.

Mr. Livingston's testimony to these ministers and the churches of the North of Ireland, at that time, is worthy of observing. Speaking of the monthly meetings of Antrim, he witnesses that there was never any jar or jealousy among these ministers, nor among the professors, the greatest part of them being Scotch, and a good number of gracious English, all whose contests were to prefer others to themselves. And though the gifts of the ministers were much different, yet it was not observed that the hearers followed any to the undervaluing of others. Many of these religious professors had been profane, and for debt, and want, and worse causes had left Scotland, yet the Lord was pleased by His word to work such a change, that he said he did not think there were any more lively experienced Christians than were these of that time; and that of good numbers, yea, of persons of a good outward condition in the world. Being but lately brought in, the lively edge was not off them, and the perpetual fear that the prelates would put away their ministers, made them with great hunger wait on the ordinances—he testifying he hath known some who have come several miles from their own houses to the communion, to the Saturday's sermon, and spent the whole Saturday night in several companies—sometimes a minister being with them—sometimes themselves alone in conference and prayer, and waited on the public ordinances the whole Sabbath day, and spent the Sabbath night likewise; and yet all the Monday's sermon not troubled with sleepiness, and so, not have slept till they went home. Because of their holy righteous carriage, they were generally reverenced even by the multitude they lived among. Some of them had attained to such a dexterity of speaking of religious purposes by resemblances to worldly things, that, being at feasts and meals, they would, among themselves, entertain a spiritual discourse for a long time; and the others present, though those men spoke good English, could not understand what they said. In those days it was no great difficulty for a minister to preach or pray in public, such was the hunger of the hearers; and it was hard to judge whether there was more of the Lord's presence in the public or in the private meetings.

In winter, 1635, the deposed and excommunicated ministers perceived no appearance of liberty, either to preachers or professors, from the bondage of the prelates. There were a number in the North of Ireland now fixedly resolved (as they had attempted before), to transport themselves to New England; and others of their friends resolved to follow them. They had got letters from the Governors and Council full of kind invitations, and large promises of good accommodation. They built a ship near Belfast, called the *Eagle's Wing* [of] about a hundred and fifteen tons burthen.* They were minded to set sail in the spring of 1636, but through difficulties that use to rise in such undertakings, in preparing the ship with other accommodations, it was September following before they set sail. They were in all passengers to go, about 140, of whom the chief were Messrs. Blair, Livingston, Hamilton, M'Clelland, Stewart, Provost of Ayr,† Archibald Campbell, David Girwin, &c.; among whom was one Andrew Brown, of the Parish of Larne, born deaf and dumb, who had been a very vicious man. But when it pleased the

---

* Others say 150 tons.

† Livingston, in his *Characteristics*, describes John Stewart, Provost of Ayr, as "a godly and zealous Christian of long standing." He stuttered, says Livingston, "so as one could hardly understand what he said, and yet I have oft heard him pray as distinctly as any man could speak."

Lord to work a change on several of that parish, a very sensible change was found on him, not only in forsaking of his old courses, but joining himself to religious people in all the exercises of God's worship, both public and private, and ordinarily, both morning and evening, he used to go alone to prayer, and used to weep. By attending sermons, and by such signs as those who were acquainted with him understood, he would express many signs of the work of God on his spirit, so that, upon his earnest desire, with the consent of all the ministers that used to meet at Antrim, he was admitted to the Lord's Supper. All the ministers were abundantly clear that the Lord approved their undertaking, and much prayer, with fasting, was gone about for a blessing to it; yet Mr. Blair and Mr. Livingston in that time often said that it was impressed on their mind that they would never go to New England.

In August, 1636, the rest of the honest ministers were deposed.* They had much toil in their preparation for so great a voyage, and both sad and glad hearts in taking leave of their friends; for they found, in the midst of outward grief, hearts well refreshed both in public and private. That which grieved their friends was, that neither could they be ready to go with them, neither could they heartily pray for a prosperous voyage to them. Yea, some of them prayed that, after the Lord had caused them to go down to the sea and be tossed a while in the depths, he would bring them back again.

At last, on the 9th of September, 1636, they loosed from

---

* In the Adair Manuscript there is at this place a parenthesis with the words, "Here remember to bring in the dispute at Belfast if it can be got." In the margin at the same place there is the following note—"This dispute was between the Bishop of Down and Mr. James Hamilton, of Ballywalter, a copy whereof Mr. Robert Dalway hath, 1721." Dr. Reid has published the document here referred to in his *History of the Presbyterian Church in Ireland*, I. 186.

Lough Fergus; and being a while detained, through contrary winds, at Lough Ryan and about the Isle of Bute, they had fair weather till they were between three and four hundred leagues from Ireland, and nearer the banks of Newfoundland than any part of Europe. But if ever the Lord spake by the winds and other dispensations, it was made evident to them that it was not his will they should go to New England; for, first they met with a mighty hurricane out of the North West, that brake one of the great master joists, made to go cross the middle of the ship. There were no waves there, but mountains of waters. They had experience of what is written Psalm cvii. They sprung a leak that gave them 700 strokes of water, pumped within the two houred glass; yet they lay to a long time to beat out that storm. In the time of the violence of the storm, he that was at the rudder and the pilot came wringing his hands, and with a lamentable voice cried "Now God have mercy upon us, for we are all gone ; the ship will not answer the rudder, it's either broken or driven off the hinges; but, however, there is no safety for us." Mr. Blair hearing this, being sore sick, and then, as frequently being led out from the cabin, did most confidently, like another Paul—Acts xxvii.—express such hopes that rather than the Lord would suffer such a company and such sort to perish, if the ship should break, he would put wings to their shoulders, and carry them as on eagle's wings—Deut. xxxii.—safe ashore. One of the company, a shipwright, hearing Mr. Blair so confidently express himself, to the great encouragement of all, steps out, saying "I will venture my life for the safety of all the rest, for if some one do it not, infallibly we are all gone." So they did tie him about the middle with clothes and ropes as he directed, and tied to him such instruments and materials as he desired, and as they judged necessary for the purpose, and then let him down to the rudder, holding in their hands a long rope tied about the middle. This man did so fix the rudder, that it not only served them all the while till they came ashore, but after this voyage the ship made a Spanish voyage with the same helm. Thus the Lord wonderfully delivered them out of that deadly danger. One morning the master and company came and told them it was impossible for them to hold out any longer, and though they should beat out that storm, they would be sure to meet with one or two more of that sort before they could reach New England. After prayer, when they were consulting what to do, Mr. Livingston proposed an overture wherewith he was perplexed thereafter— viz. that seeing they had the Lord's warrant for their intended voyage, however it be presumption to propose a sign to him, yet they being in such a strait, and having stood out some days already, they might for 24 hours yet stand to it, and if in that time he were pleased to calm the storm and send a fair wind, they might take it for an approbation of their advancing, otherwise they should return. To this they all agreed. But that day and the next thereafter they had the sorest storm that they had felt. So all almost begin to think of returning, only Mr. Blair was not yet clear to return; whereupon they all resolved to lay it over on him—that if he, after seeking God by earnest prayer, did still continue resolute to go forward, they would do so; but if he were moved to be of their mind, they should presently turn sail. Mr. Blair, hearing that the determination of so dangerous and important a business was laid over on him alone, did fall into a fit of fainting, but, shortly recovering, he was determined to be of their mind. So all of them resolved, and took it for granted, that it was the Lord's will they should return; so that next morning at daylight they turned and made good way with a main cross and a little top sail;

and, after some tossing, did at last come to Lough Fergus, November 3rd. During all this time, amidst such dangers and troubles, the most part of the passengers were most cheerful and confident. Some of them said they never, in all their days, thought the days so short as all that while, though they slept some nights not above two hours, and some not at all; but stood, most part, in the gallery and stern of the great cabin, where Mr. Blair and Mr. Livingston's family lay. For in the morning, by the time every one had been some time alone, and then at prayer in their several societies, and then at public prayer in the ship, it was time to go to dinner; and after dinner they did visit their friends in the gun-room, or those between the decks, or any who were sick, and then public prayer, afternoon, did come, and after that supper and family exercise. One aged person and one child died, and were buried in the sea. A woman brought forth a child, whom Mr. Livingston baptized and called him *Seaborn*.

Returning home, though at present they could not know what to make of this dispensation, yet they were confident God in time would let them see his mind in it to their satisfaction. Coming near Ireland, the greatest part inclined to set to sea again next spring, blaming themselves they had begun their voyage, winter approaching. But Mr. Blair said though he had been the last man who was induced to return, yet they, having made a fair offer of their service and themselves to God, and the Lord having accepted of their offer, he thought they had done enough to testify their willing mind to glorify God that way. And for himself he did not resolve to make a new attempt, seeing the Lord had, by such speaking providences, made it evident to them that it was not his will they should glorify him in America, he having work for them at home. The rest, hearing him thus express himself, both ministers and others were of his mind. That which most troubled them was, they were like to be signs and wonders, and a very mockery to the wicked, who would laugh and flout at their enterprise. But Mr. Blair, after much sad exercise thereanent, at last very confidently did assure them, that though the wicked should mock them, yet the Lord would so far incline their mind, that they should be glad at their return and welcome them. For he, lecturing on Psalm lxv. 7.—which was their last lecture at sea, and his ordinary text, said—as the Lord hath given us a wonderful proof of his omnipotency and kindness in stilling the noise of the sea and its waves; so shall the Lord as evidently give us a proof of his sovereignty and dominion over the spirits and tempers of wicked people, in stilling and calming their tumults among whom they were to live a space. And the Lord fulfilled the word of His servant, so that they were not mocked but welcomed even by the wicked. Yet the prelates and their favourers were much dismayed at their return; but neither they nor themselves knew that, within one year, the Lord would not only root out the prelates in Scotland, and after that, out of England and Ireland, but make some of them, particularly Mr. Blair, Mr. Livingston, and Mr. M'Clelland, singularly instrumental in the work of Reformation. Their outward means were much impaired by the sea voyage and blessed disappointment; for they put much of their stocks in provision for a plantation, and some in merchandize, which they behoved to sell at low rates; and had provided themselves with servants for fishing and building, whom they were necessitated to turn off, and the ministers' books were much spoiled through the sea-water in the storms. Mr. Blair did that winter dwell at the Stroane, at Belfast,* in the house of one Archibald Miller. Mr. Livingston returned to his mother-in-law's house. They

---

* The word *Strone-town* is here written in the margin—perhaps Strandtown, near Ballymacarrett.

both preached each Sabbath that winter, as they had done before, notwithstanding the prelates hounding out their pursuivants and other emissaries to apprehend them. In February, 1637, one Frank Hill, of Castlereagh, who yet came some Sabbaths to their meetings, being in Dublin, informed the State against Mr. Blair and Mr. Livingston, so that order was given for their apprehension. One night, one Andrew Young, a servant of Mr. Bell's, who did dwell hard by Mr. Livingston, overheard a pursuivant calling on a stabler to prepare against to-morrow morning two horses for him and another, because they had orders to go to the North and bring up two Scotch deposed ministers. This Andrew, immediately going to another stabler,* got a horse, and rode all that night; and in two days after brought them word. So they went out of the way, and went to Scotland.

When they came to Irvine, and to Mr. David Dickson, they learned that some good gentlemen of that country had been with him, and had desired him not to employ them to preach, for fear the prelates (they being then upon urging the service-book) should take occasion from that to put him from his ministry. "But," said Mr. Dickson, "I dare not be of your opinion, nor follow your counsel so far as to discountenance these worthies, now when they are suffering for Christ, so as not to employ them as in former times. Yea, I would think my so doing would so far provoke the Lord that I might, upon another account, be deposed, and not have so good a conscience." Upon the other hand, Mr. Blair and Mr. Livingston were unwilling to occasion trouble to Mr. Dickson, or dissatisfy any gentleman in the country. But he urged them upon such grounds that they could not refuse to preach at Irvine, or everywhere else as they got a

---

* *i.e.*, keeper of post-horses.

call; and they were always employed, either in public preaching or private meetings. All the rest of the ministers were forced to fly out of Ireland. Mr. Cunningham came to Irvine, and died, March 29, 1637. He had many great experiences of God's goodness, and much peace in his suffering. He spake much and well to the Presbytery of Irvine who came to see him; and, a little before his death, his wife sitting on a low bed where he lay, and having her hand upon his head, he was in prayer, recommending his flock in Holywood to the great Shepherd, and his dear acquaintances and children. At last he said, "Lord, I commend to thy care her who is now no more my wife," and with that he thrust away her hand, and after a while died. Mr. Blair made these verses on him, which are engraven on his grave-stone:—

> Hic Cunninghami recubat Roberti
> Corpus. O qualis genius latebat,
> Quamque divinus fragili involutus
> Pulvere in isto!
>
> Acrius nemo intonuit superbis;
> Nemo dejectos magis erigebat;
> Sed Dei laudes celebrando, vicit
> Seque aliosque.*

---

* The following is an old poetic translation of this epitaph:—
> "Here rests—O, venerable name—
> The dust of Robert Cunninghame;
> Ah! what a mind was there concealed,
> By Christian loveliness reveal'd;
> And what a soul of heavenly worth,
> Inspir'd that frame of fragile earth,
> None to the proud, with holier awe
> Thunder'd the terrors of the law;
> And none with more persuasive art
> Cheer'd the disconsolate in heart;
> But, Oh! intent his God to praise,
> He shorten'd his terrestrial days;
> For, preaching Jesus Crucified,
> He others and himself outdid."

At the beginning of the [second] Reformation in Scotland, things looking difficult and dangerous, Mr. Blair renewed his old resolution for France, and took a call to be minister to Colonel Hepburn's regiment. Prelate Spotswood, then Chancellor, had threatened he should not stay within the King's dominions. Thereupon, he embarked at Leith with a number of profane soldiers. But being vexed with their profanity and swearing, and reproving them, one of them— a Highlandman—drew his dirk and vowed to stab him. He resolved to return; and, coming over the side of the ship, his foot did slide, and he was in hazard to fall into the water; but, a rope providentially hanging over the side of the ship, he took hold of it, and hung till he was relieved. When he came to John Mein's* house in Edinburgh, he was received with great joy of his friends who had protested and prayed against that undertaking. His first wife's sister —John Mein's wife—brought him paper, and pen and ink, desiring him to write a Petition to the Council, and the good women of the town would present it; which he did, and it was given to the treasurer Traquair, as he went into the Council, by the women—a great company of godly women being present. And after [wards] things grew more hopeful, and he had a call to Ayr, which he embraced. Thereafter, at the Assembly of Glasgow, 1638, he was transported to St. Andrews, sore against his will. When he was in Ayr, and Mr. Livingston at Stranraer, multitudes of people came from Ireland to their communions, and brought their children over to be baptized.† And many took up their

---

* John Mein, merchant in Edinburgh, was Mr. Blair's brother-in-law. "He used, summer and winter, to rise about three o'clock in the morning, and always sing some Psalm as he put on his clothes; and spent till six o'clock alone in religious exercises, and at six worshipped God with his family."—*Livingston's Characteristics.*

† Livingston in his Life says—"Some of our friends out of Ireland came and dwelt at Stranraer; and at our communions, twice in the year, great numbers used to come—at one time 500 persons—and at one time I baptized 28 children brought out of Ireland."

habitation in Ayr, and Irvine, and Stranraer; things growing more and more troublesome in Ireland through the Black Oath and Black Ban*. But God ordered it so, that they, by that means, escaped the cruelty of the Irish in the time of the Rebellion [in 1641] wherein the bulk of swearing and worldly people, who regarded not the gospel, were cut off or escaped naked.

* *i.e.*, Band.

CHAPTER IV.

CONTINUED SUFFERINGS—TUMULT IN EDINBURGH, AND OVERTHROW OF PRELACY IN SCOTLAND—THE BLACK OATH—COALITION BETWEEN PAPISTS AND PRELATISTS—ABOUNDING WICKEDNESS—USSHER'S PREDICTION—STRAFFORD'S PROCEEDINGS.

BUT I return to consider more particularly the state of things after the ministers came back to Carrickfergus Lough, and laid aside their design for America. As was said, according to Mr. Blair's prediction, some had compassion on them; yet the Bishops showed no mercy to them wearied with a long and dangerous voyage, and wasted in their bodies, spirits, and estates; but grew more violent in their persecution not only of them, but of those left behind, both ministers and people. So that now it was not summoning to their courts, and taking a little money from the people for their nonconformity, nor deposing ministers; but they proceeded to excommunication of all who would not come up to their length, upon which they obtained writs, "de excommunicato capiendo," for those excommunicated, both ministers and people; and pursuivants were sent forth to apprehend them, and many people were taken and imprisoned. Yet, through God's special providence, the ministers escaped to Scotland, some of them very narrowly, and by singular stratagems of Providence, even when they were upon the water in their enemies' hands—as Mr. Colwort and Mr. M'Clelland, and before that, Mr. Blair and Mr. Livingston, mentioned before. And after the ministers, many of the people followed to Scotland with what small stocks they had; and lived sparingly upon them, as strangers in the land (though their native land), till God should give an out-gate. The ministers haunted in the west country, in Galloway, in Carrick, and about Irvine and Ayr, together with diverse of the most noted and principal professors. There were two persons at that time made singularly instrumental for their comfort, besides many others of the godly in those places. Mr. David Dickson, minister at Irvine, for his eminency in the work of God, and very singular fruitfulness and blessing following upon his labours, and refusing conformity, had been some years before that removed from his place, and confined in a little village in the west of Scotland. But, through God's mercy to that part of the vineyard, and the intercessions of persons of quality, he was restored again to his place in the full and free exercise of his ministry. He, upon the coming of those worthy ministers, Mr. Blair, Mr. Cunningham, and Mr. Ridge, did employ them to preach publickly in his church in Irvine—though, to his great hazard, things then in Scotland coming to the greatest height and crisis. This to these ministers was a great privilege, and to the people a great mercy. In the meantime, Mr. Cunningham died in Irvine, as before related.

There was a gentleman in Carrick,* called Fergus M'Cabbin, left a considerable patrimony by his father, and being able, was at that time a Gaius, who entertained ministers and professors coming from Ireland, as if he had been appointed to keep a public inn for them, and that not for a night or week, but ordinarily—insomuch that his natural friends said he would presently exhaust his estate with such dealing. But he professed and found the contrary, that he grew richer; and it always prospered better with him, not only then but to his dying day. As this was a mercy to him, so was it a special mercy to them who were entertained by him, and encouraged others to do the like. But the Bishops of Scotland, hearing

---

* In Ayrshire.

of these strangers coming from Ireland in this capacity, and driving on the same design with those in Ireland, begin to threaten them early and trouble them, insomuch that they begin to think of removing to some other church abroad; and Mr. Blair, undertaking his voyage to France, did embark at Leith, and was, by contrary winds and tempests, kept in the roads divers days, till (with other concurring occasions, as was said before) he was forced to return—others of them lurking in parts of the country, where they had relations or acquaintances.

Now comes to be recorded God's signal, and indeed wonderful appearing for his distressed people, not only for that little handful who were driven from Ireland for preserving their consciences, but for his people in Scotland, who, at that time, were brought to the point of extremity and despair as to human help; as well as those of England, who were Nonconformists. For in England, by means of Laud, Bishop of Canterbury, and those of his faction, the godly were brought to great extremity, through banishment, fining, and imprisonments; and things were running in the high road to popery—as may be more clearly seen in the histories of those times anent England, and in a little piece called "The Canterburian's Self-conviction," writ by worthy Baillie.*

And in Scotland the Bishops, after long encroachments on the liberties of Christ's church and kingdom, and bitter persecution of the godly there, had brought their designs to such height that there was a Service-book compiled in England by Laud, of Canterbury, with the help of some Scotch Bishops most infected with Arminianism and Popery; and calculated for the present state of Scotland—some things seeming more condescending to the genius of that church, but

---

* Baillie was afterwards one of the Commissioners from the Church of Scotland to the Westminster Assembly, and Professor of Divinity at Glasgow. His "Canterburian's Self-conviction" appeared in 1640.

otherwise having in it more of the poison of superstition and error than the old Common Prayer Book of England. This book being now prepared, was, by the King's proclamation, from authority, not only recommended, but imposed upon all ministers in their respective churches, to be there used within fourteen days after intimation given, and that under the highest pains. And, because the city of Edinburgh was the most eminent place of the kingdom, and where the King's council and seat of justice were kept, and the Bishops ordinarily frequenting it, they thought fit to begin the practice of this new form in that place, that it might be a leading to other places of the kingdom. And so the day is appointed, and the Bishop of Edinburgh, with his Dean, is to read it first in the High Church of that city, where the Lords of Council and Session, with the Bishop's people in the town, usually attended the public worship. Thus, when they were met, having brought the new book with them, and the Dean (after their private public devotion performed by themselves in sight of the people)* opening the book in the reader's seat beside the pulpit, where the Bishop sat with his book, there did immediately rise a noise and stir and confusion in the church from a number of well-meaning common people (who among themselves had resolved at all hazards to give a testimony against this horrid innovation) crying out and casting stools at the Dean and Bishop, insomuch that there was a pitiful noise and lamentation—many crying out and casting stools at the Bishop, others standing amazed, as surprised at such an unexpected resistance—till the provost and magistrates commanded their guards or

---

* Adair here refers to a practice common in the Church of England, in conformity with which each individual offers up a private prayer when he appears in the congregation, at the commencement of public worship. Many conceive that such a practice is condemned in Mat. vi., 5, 6, and that secret prayer should not be thus ostentatiously presented.

halberdmen to run amongst the people, and by force drive out of the church all who made any stir. Of this I, being a boy, was eye-witness. And many other passages fell out that day evidencing the people's antipathy to the Bishops and their new Service-book, insomuch that the Bishop and his clergy with great difficulty escaped safe without a mark of God's just judgment upon them for being instrumental in overturning the purity of worship and government in a church where it had been so delivered. However, this was a rash and precipitant act in the multitude, which, in all respects, could not be defended as to the manner of it.* Yet the wonderful Counsellor and Worker brought order out of it; for this beginning of resistance in Edinburgh did so animate the lovers of the Truth in other parts of the kingdom, especially in Fife and in the West country, that within a few days gentlemen of diverse ranks and qualities, and faithful ministers, flocked into the town, and, after consultation among themselves, did petition the King's council against these innovations. Thereafter noblemen did own the cause; and by degrees it grew till they resolved on the renewing the national covenant of Scotland, compiled in that year. And, after that, the Lord carried on that work against much opposition and through many difficulties, which I leave to other histories; only I shall observe this one thing:—That as that famous reformation first begun by Luther was not designed by him at first, but he was led on, step by step, by the special hand of Providence, so it was here. For this first attempt against the book was only by some inferior simple sort of people and well-meaning women, who, for a little time, were punished, and suffered for it. But

---

* It is evident, from the statement here made by Adair, that, so far as he could ascertain, the more sober and influential Presbyterians had no share in this uproar. Janet Geddes and her colleagues acted on their own responsibility.

thereafter God put it in the hearts of others somewhat more considerable to own that affair, and after that in the hearts of the generality of the nation to own it with the hazard of their estates and lives; and, whatever have been the malicious reflections of some men against the proceedings of that church and nation in those times, yet it cannot be denied but God wrought wonders for his people, even as sensibly as he did when he brought Israel out of Egypt and Babylon, and when he brought the church in Luther's time from spiritual Babylon. It cannot be with reason denied (except people will shut their eyes against God) that the fruits of this reformation have been such as manifest it to be from God, [judging] by pure church ordinances erected, the course of Popery stopped, the church purged from errors, and from superstition and idolatry, which were running in like a flood, and many thousands of souls brought to God through the blessing upon the purity and power of ordinances which followed thereupon—yea, such a foundation laid and farther fixed in these nations that the gates of hell shall never prevail against or overturn it.

But to return to what concerns Ireland. Upon occasion of this revolution in Scotland, it becomes a shelter for those of Ireland who had been forced from it. The ministers not only were specially instrumental in these beginnings of reformation together with other worthy ministers in Scotland, but in a short time were fixed in congregations. Mr. Blair, in Ayr for a time, was thereafter by the Assembly transported to St. Andrews, as a place of greater note, and more difficult to find men fit—for being the seat of the Archbishop and Metropolitan of Scotland, and much infested with the corruptions of these times; and also, being the place of two philosophy colleges, and one of divinity. He was planted there as first minister of the principal church, and remained a shining light till his old age, together with the learned and eminently godly Mr. Rutherford,* to whom also Mr. James Wood, a pious and very learned minister, was added thereafter—yet with very small fruit of their ministry in that place.

Mr. Livingston was settled for divers years in Stranraer, where his ministry and holy conversation proved not only a mercy to the place, and to many exiles from Ireland who sojourned there for a considerable time, but a mercy to the country about, the special of whom did attend frequently on his ministry. He was thereafter, by the Assembly, transported to Ancrum, in the South of Scotland—a considerable parish where the Lord did much seal his ministry, by reducing an ignorant and almost barbarous people to the knowledge of Christ; and had many converts. Both Mr. Blair and he died sufferers for that truth they had so long owned—Mr. Blair banished from St. Andrews, and Mr. Livingston in Rotterdam, in Holland; both of them full of days and true honour amongst the godly, flourishing and ripening in their old age; and so came to their graves as a shock of corn in its season.† Mr. Colwort was settled in Paisley, where he lived long an honest minister. Mr. Hamilton—first at Dumfries, and then transported to Edinburgh—lived a long time with universal love and approbation of the godly, and died a sufferer for the truth he had so long owned.‡ Mr. M'Clelland settled at Kirckcudbright, became an eminent minister of Christ, and so lived for a considerable time; yet died before the sad revolution came on the Church of

---

* This was the famous Samuel Rutherford. He was Professor of Divinity at St. Andrews, and afterwards one of the Commissioners of the Church of Scotland to the Westminster Assembly.

† Blair died in 1666, at Meikle-couston, in the Parish of Aberdour, in Scotland. Livingston died in 1672, at Rotterdam, in Holland.

‡ He suffered with his brethren at the Restoration, and died in Edinburgh in 1666.

Scotland. It may be said he was endued with a more than ordinary spirit, not only of ministerial authority and boldness in his Master's work, but of a singular sagacity, whereby from Scripture he did frequently foretell events anent the church and particular persons who were enemies to the church of God; insomuch that his ordinary hearers, observing his warnings coming to pass, would declare it was dangerous to provoke Mr. M'Clelland to speak against them.

There were also many honest people removed at this time, from Ireland to Scotland, partly to enjoy the ordinances, being forced away through persecution; and withal, foreseeing sad things to come on this nation—who continued there a considerable time, in the west country especially. But, in the meantime, during this comfortable respite which the ministers and they had in Scotland, the condition of those remaining still in Ireland grew more hard. For Deputy Strafford, then ruling in Ireland, being a man not only opposite in his principles to the course now on foot in Scotland, but of a severe and jealous temper, began to be jealous of the whole Scotch nation in Ireland, and particularly in the North, [suspecting] that they were on the same design with Scotland, because they went under the same profession of Nonconformists, and were known to be well-wishers to the cause undertaken there; and many of them had gone over there, and joined with the rest in Scotland. This jealousy was not hid from two Scotch Lords (Ards and Claneboy), in the North—on whose lands many of these ministers and people had dwelt,—who found themselves and estates in hazard. And to vindicate themselves that they had no hand in the business of Scotland, there was an oath framed to be imposed on the country as a test of their loyalty (as it was called), wherein they were to abhor the work in Scotland, or any such thing, and obey the King's royal commands. This oath, called by the people "the Black Oath," was (it is said) framed by these two noblemen, and recommended by the Lord Deputy to be urged by authority on the country—which was done with all rigour. The generality did take it who were not bound with a conscience; others hid themselves or fled, leaving their houses, and goods; and divers were imprisoned and kept in diverse gaols for a considerable time. This proved the hottest piece of persecution this poor infant church had met with, and the strongest wind to separate between the wheat and the chaff. However, God strengthened many to hazard all before they would swallow it.

In the County of Down, not only divers left their habitations and most of their goods, and followed to Scotland; but others were apprehended and long imprisoned; amongst whom, as an encourager of the rest, was one Margaret Stewart, a woman eminent for piety and zeal for God, not without Christian discretion; and they were kept long in the prison, till thereafter Wentworth was executed in England. In the County of Antrim, likewise, many were necessitated to flee, wherein they sustained great loss in the goods they left behind them; and yet were provided for, and lived sparingly in Scotland under the Gospel; and those men who were fit for war were made use of in the levies of Scotland about that time. One Fulk Ellis,* an English gentleman, had the most considerable company of soldiers under his command in the whole army, consisting of above one hundred men, who were both resolute and religious, all banished out of Ireland.

The like sufferings befel those of the Scotch nation who were godly in the counties of Tyrone and Londonderry; fewer of them going at first to Scotland, they were subject

---

* Captain Fulk Ellis was the eldest son of Edmond Ellis, of Carrickfergus, an English colonist.—*Reid*, I. 243, note.

to the more suffering. Upon refusing the oath, they had their names returned to Dublin, from whence pursuivants were sent to apprehend those who were refractory. Divers were apprehended and taken prisoners to Dublin, amongst whom was worthy Mrs. Pont*, who remained prisoner nigh three years, and her husband escaping was forced to flee the country. Others, though sent for, yet by special and very remarkable providences, escaped the pursuivants who were most earnest to apprehend them. John Semple (afterwards an honest zealous minister in the Church of Scotland for many years) and Mr. Campbell, of Duke's Hall, a godly man, and the Laird of ——,† were so nigh to be taken by the pursuivants divers times, that it appeared to be more than ordinary providence that they escaped. Particularly one time, John Semple met a pursuivant by the way, who was sent to take him, and John Semple inquired the way; yet the man, having formerly a description of him, did not know him. Another time, the Laird of ——, with Major Stewart and John Semple, came to Newtonstewart together about their affairs. Stewart and Semple lighted at one house, their usual quarters, and the Laird at another. While the former were taking a drink, it was presently told them that three pursuivants were at the door, upon which Major Stewart mounted John Semple on his horse, and gave him his hat, who, being mounted, and riding by the pursuivants, inquired whom they were seeking? They said, " If you will tell us where they are whom we are seeking we will give you a reward." He answered, " It may be I will." " Then," said they, " we are seeking the Laird of —— and John Semple." Then, putting spurs to his horse, he answered, " I

---

* She was the wife of a minister in the neighbourhood of Derry—perhaps the minister of Ramelton. Both husband and wife were zealous Nonconformists.

† There is here a blank in Adair's MS., but the gentleman intended was the Laird of Leckie.—*See Reid's Hist.*, I. 244.

am John Semple, you rogues." While they were calling others to help them to follow him, the Laird took his horse and escaped, and Major Stewart also. The pursuivants, being disappointed, said, "All the devils in hell will not catch these rogues."

Mr. John M'Clelland, being excommunicated by the court in Down, retired up the country to Strabane; and being lodged one night in the house where the woman was a Nonconformist, and it being noticed thereafter, her husband, called William Kennah, was fined in £5 for lodging an excommunicated person one night.

There being a young man, a merchant in Strabane, a Nonconformist, the Bishop of Derry, Bramhall, coming to that place, enquired of the provost what [sort of] a man he was. The provost answered he was a young man, a merchant of the town; the bishop answered, "A young man! he is a young devil." Thus that spirit raged amongst them before the rebellion, persecuting and imprisoning all who would not conform and take the black oath. And there were divers women, eminent in suffering, with patience and courage which become the godly.

There was, about a fortnight before the rebellion broke out, a meeting at Raphoe, at which were the two Leslies, prelates of Raphoe* and Down, and Bishop Maxwell, now made Bishop of Killala, who had been Bishop of Ross, in Scotland, at the beginning of the stir there (who came

---

* John Leslie, Bishop of the Isles, was translated to Raphoe in 1633. He possessed great energy of character, but was more remarkable for his bravery than his piety. Though very far advanced in life at the Restoration, such was his anxiety to be among the first to welcome Charles II. on his arrival in England, that he performed the astonishing feat of riding from Chester to London, a distance of 180 miles, in twenty-four hours. See *Harris' Ware's Bishops of Clogher*. He died Bishop of Clogher in 1671, aged, it is said, one hundred years. He was the father of Charles Leslie, the author of a *Short and Easy Method with the Deists*, and many other works; and from him the Leslies of Glasslough, Co. Monaghan, are descended.

here in a disguised habit,) and others of their own sort, together with Cullenan, Popish Bishop of Raphoe. Their clandestine consultations were kept close—concerning which, Sir William Stewart did propose some necessary queries to the Bishop of Raphoe, in the name of the country, at a meeting of commissioners of the country, which were never yet answered. Whatever consultations might be amongst them, it is certain there was in those times more fellowship and intimacy between the Popish clergy and these bishops with their curates, than could well consist with Protestant principles. It appeared, by a declaration of the lords and gentlemen of the Pale, when they first took up arms, that therein they declared themselves friends to the conformable Protestants, and that they intended no harm to them in their persons, religion, or estates, but only did take up arms to subdue the Puritan party, who owned the actings of the parliament of England and Scotland. The same they declared in a petition they sent over to the King about that time. Yea, a learned pen, about that time, gloried in print that the face of the English church began to alter, and the language of their church to change, so that if a Synod were held without mixing Puritans, there would soon be an agreement.

The managing the war was by the King committed to the Parliament of England at the beginning of the rebellion, and the Parliament, with the King's consent, pursued the rebels with force of arms. Providence so ordered it that what destruction the rebels made at their first breaking out or thereafter, fell upon those alone who were not Puritans (as the more religious and stricter sort of people were then nick-named); and those called Puritans escaped the stroke, having before the rebellion generally repaired to England and Scotland to evite the sharp persecution of the Bishops; and the few who were left were hid from the bloody hands of the murderers, not without the singular providence of God appearing in their preservation, whereof divers instances may be given very observable (of which we may speak more hereafter).

And surely it should not be passed without a special remark, and an awful observing of the holy God in this dreadful stroke, what was the state of the kingdom in this time of the breaking forth of the rebellion. For not only had the Bishops, specially in the North parts, persecuted and driven away the Nonconformist ministers, and others who durst not comply with their sinful courses, but the country was generally overgrown with profanity, luxury, and settling in one external form of religion mixed with superstition, and daily growing in a further tendency to Popery (as it was in England and Scotland at the beginning of the revolution there), and the people remaining in the land unconcerned for persecuting the godly, or markers of them and enemies to them, specially in Ulster, where the persecution was greatest, and the stroke lighted sorest and soonest. The people there had been witnesses to the power and purity of the Gospel for divers years before that; and the bulk of them had not received the love of the truth, but embraced this present world, and went along with the times, without regard of the interest of Christ. There was the guiltiness lying on the country of a wicked oath, taken generally by the people, contrived in opposition to the work of reformation in Scotland; yea, they bound themselves to obey all the King's royal commands, *i.e.*, whatever the King from his royal breast should command them, without reservation and subordination to the word of God.*

---

* The following is a copy of the oath called the Black Oath :—" I,——, do faithfully swear, profess, and promise, that I will honour and obey my Sovereign Lord King Charles, and will bear faith and true allegiance unto him, and defend and maintain his Royal power and authority; that I will not bear arms, or do any rebellious or hostile act against him, or protest against any his Royal commands, but submit

Besides, there was a sinful mixing with the Papists in all things, except the outward form of public worship; Protestants being equally profane and ungodly in their carriage with Papists, and in their religion coming toward the Papists; leaving off the former sincerity and soundness in their doctrine and worship, which sometimes had appeared among the conformable Protestants, both clergy and people, in Ireland, in opposition to popery; and the people generally becoming unconcerned in religion; conforming ministers and popish priests using all familiarity together, and that even on the Sabbath-days after their service and mass, drinking together and spending the time idly; which the people also followed, as occasion served; and under all this a general deep security without any sense of sin in ministers or people, or apprehension of the approaching anger of God.

There was also another procuring cause to this sad stroke proceeding from the indulgence and favour shown to the Papists by the magistrate. They for a long time had had no restraint of their idolatry—as openly and avowedly practised as the Protestant religion,—yea, they were indulged and favoured, when the better and more sincere part of Protestants were restrained, and persecuted, and forced out of the land (as before related). Besides, the Papists were admitted to all offices of trust, civil and military, where orthodox and pious Protestants were discountenanced. They were justices of peace through the country, lawyers, sheriffs, privy counsellors, and parliament men, and swayed

---

myself in all due obedience thereunto; and that I will not enter into any covenant, oath, or band of mutual defence and assistance against all sorts of persons whatsoever, or into any covenant, oath, or band of mutual defence and assistance against any persons whatsoever by force, without his Majesty's Sovereign and Royal authority. And I do renounce and abjure all covenants, oaths, and bands whatsoever, contrary to what I have herein sworn, professed, and promised. So help me God in Jesus."

most in that Parliament which was in being (though prorogued) the same time when the rebellion broke forth, and whole lands were granted them a while after James came to the Crown of England—whereas it had been otherwise in the time of Queen Elizabeth—the King thinking thereby to engage them to peace and loyalty, did, notwithstanding of the many proofs they had given of a rebellious and treacherous disposition, yet labour thus to gain them.

It is worthy of observation what is recorded in the life of famous Bishop Ussher, and which I have heard from divers ministers and others long after the rebellion, that forty years before the rebellion—viz. anno. 1601 or 1602, that Bishop Ussher, being then young, and preaching before the State upon the text,* Ez. iv. 6, and being grieved at a late connivance and indulgence the Papists had got, applied the text thus :— " From this year I will reckon the sins of Ireland, that those whom you now embrace shall be your ruin, and who shall bear this iniquity." The cause of this holy man's grief at this time was, that before this year the laws against the Papists were severely executed, and an High Commission erected thereto, and the State had appointed ministers to expound the grounds of the Protestant religion and the errors of Popery, where those who were Papists must be present. The Papists, being thus put to it, did generally attend the sermons, especially in and about Dublin, the greatest and most considerable of them, and professed satisfaction; and so there were great hopes of gaining them, if these courses had been followed. But so it fell out that, notwithstanding these hopeful beginnings, suddenly the

---

* " What a continued expectation," says Dr. Bernard, " he had of a judgment upon his native country, I can witness from the year 1624, when I had the happiness first to be known to him, and the nearer the time every year the more confident, to my after wonder and admiration, there being nothing visibly tending to the fear of it."

statute was suspended, and the power of High Commission was withdrawn, at which the Papists withdrew themselves again from the Church, the ministers were disregarded, and good men's hearts grieved. This was towards the beginning of the reign of King James, very nigh or about forty years before the breaking out of the rebellion. However, it holds that, within forty years after that, the Papists became Ireland's ruin—whether it were in the year '41 or '42—in both which years the Papists proved the ruin of Ireland, and the great misery and trouble of it many years after. Yet, whatever is said of the sins procuring this stroke by the bulk of the inhabitants at that time, yet we must not doubt there were many godly persons in the land, and a seed of true Protestants that had not gone either to England or Scotland, or, it may be, went not under the name of Puritans, specially in those parts of the land where the Gospel had not been in that purity and power as it was in the North. That there were even many such, not only Christian charity allows amongst such a bulk of Protestants as were then in Ireland, but it did appear in the steadfastness of many of them, who being offered their lives if they would go to mass, did refuse it, and rather chose to be murdered by the bloody Papists than prostitute their consciences to that idolatrous worship. Wherefore, it is charitably to be supposed that the gracious God made use of that affliction to waken the consciences of many who formerly had been sleeping in security, putting them to some sense of sin and crying to God.

Besides the business undertaken in Scotland going on, and armies being raised for their necessary defence, Strafford, by the help of four subsidies from the Parliament in Ireland, raised an army of Irish, and some profane and ignorant of the British, of 8,000 foot and 1,000 horse, and sent them down hither to the North (in order to the invading of Scotland), where the Earl of Antrim had engaged to get them supported. They stayed a considerable time quartered in this country, much oppressing it, and were, both for their design and carriage amongst the people, called "the Black Band." However, thereafter upon a pacification made between the King and his subjects in Scotland, and at the desire of the Parliament of England, and with the industry of the Lords Justices in Ireland, that Black Band was disbanded in August, 1641, their arms being lodged in 'the King's storehouse, in Dublin—which was one piece of providence for that city on the breaking forth of the rebellion.

There were also at this time sent forth certain persons as spies, under pretence of friends to Nonconformists, to search and sound, by private conference, who were favourers of that business in Scotland.* However, the Lord ordered it so that most were upon their guard, and none found prejudice that way except one Trueman, who was trepanned at Larne, and brought to Carrickfergus, there tried, and condemned and executed as a traitor, for speaking some words in defence of the business in Scotland—which was intended for many others if they had been found of the same principles, but Providence ordered that the design was prevented.

---

* He refers here, and in the foregoing pages, to the adoption of the National Covenant in 1638, and to the other movements connected with it.

CHAPTER V.

HORRORS OF THE IRISH REBELLION OF 1641—PRESERVATION OF DUBLIN CASTLE BY OWEN O'CONNOLLY—PROCEEDINGS OF THE LORDS JUSTICES.

HUS this country remained for a short time, till the rebellion broke forth, October 23rd, 1641, of which shall be here given but a short account as to particulars. But in general are to be considered and never to be forgotten—(1) their inhuman cruelty in it, and the sad case of the people; (2) their designs, pretences, and encouragements; (3) the means they used, notwithstanding of difficulties and disappointments, and their constancy in their first resolutions; (4) the provoking causes from God; (5) the means how their design was frustrated; (6) God's visible judgment on them thereafter; (7) how this rebellion made more way for the interest of Christ in this land.

For the first, it cannot be denied by any having any sense of humanity in them that the cruelties exercised by these barbarous people upon their surprised and secure neighbours were beyond the ordinary wickedness that human nature doth reach to, in not only killing and massacring many of them, but torturing their neighbours living friendly beside them—men, women, and young children—devising ways to put them to painful deaths, as was not only generally known in the country, but attested upon oath by hundreds of persons eye-witnesses to it, many of whom did bear the marks of their cruelty. It is true this inhumanity was not exercised in all places alike, but somewhat according to the disposition of the actors. For some did proceed at first in a more cunning way, coming in unto their neighbours' houses and first only disarming them, then taking their goods, then stripping them naked, and shutting them out of their houses, and exposing them to the misery of hunger and nakedness in the open fields in the winter season, and a season which was more than ordinarily tempestuous. And many of these so sent out of their houses—it may be with old rags covering a part of their nakedness—were met by others, and either killed or the remnant of their rags taken from them, insomuch that many women and children in that case were put to wander through mountains covered with snow for many days, and had nothing to feed upon but snow. And yet, some whose lives were spared by the merciless Irish met with miraculous preservation from the immediate hand of God, which I refer to other histories, wherein some of these instances are given.

After this manner they did proceed at first in Ulster, without resistance against a surprised and amazed people; and had, in a few days, not only surprised the houses and goods, with the persons of their neighbours, but by treachery, and under colour of friendship, in one night, got into their hands the strongholds and castles belonging to the King. And where any of the inhabitants got into a place of any defence, so that the barbarous rebels could not easily, and without some hazard, reach them at first, sometimes they pretended to give these people some tolerable conditions till they got them out, and then either killed them, contrary to express conditions (as was done in diverse places) or, if they let them go, they appointed other companies of rebels not far off, to meet them and destroy them—which many met with in their way towards Coleraine, Derry, and Dublin.

But this looking somewhat like the ordinary way of enemies, did not last long. For after a little time when they were baited with blood, they did not come to people with any pretence of civility; but at once murdered and massacred and tortured all who came in their way. Some numbers in some places ran to churches or houses; partly for shelter from the storm—partly for some present defence; and divers of these places they put fire to, so that the poor people were burnt quick—as divers hundreds of them in Armagh. Those whom they did apprehend, they brought to steep places and bridges, and forced them into the water, and by force kept them from endeavouring to swim, or scramble to the brink of the river, with their pikes. They also set themselves to destroy the victuals and corn of the country; and the beasts they exercised much inhumanity on, that they might not have an English beast, nor any breed of that kind preserved. Finally burning, killing, destroying all persons, houses, and whatever came in their way was the thing they delighted in.*

This endured in Ulster for a month or thereabout, not being yet seconded by their confederates in other provinces, occasioned by their disappointment in their intended surprise of the Castle of Dublin. Meantime, the persons spared or escaping in Ulster were in such consternation that they knew not what to do, and were in a manner petrified. But within a little time the other provinces broke out, and followed the Ulster rebels in their cruelty—first Wicklow, then Wexford, and Catherlough †—not pretending to any civility, but falling on with inhuman cruelty at the first upon women and children, and with all the malice hell could invent, as was suitable to the anti-Christian crew against those who

---

* The reader must recollect that Adair settled in Ireland about four years after the rebellion, so that he must have heard much of its horrors from eye-witnesses, or sufferers. Though he over-estimates the numbers killed, his testimony as to its sanguinary character in that part of the country with which he was connected, cannot fairly be rejected.

† *i.e.*, Carlow.

adore not the Roman beast. And if through some special considerations of their own they spared the lives of any, either they kept them prisoners in much misery for that time, and thereafter when they began to be resisted and received disasters from the British forces, they returned upon their poor prisoners with a spirit of revenge; or, if they let them go, pretending to dismiss them to the towns or cities they desired, these poor people that were let go were in some respects more unhappy than those who were immediately murdered; for, besides the insufferable miseries they met with by the way, they came naked and starved to these places (if, indeed, they came where they intended). Dublin and other places they came unto were not all able to contain the numbers and supply their wants. Multitudes died in the streets and corners of Dublin, Coleraine,* and other towns through hunger, nakedness, and nastiness in their rags after sore travelling. Yet some who might have had some supply from persons who particularly knew their former case, were so distracted with their injuries that they neglected their own supply, and in a kind of desperate way gave themselves up to death and starving. For their misery came on them in such a sudden, and they had been before generally living in such peace and plenty, and not expecting in the least any such desolation and calamity, that it did overwhelm their spirits, and swallow them up in grief and vexation.

The city of Dublin in this time, though at first preserved from the design of the enemy in some sort, yet was not

---

* Temple has published the following deposition:—" James Redferne, of the County of Londonderry, deposeth that in the town of Coleraine, since the rebellion began, there died of robbed and stripped people that fled thither for succour many hundreds, besides those of the town who had anciently dwelt there, and that the mortality there was such and so great, as many thousands died there in two days, and that the living, though scarce able to do it, laid the carcases of those dead persons in great ranks into vast and wide holes, laying them so close and thick as if they had packed up herrings together."—*Hist. of the Gen. Rebellion in Ireland*, p. 138. Cork, 1766.

without great fears and troubles, as well as the other parts of the kingdom not yet destroyed. For there was a very considerable part of the city itself ready to join with the rest of the rebels, and not at all to be trusted. And there were daily fears and appearances of the enemy's assaulting the city, men's hearts failing them with fear of the Irish assaulting on all quarters, insomuch that the very face of the city was changed, and had a ghostly aspect. Many Protestants went to England, and though beaten back by many storms, yet would not venture to set their foot on shore again—yea, Papists themselves went out of the city, fearing its surprisal, and a general massacre, wherein they might not be at first distinguished from others. By this case of Dublin, wherein appeared the only probable safety to Protestants in Ireland, we may easily gather what was the case at this time of all other parts of the kingdom where the enemy raged and ruled without any resistance for a time. For though there had been a standing army in Ireland for many years, yet at that time it was become insufficient for opposing such a general insurrection of bloody rebels, there being only about 2,300 foot and about 900 horse, and many of these Irish and Papists, and more of no religion at all. And, besides, they were so scattered in garrisons in divers places that they could not come together without hazard of being cut off by the numerous parties of Irish then in arms. And if men could be had, there was then no money in the exchequer to induce men withal. Besides, in the North, amongst the Scotch, their arms had been taken from them before by Strafford, and so they were rendered unable to defend themselves in any kind, except by a few sent from Dublin.

This was the sad case of the kingdom at that time, the Irish nation and English Papists turning mad, raging as bears bereaved of their whelps, and destroying all before them, burning and consuming men, beasts, corn, and the

British and Protestants partly destroyed and put to death, partly left in a worse case than death itself, and others standing amazed. It is attested by some worthy persons and well acquainted with the case of these times, that there were about 300,000 persons,* men, women, and children, destroyed one way or another.

Next, of that which might be supposed to provoke the Irish to this rebellion, and their designs and encouragements, no doubt there were various grounds which Satan and their own wickedness suggested to them. For, first, as they were natives of Ireland, and conceiving themselves and no others had any right to this country, they retained from the very beginning of the English Conquest, and thereafter from the time of the Scottish denization and naturalizing in it, an implacable hatred at both. They saw themselves generally poor and miserable, which was through their idleness, unskilfulness, wasting disposition, and evil managing; and the British living in prosperity in the land which they counted their own, through their frugality and the blessing of God. Besides, it provoked their evil disposition that they were under the power and government of another nation, and punished frequently for their thefts and robberies. Laws were made against their idolatry and superstition, though these laws for a long time before the rebellion had been very faintly executed, and they had liberty of conscience, as well as other encouragements, as subjects under the King's majesty, and at his special allowance; but there remained always a grudging in their hearts against the British, as their enemies and oppressors. Yet their ingratitude in this may appear, if we

---

* According to a statement in Sir John Temple's *History of the Rebellion*, 154,000 of the British were wanting in Ulster alone. But this statement, as well as that in the text, is now generally considered too high an estimate. The manner in which Lingard, in his *History of England*, passes over this Irish massacre, betrays a sad want of candour.

consider the King of England's ruling over them was confirmed by their general consent—renewed and confirmed in divers ages. Yea, they did submit to the English government with all seeming condescendency and willingness. And surely, if they had been capable of being happy, they might have lived exceeding more happy under the English government than ever they had done before, under their petty kings of Ireland, where the bulk and multitude met with nothing but barbarous tyranny. None knew what was his own property—exposed to continual blood and confusion through mutual wars amongst themselves. And now they were brought under the protection of the British laws—every one of them enjoying their own estates and properties, in peace and tranquillity. Yea, a little before this rebellion, some pretended grievances had been taken off by the King's special gift to the commissioners sent to London from the parliament of Ireland, no restriction being on them in the business of religion. Finally, at this time they were in the happiest condition that ever they had been in, since they were a nation. But that which mainly instigated them to this wicked course, was, that they were Papists under the power and conduct of the Roman Antichrist—that Whore of Babylon, and bloody persecutor of all who worship not the Beast —who could never be satisfied with the blood of those who own the truth of Christ against Antichrist. Their education and principles in this bloody religion did especially stir them up—being thereto animated by their priests and churchmen —and therein following the track and course of Papists in other parts of Europe against the Protestants; who, a few years after the reformation in Luther's time, as histories record, did kill and massacre 900,000 and upwards of Protestants — besides the many hundred thousands that were destroyed before these times under the profession of ordinances in France, Italy and Spain.

There was also another consideration and encouragement which moved them at this time to design the destruction of the Protestants, and the recovering their own land, as they pretended. They were grown a very numerous and considerable multitude in the kingdom, able to raise considerable forces, and much in strength and multitude of people beyond the British inhabitants. Besides that, they had, by their emissaries abroad, contracted a kind of alliance with the Popish party in divers nations abroad — especially France, Spain, and Flanders—from whom they were promised aid of men, arms, and money, insomuch that some of them boasted to their opposers that they would not only regain Ireland, but conquer England through these aids, the Conclave in Rome having a special influence in these transactions as the first mover therein, and cunningly carrying it on, not only in Ireland, but in those other kingdoms, not without encouragement and promise from those who had the government therein. All which appeared by divers testimonies and examinations given thereafter unto the Council of Ireland, and before the Parliament of England.

They did also, at their rising in rebellion, publickly present an allowance and commission from the King, which his Majesty, being informed of, did, the 1st of February, thereafter issue forth a proclamation highly resenting the rebellion, and declaring those engaged in it to be traitors and rebels, and thereby charging all under his command and authority in Ireland to prosecute them as such. This came to the hands of the Lord Justices the 10th of January, and the King also appointed a fast to be kept for the case of the Protestant subjects of Ireland through England and the dominion of Wales. Yet, at this time there was another occasion that did seem to invite them at this juncture. There were unhappy differences beginning to appear between the King and his subjects both in England and

Ireland, which then were drawing to some height, and thereafter came to greater height. And, though at their breaking out into this rebellion things were not come to a height between the King and Parliament of England, yet they did strangely conjecture and, beyond appearance of reason, seem to know what was coming; so that they, in their first rising, did encourage themselves in this, that England should not be in a capacity to send forces against them as formerly. And, withal, the old standing army in Ireland was not significant, as was said before, and Scotland about that time had gotten conditions from the King.

The special things they pretended for their rebellion were, (1), the obtaining their liberty, estates, land, and country, which was, they said, their right, together with the liberty of propagating their religion in Ireland; (2), the King's prerogative, which, they said, was opposed by the Puritan faction in England and Scotland; and therefore, they said, they designed to cut off the Puritan faction especially— though it is observable, that in executing their cruelty, they made no difference among Protestants. For though Satan had a special anger at the godly party, who then went under the name of Puritans, yet, their interest being complex, and not only for their religion, but that they might enrich themselves with the spoils of others, they did promiscuously spoil and destroy all British inhabitants who had but the name of Protestants. And it is remarkable that, whatever was their special envy against the Puritans, yet fewest of these met with the stroke. For very few Nonconformists were then in Ireland, except in the North and in a few counties there, and these had been driven away into Scotland, and some few to England before, through the persecution of. the prelates at first, and then by the Black Oath, so that few of these persons came into their hands. But in the time of the rebellion they are preserved, under God's protection, in Scotland, and some of the English in England. So that the severity of the Bishops was, under Providence, made a means to prevent that stroke upon those specially appointed to destruction; and it lighted upon those who were either persecutors or neutrals, and went on with the iniquity of the times.

It is worthy of observation that, though the Irish are not counted a politic people—as the course of their living and their actions declare them to be rather barbarous and unpolished—yet, in this design they carried with much policy and secrecy in the first contrivance of it, and in their first attempting it, till the only Wise God blasted their endeavours. For by all the enquiry and conduct the Council of Ireland could use to find out the first plotters particularly, they could not find them out; and it seems to have been the policy of those who first hatched it, so to conceal and hide this work of darkness with dreadful oaths of those whom they first made acquainted with it—that whether it went on, or miscarried, their names should not be particularly known, and be so execrable to posterity.

However, it doth appear, not only from the nature of the thing itself, and the constant course of the See of Rome, but from divers examinations taken in Dublin, that the Popish clergy were among the special and first contrivers of it; and probably it bred first at Rome, and was fomented by those of the same profession here in Ireland, under the clergy residing there; and especially by the emissaries who were continually sent abroad by their superiors in Rome, to use all means whatsoever, good or bad, to propagate that interest, and to deliver it where it had been suppressed. For before those times, multitudes of these sorts swarmed in Ireland, and haunted with great liberty among the Irish. The laws against the Popish clergy having been for a long time suspended, though they were severely executed against the Nonconformists in the reign of the bishops, who have still been in their practice in these nations, more severe against those who differ from them in their hierarchy and ceremonies (called by themselves indifferent things), than against those who are professed worshippers of the Beast, and who go a-whoring after Romish idolatry and superstition — though the one partly be acknowledged by themselves orthodox in doctrine, and differing in nothing but ceremonies, and godly and approved both in their subordination to Christ and the magistrate—and the other, partly known to themselves, to be idolatrous, corrupt, profane, and of murdering principles toward Protestant kings and other magistrates.

It did also appear, upon some examinations, that the cursed work was long in contriving, some of the Irish confessing that they knew of such a design intended seven or eight years before the execution of it, and that, all that time, meeting with disappointments, and things not succeeding as they would, they continued their design notwithstanding, and, for that end, kept up correspondence with their party in France, Spain, and Flanders, wholly managed by the Conclave of Rome. And all this time it was kept close by these contrivers till about January, 1640, at which time it was communicated to some Irish gentlemen of Ulster, as was testified by the Lord Maguire (of Fermanagh) in the town of London, of whom more thereafter.

At this time one Roger Moore, a gentleman of a broken fortune and Irish descent, but honourably allied to some noblemen of the English Pale, did communicate it to them also, as a thing agreed upon by many not only in Ulster, but in Leinster and Connaught. And it was then proposed by the said Moore, and agreed on by the rest, that every one of them should acquaint their friends and their own counties, and engage them at once, and thereafter acquaint their friends abroad, that they might be ready to assist them, as necessity required. And [it was arranged] the time for beginning it should be near winter, that the English might not be able to send supplies to the Protestants here till next spring, against which time they might also have help from their friends abroad. And thus they continued their consultations till October, 1641, and resolved to rise then at once, surprising not only their secure neighbours, but the Castle of Dublin, and other of his Majesty's forts and castles through the kingdom, which they got delivered—except Dublin, and some very few other places.

How they did begin this tragedy we did speak before, with some pieces of their policy in first carrying it on. For first they pretended a kindness to the Scotch nation in Ireland, and that their quarrel was only against the English who had subdued them, and who ruled over them—whereas, the Scotch were but strangers, and in their own condition under the English Government—thinking by this pretence first to cut off the English, and then to fall on the other. But this lasted not long, for the Scotch neither expected nor found any kindness from them, and so they made no difference wherever they came.

The Lords of the Pale,* who were always English and Papists, and the other gentlemen with their followers, did at first pretend great loyalty, and came in willingly to the Council, clearing themselves by oath of having any hand with these rebels of the North. And thus they continued a while, and got arms from the Council, and command over

---

* By the Pale was understood that part of Ireland which acknowledged English law. In the beginning of the sixteenth century it was confined to part of the Counties of Dublin, Meath, Kildare, and Louth. The name remained after English law asserted its supremacy throughout the island.

the country to keep all in peace, and subdue any who should rise in arms. Yet, thereafter they met with those of the North, and openly declared themselves; and after them, those in other parts of the kingdom who had, till that time, sat still, broke forth in the same cruelty with the Northern rebels. And it shows how fatally and desperately they were guided that they did thus join after their great disappointment of the city and castle of Dublin—after some resistance made to the rebels of the North—and after the Parliament of England, with the King's consent, had declared against this rebellion, and were preparing forces against them. But they were so deeply engaged in the first contrivance that they could not resile, and they had great confidence in their aids from abroad. Thus the Lord brought forth their long-hidden wickedness, though they purged themselves of it at first by oath, that so the treachery of the Antichristian crew might still appear, and that more ruin in the end might come upon themselves.

But it is to be observed, that in order to this rebellion were employed both Irish lawyers, and Parliamentmen, and Churchmen, to prepare the people for it. For their Parliamentmen (many of whom were lawyers, and who were admitted to sit in Parliament) stirred up all the country, and did complain of the taxes of the country exceedingly in Parliament, and laboured to sow seeds of division among members of Parliament, otherwise not evil-minded, and Protestants, upon account of the grievances of the nation. And Churchmen [Clergy] did generally, at their mass, aggravate the persecution (though they had no ground) and their oppression by the Protestants—yea, they spread great calumnies of the Protestants in England that they used all cruelty in their new beginning of reformation against the Catholics there, and that the same would be their case ere long. They used, a little before the rebellion, in their public prayers, to commend to God a great and glorious design then on hand for propagating the Catholic cause and religion. Yea, immediately before it, they gave the people leave, in their dismissing them from mass, to go and possess themselves of what the Protestants possessed; and told them it was the best service to God they could do, to destroy and kill and drive them off the face of the earth, as being enemies to the Catholic cause.

Thus they fell on their bloody work, designing in one night to surprise all the King's castles in Ireland, and so to fall upon their secure neighbours, living peaceably and confidently among them. The chief command in Ulster was, by the common consent, given to Sir Phelim O'Neill, nearest in blood to the former Earl of Tyrone; a person of small parts and base carriage, yet bred at the Inns of Court in England a while, and professing to be a Protestant while he was there; but, returning to Ireland, he changed his profession, and was employed by the more cunning contrivers of the rebellion, to act the falsehoods and cruelties they had devised—being popular among the Irish in Ulster, because of his relation to the great O'Neill. This Sir Phelim did, the first night of the rebellion, surprise the castle of Charlemont—getting entrance with his train of rebels under pretence of a friendly visit to my Lord Caulfield—that lord and none else in the country having any jealousy of the Irish. The same ways were followed in many other places of the country, where any castles or strongholds were. So that within a few days Sir Phelim and others, his confederates, had not only overrun all open places of the country where there was no resistance, but had obtained possession of the castles and strongholds.

Meantime, the contrivers of the rebellion having resolved to seize the Castle of Dublin the same night on which

Sir Phelim O'Neill seized Charlemont, and having the persons assigned for that service present in town, one of them—Colonel M'Mahon, grandson to the old traitor Tyrone, and who had been under the King of Spain's service—did communicate the design to one Owen O'Connolly, of purpose to have him concur in this design, knowing him to be an Irishman, and to be of a close, confident temper, fit for any undertaking of that nature. He knew him to be a Protestant, but not that conscience had bound him to the Protestant interest. This Owen O'Connolly having, the very evening before the Castle should have been surprised, received information, did seem to comply with the motion, and drunk heartily with this M'Mahon; but thereafter stole from him, and acquainted Sir William Parsons with what he had information of, which Sir William, not giving much credit to (perceiving him in some disorder through drink), sent him to inform himself better, commanding him to return. Upon which, returning to the lodging where he had been with this his informer, the informer began to suspect and threaten him, especially if he stirred from the house till the occasion came of surprising the Castle, which he, seeming not to decline, after a while pretended necessity to go out to ease nature, left his sword on the table, and had a servant sent to watch him. However, with difficulty, he got from the servant over some pales and a wall, and with as great difficulty got through the guards unto the Lords Justices, where he further assured them of the business in hand. And they immediately called as many of the Council as they could get together, and gave orders for watching the Castle and city in the meantime, and, withal, for apprehending as many of the conspirators as were in the town that night. But most of them escaped, having many Papists in the town to conceal them, and quietly convey them away; only the Lord Maguire and Colonel M'Mahon were apprehended. It is worthy of observation that this Owen O'Connolly was at first a poor Irish boy admitted into the family of Sir Hugh Clotworthy, at Antrim—a religious and worthy family; and there was educated and taught not only the principles of the Protestant religion, but, through the blessing of God upon that education, and the power of the Gospel in that parish of Antrim, he became truly religious, in heart and conscience bound to the truth, and to those who were truly godly. He was not only a Protestant, but a Puritan* (as was the style in these times)—which the Irish did not know, having now left that family of Antrim. And thus God, in his merciful Providence, not only to the city, but to all Ireland, did make use of the sincerity that was in him for preventing the surprisal and massacre intended against Protestants in Dublin, and in some degree to be an instrument for the safety of the remainder of the Protestants in Ireland, and preserving a seed in it. This may encourage such families to endeavour to procure religious servants, or to make them religious, so far as they can, by example and instruction. The honesty of this one man, though a mere Irishman (being well educated), proved a great and singular mercy to the whole Protestant Church.

But to return. However the surprisal of the Castle of Dublin was happily prevented, and proclamation issued out to warn all to be on their defence, yet fears were not over even in Dublin. The Lords Justices and Council used all means to fortify the Castle—victualling it, whether against assaults of the Irish now risen in other parts of Ireland, or against the treachery of the Papists within, though they

---

* Mr. M'Bride, Mr. Patrick Adair's immediate successor in the ministry in Belfast, states that O'Connolly was an elder in the Irish Presbyterian Church, and that, as minutes still extant in his time testified, he often sat as such in meetings of Presbytery.—*A Sample of Jet Black Prelatic Calumny*, p. 174.

carried with great prudence and wariness toward all the Papists who at first did not rise in rebellion, not having jealousy of them, but putting trust and confidence in them, giving them arms and commission against those who had appeared in rebellion. Especially this they did with the lords and people of the English Pale, who, though Papists, yet their ancestors had been English, and had stood fast to the Crown of England in former rebellions of the Irish. Therefore, the Council thought they might still prove loyal (not then knowing the long and deep contrivance of this rebellion); but the Popish lords and people of the Pale, though at this juncture they made many great professions of loyalty to the King, and abhorrence of the rebellion of the Ulster Irish exercising much cruelty at that time, and that they intended no harm to the Protestants; yet, within a little time, they discovered themselves, and joined with the Northern rebels. They were at first dashed with the disappointment in surprising the Castle of Dublin, and waited to see the event in other parts of the kingdom; and, when they understood the rebels in the North had such success in their undertaking at the beginning, they were encouraged to own them, palliating their wickedness with pretence of fear from the Government and the Protestants, wherein they alleged many palpable untruths, and reflected on the Lords Justices and Council as if they had forced them to take arms in their own defence—which passages, in particular, we leave unto their proper histories.

Meantime, the Lords Justices and Council did acquaint the King, then in Scotland, with these beginnings of this rebellion, and despatched Owen O'Connolly to the Parliament of England, not only with information of the business, but with a recommendation of that person who had seasonably discovered the plot to them—and so had been instrumental to preserve Dublin. The Parliament not only did at present gratify O'Connolly with £500, but resolved to put a mark of their favour on his posterity. And they did immediately fall upon the consideration of the case of Ireland, to prevent the utter ruin of the British and Protestants there with all expedition. These designs and endeavours produced not that seasonable or effectual supply which necessity called for, and was expected—through the unhappy misunderstandings and counteractings that shortly fell out between the King and Parliament. At length, however, some supplies in men and money and other necessaries came, when the fate of Ireland was expiring; and which, through the mercy of God, and a signal blessing on their sent forces, proved in a short time a relieving of the Protestants in all the counties about Dublin—a particular account of which is not proper for this short narrative, but I must refer those who would be more particularly informed, to other histories that relate at length these passages.

The Lords Justices and Council, when they sent information to the King and Parliament, did, at the same time, issue out their proclamation through those parts of the kingdom to which there was access, that the British should stand on their own defence, resisting them as such, yet so as those who would immediately come in and submit might be spared and protected, except those who should be found to be special actors and contrivers of that rebellion. They also sent commissions to the Lords Claneboy and Ards for raising men, with some help of arms as they could spare—who made use of that power as the present case of the country could admit, and were not unuseful. Withal, commissions were sent to the Lagan to Sir William and Sir Robert Stewart to raise two regiments, consisting of officers who were worthy and gallant gentlemen, and two troops of horse. These small forces in the Lagan,* bordering on multitudes of the rebels on all hands, were successful against them to admiration in many encounters they had; and usually the British (not the third of the number of the rebels, sometimes not the fourth) did overcome, and constantly routed and overcame them, taking great preys from them, and what castles and strongholds they had surprised. The like victory had Sir William Cole with his regiment and troop against the rebels near Enniskillen; and likewise Sir Frederick Hamilton in the country where he lived. I might relate, in particular, many remarkable instances of the Lagan from the narrative of one who was an eye-witness and special actor, and a faithful narrator; and of those in and about Dublin from the histories extant of the rebellion of Ireland. It is not, however, my design to give a narrative of particular passages of that nature, but to observe the Lord's merciful hand toward His sinful people, that, after He had by such a surprising and overflowing tempest manifested His anger against those who professed His truth and walked not suitably to it, He would, in the midst of wrath, remember mercy, and let them see that, when they were in any measure awakened out of their carnal security under their sin, He could put a difference between them and their enemies, giving spirits, courage, conduct, and success to them, and visibly depriving their bloody treacherous enemies of His assistance. However, the Lord did not for divers years thereafter remove their trouble and difficulty, but kept the British at work and in suspense in reference to their comfortable settlement in the country.

* This name was formerly given to a district in the neighbourhood of Derry.

CHAPTER VI.

THE SCOTCH ARMY IN ULSTER—THE FIRST PRESBYTERY MEETS—SESSIONS ERECTED AND MINISTERS APPOINTED—DISCIPLINE OF THE PRESBYTERY.

IN May, 1642, the Scotch army came over, consisting of, I suppose, 10,000 men (though Burleigh says but 2,500) under the command of General Leslie—though he came over but once, and staid a little while setting matters in the best order he could, and left the government of the army to Major-General Robert Munroe. This army was sent by the States of Scotland as their immediate masters, who ordered them to this service upon a treaty with the Parliament of England; unto which, it is said, the King was at first averse, yet, by the Parliament's importunity, he was prevailed with to give his assent, at Windsor, January 17th, 1642.

This army for their chief garrison, had the town and castle of Carrickfergus, where their chief commander resided with his regiment. The other regiments were quartered in such places of Down and Antrim as the British regiments could spare. Many in England and Ireland have taken liberty to represent this army as having done little service in the country, and not worth the pay they had from England. But all representations of that kind, coming from emulous, envious pens and tongues, ought not to be received. It is most sure it consisted of officers who generally were men of courage and conduct; many of them had been bred in foreign wars, and were bred soldiers; others, who had not been abroad, were men of gallant, generous spirit, who thereafter proved eminent. Some who were then but majors to regiments and captains of companies, became thereafter generals and lieutenant-generals in foreign kingdoms. Doubtless, the fault of most of these officers was want of piety rather than courage, or any accomplishment for that undertaking—though there were also a great many officers in that army truly godly. It is also certain they did many considerable services against the rebels in Ulster, so that they became a terror to them; and most of them laid down their arms, and came in and sat down under their mercy. The truth is, this army was irritated for want of the pay promised them; matters then falling into confusion in England, and the Parliament not being able to support so many armies at home and in divers places of Ireland, they were much neglected, being strangers, and quartering upon the Scotch in Ulster. And no wonder, when the forces sent over by the Parliament, in and about Dublin and Munster, did as grievously complain at that time from want of supply, though they were in greater hazard from the rebels. Upon this, they were not only disabled from service, but were forced to take free quarters off the country, in doing which they restrained the officers to a small maintenance, and the common soldiers to a pitiful allowance which was not sufficient for their comfortable subsistence. Yet, their coming over upon a wasted country, where people had generally little or nothing left to themselves—this taking off the country for their mere necessity—became intolerable to the people, and they were reflected on as oppressors—yea, as doing nothing but lying in their quarters and oppressing the country. And yet they themselves were discouraged, and the soldiers just starved—insomuch that some regiments went over to Scotland, without the consent of that State, nearly in a mutiny, and upon mere necessity. And others, such as Hume's and Sinclair's regiments, were content to take a call from the State, a little after, to engage against Montrose, then victorious and carrying all before him in Scotland, and most of them were cut off. So that as the country was weary of them, so they were as weary of the country. And indeed in the end, though they had spent much blood, besides travel and misery in the service of Ireland, the remainder of them were badly requited, being forced out of Carrickfergus and Coleraine by Colonel Monck—then under the Parliament of England—and disbanded, without satisfying their arrears (as we may see hereafter). It is certain God made that army instrumental for bringing church government, according to His own institution, to Ireland—especially to the Northern parts of it—and for spreading the covenant, as shall be recorded hereafter. The Scotch army coming hither in the Spring of the year 1642, found much of the country wholly desolate, except some parts of the County of Down, where there had been two regiments formed by Lords Claneboy and Ards, and so had, in some measure, kept off the force of the enemy. Likewise, some towns in the County of Antrim were preserved, as Belfast and Carrickfergus, with Lisnegarvy* and Antrim, through some defence which had been made in these places. But generally in the country, through the County of Antrim, all was waste, and more in other counties, as Armagh, Tyrone, &c. Most of Londonderry had been preserved, by the great blessing of God upon the defence made by the British, Scotch, and a few English there under the conduct of Sir William and Sir Robert Stewart, who obtained signal victories there over the Irish in those parts, a very little after the rebellion began, the particular passages whereof we refer to their proper histories, this narrative being intended only for recording the providence of God toward His church in the North.

---

* *i.e.*, Lisburn.

It is to be much observed, that the Sovereign Holy Lord in his providence, by this rebellion, made way for a more full planting of the Gospel even in those parts which had met with the greatest cruelty; and where the people had been, against whom the Irish intended greatest mischief and cruelty, both to their persons and professions. For it was so ordered by Divine Providence, that the country being laid waste and desolate in God's righteous judgment for crying sins in the bulk and generality (though most wickedly and treacherously on men's part), the Lord made use of that overflowing scourge not only for emptying the land of many profane and wicked men—haters of godliness, and yet under the name of Protestants—but the Irish themselves were greatly wasted in a few years thereafter by sword and famine, so that the land was much emptied of them, except of some who came in upon protection. And others came out of Scotland in their room who were lovers of the truth—even as it had been ordered before in the time of Queen Elizabeth and King James. The land being overgrown with idolatry and barbarousness, they did rise in divers rebellions, and God made use of that to lay them desolate, and make way for others who professed the Gospel, though only in the way of conformity, yet the truth was preached and many believed. And the Lord had his hidden ones at that time—as appeared in Bishop Ussher and many others—both preachers and professors in and about Dublin; the effects whereof did appear, as formerly hinted, in the Articles of Ireland.* But now, God made way for a more full reformation; and as the foundation of a plantation in the country, Providence ordered it so

---

* In 1615 a Convocation was held in Dublin, and under its direction, Ussher, then Professor of Divinity in Trinity College, drew up a collection of articles for the use of the Church of Ireland. These articles inculcate the Calvinistic theology, and the divine authority of the Lord's Day.

that several officers and soldiers were forced to labour the ground, and keep stocks of cattle in the country; and others, probably inhabitants who were left, did the same. After them, within a while, the inhabitants grew more numerous, partly through the increasing of these in the country, and partly through others coming from Scotland. Meantime the country was destitute of ministers; for the bishops and their party were generally swept away by the rebellion, and now began to be also discountenanced by the Parliament of England. So that from that time forth the Lord began more openly to erect a new tabernacle for himself in Ireland, and especially in the northern parts of it, and spread more the curtains of his habitation. The methods and ways of providence therein, together with the difficulties met with, and His carrying His work through these difficulties, and over the oppositions from Satan and his instruments (His ordinary way in such cases), shall be the subject of our following narrative, so far as great weakness can reach the declaring of God's great works towards His Church.

The first means God used for this end was the sending over of the Scotch army, consisting of about ten regiments, with whom there came from Scotland divers ministers who were principled and inclined toward the doctrine, worship, and government at that time in the Church of Scotland: as Mr. Hugh Cunningham, minister to Glencairn's regiment; Mr. Baird to Colonel Campbell's; Mr. Thomas Peebles to Eglinton's; Mr. James Simpson to Sinclair's; Mr. John Scott, Mr. John Aird, and others. They, coming along with the army, found it their duty to erect themselves into a Presbytery, and to have their meetings, in order to which they found it necessary to choose ruling elders in the regiments for helping them in carrying on discipline in the army, which the dissoluteness of soldiers did much call for. This motion being communicated to the Major-General, the commander-in-chief of these forces (and to the officers of the several regiments), he did embrace the same, being a man not alienated from the reformation in Scotland, and besides having been sent over by the State of Scotland, who, he knew, at that time did favour the government of the church—yea, some special noblemen of Scotland who then had great rule there, being colonels of regiments over whom he commanded in chief. They (not being in Ireland themselves) having placed officers over their regiments who were also inclined that way, the motion went on without resistance among, and by the consent of, all the regiments. It is true there were in most regiments of the army (especially in the Major-General's own regiment) officers of bad principles, and worse inclinations and practices, no favourers of religion, nor of the Presbyterian government, nor of the work of reformation, but (as was the title given them in these times) malignants, royalists, cavaliers, &c., much abhorring the setting up of discipline in their bosom, which might have power to censure them for their drinking and whoring. Yet, through the terror of God upon men in these times, they made no open resistance.

The first Presbytery was held at Carrickfergus on the 10th of June, 1642, where were only five ministers of the army and four ruling elders from the four regiments, who had then erected sessions — viz. Argyle's, Eglinton's, Glencairn's, and Hume's. One of their number (Mr. Baird) preached, by desire of the rest, and by appointment beforehand, on Psalm li. and last;* another was chosen Moderator; and Mr. Thomas Peebles was chosen Clerk, in which office he remained during his life.

---

* This is evidently a mistake for Psalm li. 18. "Do good in thy good pleasure unto Zion ; build thou the walls of Jerusalem."

They began with appointing divers of their members to speak to the Colonels and Lieutenant-Colonels of those regiments, where there were not sessions, together with the rest of the officers and others concerned in the regiments, that sessions might be erected. Withal, they appointed each minister to begin examination in his charge; and appointed, also, a fast to be observed the week after, and to be intimated next Sabbath—wherein they were to sympathise with the case of the churches abroad in Germany and Bohemia; the present distraction of England and hazard of God's work there at that time, through the difference beginning between the King and Parliament; and the people of this poor land, who were scarce as brands plucked out of the fire, yet security and profanity remaining among many both in country and army—and that God should be cried unto to bless the country with a spiritual ministry, and for a blessing to the going out of the army against the Irish, &c. All these were immediately performed, and so the Presbytery did meet almost weekly, though few in number. There were, besides these ministers of the Scotch army, two preachers in the country before, Mr. John Drysdale, and Mr. James Baty, the one preached to Lord Claneboy's, the other to the Lord of Ard's regiment.

The Presbytery had, upon their first meeting together, written to these noblemen that it were fit these their preachers, being of the same principles with them, should be present. Upon which Lord Claneboy wrote a letter, and Ards sent one of his captains, thanking the Presbytery for their letter, and professing their great willingness to join in that government, and to have these men admitted to be ministers of their regiments upon that account, and did, during their short continuance thereafter, countenance the Presbytery and these ministers sent from Scotland. Thus, these lords seem to have been convinced of their error two years before in being instruments in pressing the Black Oath—which was soon followed with a sad judgment on the land: and shortly after that they both died.* However, these two men† passed their trials before the Presbytery, and were admitted ministers, first to the regiments, and thereafter, upon serious deliberation, were placed in parishes of the country which were best planted, and where also the soldiers resided. The ministers, also members of the Presbytery, were appointed to produce their admission to the several charges or regiments, by virtue of which they sat as members of the Presbytery—which they all did; as also the ruling elders, that sat in every Presbytery, produced their commissions from their respective sessions. The Presbytery being informed of a minister's practice, who had been a Conformist before in the country, and now had taken the Covenant, that he used to baptize privately, brought him to acknowledge his fault (which he said he knew not was so), and to promise to forbear that practice. Divers ministers and others who had taken the Black Oath, and been instrumental in ensnaring others in it, and had gone on in a course of conformity and defection, upon an intimation from the Presbytery, did come and own their sinful defection, and made the same acknowledgments in those places where they had been particularly scandalous, as Mr. Nevin, at Dunody, &c.

In September, 1642, there were sent over from the General Assembly in Scotland, the Rev. Mr. Blair, and Mr. Hamil-

---

* It would seem that Lord Claneboy, in pressing the Black Oath, was very much influenced by the fear of Laud and Wentworth. It is stated in the *Hamilton Manuscripts*, as quoted by Dr. Reid, I., 242, note, that he "had secret friendly correspondence with the ministers and others that were persecuted for conscience' sake—yea, some hid in his house when his warrants and constables were out looking for them."

† *i.e.*, Drysdale and Baty.

ton, with a commission from the Assembly. They sat in the Presbytery and proceeded as they were chosen—their commission being inserted in the Presbytery-book as fit to be recorded. By this commission may be seen the earnestness of the people of the country for having the Gospel planted amongst them; and also, the zeal and care of the Assembly of Scotland for this poor church, to nourish and encourage it in its beginning, being as a brand plucked out of the fire.

But the occasion of this commission and sending of these worthy and reverend men from Scotland is to be remembered. For, immediately upon the ministers forming themselves with the ruling elders into a Presbytery, the people planted in the country became importunate with the Presbytery for help in preaching to their congregations, where were any stock of people planted in places that the army were not in, as they could overtake this work. Upon which the Presbytery moved that there should be elderships erected with the consent of these congregations, and that by their help a present supply might be procured, and in due time ministers be settled among them. This motion of the Presbytery was very acceptable to these congregations, as appeared by their immediate and earnest address to the Presbytery for ministers to be sent for that effect, which also was readily done by the Presbytery, who sent ministers to divers congregations who were first in a case for elderships—viz. Ballymena, Antrim, Carncastle, Templepatrick, Carrickfergus, Larne, and Belfast, in the County of Antrim; Ballywalter, Portaferry, Newton, Donaghadee, Killileagh, Comber, Holywood, and Bangor, in the County of Down. And, the elderships being erected in these places, there began a little appearance of a formed church in the country. Upon this there was a motion that commissioners should be sent from this country to the General Assembly in Scotland, supplicating their help for founding and promoting the work of Christ in this wasted church now beginning to rise out of the ashes; and they were sent to the Assembly, at St. Andrews, July, 1642. Upon this petition, these two worthy ministers—Ireland's old acquaintances—were sent with the commission formerly mentioned. And it may be judged how refreshful and useful in the country they were, who formerly had been eminently instrumental in laying the first foundation there, and for their faithfulness had been driven away, and at their departure such calamities had come on; and now they were witnesses of a new reviving and a rising work out of the rubbish.

The people were very hungry in receiving the Gospel—which before these times had been preached with so great success, and for which both ministers and people had suffered so much—and which was now again reviving out of the ashes. Surely this was a time when the people's joy trysted with the great poverty and deep affliction which lay upon them, having a considerable army quartered among them in a country yet but waste. And though they had some supplies for the army from Scotland and England, yet these did but answer their necessities; happily, they had a bountiful supply from Holland, as a gift and gratuity in these their extraordinary straits. However, the Gospel was sweet to many.

Any persons who at that time were under scandals of any kind, and not properly under the ministry of any in the Presbytery, were received, upon their own free offer, to public repentance; but were not compelled, till they became members of some formed congregation—except in case that they required the benefit of sealing ordinances, or in the case of those who had been Conformist ministers and were now taking on themselves to preach. These the Presbytery by an act

G

appointed the people to be warned from hearing or countenancing, till they gave satisfaction, which divers of them did—some before Mr. Blair in Bangor, Donaghadee, and Killileagh; and others before Mr. Hamilton. In this the hand of the Lord is to be observed, that these men who a few years before were deposed and driven out of the country for refusing conformity, should be the first now to receive the acknowledgment and repentance of Conformists. A few who were left from the general scourge, and were more ingenuous than the rest, did willingly appear and maké their acknowledgments publickly, both ministers and people. Moreóver, Mr. John Drysdale and Mr. James Baty—who had preached for a while to Claneboy's and Ard's regiments, and were on their trials in order to ordination, with the concurrence of Mr. Blair, who presided at the ordination of Mr. Drysdale, and Mr. Hamilton presiding at Mr. Baty's admission (with the army ministers)—were settled in the parishes of Portaferry and Ballywalter, upon an unanimous call from these parishes, rather than among the army. Only in Ballywalter there was a reservation of Mr. Hamilton's interest there, if God should clear his return to that place where he had been minister before. Thus these two ministers, Blair and Hamilton, who had a while before been deposed from their ministry by the bishops, are now employed as the instruments for first planting ministers in the country according to the purity of the Gospel—who were also useful in the army's Presbytery, and were the beginning of a settled ministry in the country.

At this time also, with the assistance of these two worthy men, the Presbytery, upon information of the danger of separation, and the beginning of some heterodox opinions spreading about Antrim by one Thomas Cornwall and one Vernet, did order Mr. Blair, in his visiting these places, to obviate these dangers by warning the people and publickly declaring against them. Also all the ministers were appointed in public to give warning to the people against those snares. They also summoned the said persons to appear before the Presbytery to give a confession of their faith—but none did appear. Thomas Cornwall said he was not subject to the Presbytery, but was a stranger, and ready to depart; others, in private conference, did give satisfaction; some were otherwise hindered. However, these opinions did not spread.

There was at this time another fast appointed to be kept on the Lord's Day, November 27, 1642, and the Thursday thereafter, for the troubles of churches abroad; the sad distractions in England whence help only could be expected to this country, under God; the discouragement of soldiers through want of necessary supplies, and of the country through their poverty and oppression; the enemy's strength and cruelty yet much remaining; general carelessness and security, with little life and zeal among people; many gross sins breaking forth among some; want of faithful ministers residing in the country to encourage the people and stir them up; and the sinfulness of the army, who should be instruments of deliverance. These days were accordingly kept.

The Presbytery at this time did impose public evidences of repentance upon scandalous persons in their parishes, and, where elderships were erected, with as great severity as had been done at any time in the Church of Scotland. And these persons did submit themselves thereunto, though the most part were not properly formed into congregations as yet, nor under the inspection of ministers.

And, whereas, some ministers who had been Conformists, and had come and submitted to the Presbytery, did use private baptism and private marriage, the Presbytery discouraged such practices in those ministers, which they promised to forbear. Yet those ministers, who had given satisfaction for their conformity and oath, were not received members of the Presbytery, except they were first received and settled in congregations in an orderly way, though permitted to preach where they were invited. At this time, there being one Mr. Black, preacher in Belfast, who intended to give the Sacrament after the way of the Common Prayer, the Presbytery, being informed of it, sent to Colonel Chichester and Earl of Donegall desiring forbearance of that way, in order to prevent scandal and inconveniences among the people. The said Colonel Chichester interposed with him to forbear. They also appointed Mr. Baird to preach every third Sabbath in Belfast, there being the third part of a regiment under his charge quartered there.

The Presbytery also wrote to the commission of the General Assembly in Scotland to hasten over the supplies of ministers appointed by the last General Assembly according to the turns appointed them, the first two being gone. The Presbytery, too, was earnest with the regiments who wanted ministers to supply themselves; and, accordingly, as ministers were presented to the Presbytery, they were put on their trials, and some rejected and some admitted.

At this time, February, 1643, the army being in great straits for want of pay, and the country under great burdens by them, the Presbytery appointed a fast on a week-day and the Sabbath following for an outget for the distressed army and country, and had the reasons contained in the causes of the other fast that was kept. The Presbytery all these times began with preaching before they went about their business, and chose for this time in ordinary the Prophecy of Isaiah.

On May 24th, another fast was appointed to be in places on a week-day, and on a Lord's Day thereafter, for the former causes, and especially the sinfulness of the army and country continuing, notwithstanding the great distress on both, and that God would bless the expedition of the army going to the field this summer. The Presbytery also sent over one of their number to the Assembly of Scotland, with commission to own their bounty in sending over one supply already, and to supplicate the continuance of the same according to the intention of the Assembly—who did accordingly, and a new supply is appointed by the Assembly, upon which comes over first Mr. Matthew M'Kail.* A new fast was appointed in January, 1644, on a week-day and Sabbath following for the causes formerly mentioned, and besides, that God would enable the army gone from Scotland to England to support the work of God there against the Popish and prelatical party who were now prevailing much against the forces of the Parliament there. In February thereafter Mr. George Hutchinson came over by the appointment of the Assembly; and visitations of congregations were used in the ordinary way, both in the army and the few places of the country where ministers were.

* Mr. M'Kail was minister of Carmanoch.

CHAPTER VII.

THE COVENANT ADMINISTERED IN ULSTER—TAKEN AT CARRICK-FERGUS, COMBER, NEWTONARDS, BANGOR, BROADISLAND, ISLAND-MAGEE, ANTRIM, BALLYMENA, COLERAINE, DUNLUCE, DERRY, RAPHOE, LETTERKENNY, RAMELTON, AND ENNISKILLEN.

IN March, 1644, the Scotch army, through discouragement and want of maintenance, purposing to return to Scotland, were taking an oath which the Presbytery judged ambiguous, scandalous, contrary to the covenant, and a divisive motion. They sent two of their number to the meeting of officers at Carrickfergus, to declare the same to them; and withal, they wrote to the commission of the Church of Scotland concerning the present state of the army and that oath, with their declaration against it. After this came over by the Assembly's appointment, Masters James Hamilton, William Adair, John Weir, and Hugh Henderson, very soon after one another. They were all present at the Presbytery, held Monday, the 1st of April, 1644, showing their commissions, and bringing a letter from the commission of the General Assembly, directing the ministers of the Scotch army to administer the solemn League and Covenant to the army. This was accordingly done. The ministers who had charge of regiments as their congregations, did administer it to these regiments; and the regiments who had no ministers received it from the ministers who had come from Scotland; and all entered into that oath with great appearance of desire and affection—some really—and others went along. I have heard that none refused it but Major Dalzell,* in the Major-General's regiment, who

---

* Dalzell has acquired an unenviable notoriety by hunting down the Presbyterians of Scotland after the Restoration. His infamy as a persecutor is almost equal to that of Claverhouse.

then, and all his days thereafter, proved an atheist, and an open enemy to the work of God. But though the army-ministers had no commissions, except for the army, yet in those places where the covenant was administered to the army, the whole country about came and willingly joined themselves in the covenant—a very few excepted, who were either some old Conformist ministers, or known profane and ungodly persons—so that there were more of the country become swearers than were men in the army. Yet, because the Black Oath had been generally pressed and taken by many in the country a few years before, those who had taken the Black Oath were not admitted to the covenant till they at first publickly declared their repentance for it. It was reported by the worthy Mr. Weir—who administered the covenant at Carrickfergus, where least was expected—that there were 400 who had renounced the Black Oath publickly, and taken the covenant; and 1,400 of the army and of towns and places about, besides women, who had not taken the same, and now entered into the covenant. And there were in other places large equal proportions, and more people running into it where it was administered—as in Belfast, Comber, Newton. Bangor; also in Broadisland, Islandmagee, and other places in the County of Antrim, not only where soldiers were quartered, but where they were not quartered. The ministers from Scotland, on their own invitation, did visit them, and administered the covenant unto them.

The covenant was taken in all places with great affection; partly with sorrow for former judgments and sins and miseries; partly with joy under present consolation, in the hopes of laying a foundation for the work of God in the land, and overthrowing Popery and prelacy, which had been the bane and ruin of that poor church. Sighs and tears were joined together, and it is much to be observed, both the way ministers used toward the people for clearing their consciences in order to the covenant, in explaining it before they proposed it to the people, and from Scripture and solid consequences from it, clearing every article of it—and thereafter offered it only to those whose consciences stirred them up to it. Indeed, they were assisted with more than the ordinary presence of God in that work in every place they went to, so that all the hearers did bear them witness that God was with them. And the sensible presence and appearance of God with them in these exercises did overcome many of those who otherwise were not inclined that way, so that very few were found to resist the call of God. The solemnity and spirituality of carrying on this work was like the cloud filling the temple, there being a new tabernacle erecting in the land. And those who had not seen those things before, nor were well acquainted with them, said (as the people in Christ's time), "We have seen strange things to-day." Yea, even the malignants who were against the covenant durst not appear on the contrary, for the people generally held their ministers as servants of God, and coming with a blessed message and errand to them. Only at Belfast there was no liberty granted to offer the covenant; but with difficulty it was granted them to preach, and that text was insisted on—Isaiah lvi. 5, 6, and 7. Many people, who had been at Holywood the day before, were present, and divers well-wishers in Belfast itself, though the generality of people in it had no such affection. It is observable of that place, that, though there was long much opposition to the work of Christ in it, yet by degrees the Lord did wear out the opposers, and made them and their posterity altogether insignificant in the place,* and brought in a new people from divers places who do entertain the

---

* The same remark may be repeated at the present day.

Gospel, and own Christ's interest with equal affection as others.

Thus, the ministers having gone about that work in all places in Down, and several places in Antrim, where the Scotch army were quartered, they resolved to go to Coleraine and the Route also for that purpose, and, according as they had clearness, to go further toward Derry. Mr. Adair and Mr. Weir visited first Antrim, and after that Ballymena, then a small garrison. In both places God was signally present with the ministers and people, the Lord assisting the ministers in the work of preaching and explaining the covenant, and the people with much affection to receive it. The ministers were directed to insist on sweet and suitable subjects thereon—as Ezra viii. 23, and Psalm cii. 13.

From Ballymena they went with a guard of horse toward Coleraine, under one William Hume, of General Leslie's regiment. They went the next day (being Thursday) to the church, and few being present except the soldiers of the garrison, they explained the covenant to them, and left it to their serious thoughts till the next Sabbath, being also Easter day. On this Lord's day the convention was very great from town and country. They expounded more fully the covenant, and, among other things, told the people that their miseries had come from those sorts of people who were there sworn against, and specially from the Papists. The righteous hand of God had afflicted them for going so near the Papists in their former worship and government in the church; and whereas, the episcopal party endeavoured peaceableness with the Papists, by symbolizing with them in much of their superstition; the Sovereign Holy Lord had turned their policy to the contrary effect for their conformity with idolaters—going on in a course which had a tendency at least that way. The first who publickly entered into covenant was the preacher in that town, Master Vesey, who did solemnly acknowledge the sin of the Black Oath, and the cursed course of conformity with the former times. Such was the day of God's power on men's consciences. For this man proved not sound or steadfast thereafter, nor ever joined with the Presbytery, and upon the restoration of bishops did again conform to episcopacy, and died Archbishop of Tuam.*

Next, the whole people of the country present did solemnly acknowledge the oath, and by lifting up hands to God entered into the Solemn League and Covenant, with which were mixed prayers and singing of psalms, after the ordinary exercise of preaching was over. There were few of the townsmen who entered into the covenant the first day, but they gave the ministers knowledge that their purpose was on Monday to enter into it. The ministers, first commending them for their deliberate way of doing such a thing, observed the Monday, and received them into covenant, both the Mayor and others of the town, they desiring to do it by themselves, but so that in their entering into the covenant they did abjure their former corruptions, and renounce them. So did the ministers and people of Route, who were all of them convened in two places—Billy and Dunluce. In the one was Mr. Adair, and in the other was Mr. Weir, where the former ministers followed the same way, with others before them, and the people also. Mr. Adair and Mr. Weir took occasion from the ministers' repentance to show the people in public how dangerous it was to credit ministers without ground from Scripture.

But as this work had little or no resistance hitherto appearing, so now some were stirred up against it. Colonel

---

* Dr. Reid has remarked that Adair has here fallen into an error. It was the son of this Vesey who became Archbishop of Tuam. His name was John Vesey. He was born at Coleraine in 1637—was made Bishop of Limerick in 1672, and Archbishop of Tuam in 1678. He died in 1716.

Mervyn began occasionally coming to Coleraine, and reflecting upon the people taking the covenant, and had almost discouraged and dissuaded some who were upon the way of taking it. Then one Mr. Philips, about Ballycastle [Ballykelly?] (near Newtownlimavady), set himself against it, and did endeavour to dissuade the garrison thereabout from it. And Sir Robert Stewart, with Mr. Humphry Galbraith, were using the same endeavours about Derry, having heard that the ministers, upon invitation from some people, were coming there.

But a greater opposition met them from Derry; for, coming the length of Muff, they received a message and letter from the Mayor of Derry, one Thornton, and from Colonel Mervyn, prohibiting their coming there upon their peril. Yet, they considering they had invitation from a well-affected people to go there, and that God had signally appeared for them in carrying on that work in all places they had been in, went forward, not intimating to their company their discouragements. Whereupon their convoy leaving them, they went on, and being met by Captain Lawson* (one of those who had invited them), they were brought over the ferry to his house, which was without the wall, not knowing how to enter the town. But Providence appeared for them; for Sir Frederick Hamilton, a bold man, and one of a great interest in that country, then occasionally being in Derry, came to the wall, and sent for them and brought them unto the gates to his own house, much encouraging them, and commending their coming forward, notwithstanding the threatenings they received. As they went toward his lodging through the streets, there seemed to be a commotion among the people, some by their countenance and carriage declaring

---

* This Captain Lawson was the son-in-law of Mr. Barr, of Malone, near Belfast, who was a staunch Presbyterian. Captain Lawson had distinguished himself at the breaking out of the rebellion in defending Belfast and Lisburn.—See *Reid*, I., 300-3.

their indignation—some their affection. Others were surprised at the so sudden coming of these worthy men. For Providence ordered it that they came before they could be expected, and it was then told them by Sir Frederick that he heard there were means used for laying wait for them by the way, and using violence to them. Sir Frederick did commend them for their policy in preventing a knowledge of the time they might be expected; but they referred it wholly to Divine conduct, for they neither imagined nor knew any such thing. And so after they had supped with him in another house near his own lodging, he left them. They were much encouraged and refreshed by the experience of God leading them that day. Next day the Mayor, with the Aldermen, who were also Town Captains, came to their lodging, reminding them that he had written to them the day before not to come there, lest they bred division in the garrison and town. They told him they came for a happy union in that division, and they were so far on their way before they received his letter that they could not with any conveniency return. He questioned them by what authority they came there with the covenant? They answered—1st, upon a petition from the British in the North of Ireland for ministers to come and visit them from the Assembly of Scotland; 2nd, that the Assembly had given them commission to give the covenant to the Scotch army and others who willingly should receive it; 3rd, upon a petition from the British of Ulster to the States of Scotland, desiring help in divers things, particularly in victualling and ammunition for Derry, which they desired earnestly—and, above all, also the Solemn League and Covenant to be sent over to them, unto which, as the States of Scotland had respect, according to their capacity, to the rest of their desires, so particularly unto this in these words:—" And the Committee of Estates do embrace their desire to enter into the covenant, and will take care to send the same to Major-General Monroe to be presented both to the Scotch Army and the British, as a firm ground of their union in this cause." The ministers did return to the Mayor a copy of this order subscribed by the clerk's hand. He answered that was no legal warrant for them to take the covenant. They replied, these things put together, there was a sufficient ground for them to offer it, though they would press it on none, and *volenti non fit injuria*, since themselves by petition had sought it; and there were also letters from the Parliament of England to the same purpose. It could not be offensive nor a-wronging the people to offer that to them, which themselves had petitioned for, being a thing in itself so lawful, and recommended by the States of Scotland with the Parliament of England, and binding them to their duty both to God and the King. Notwithstanding all this, the Mayor did request them to forbear administering the covenant in that place. They again did entreat him to suffer them publickly to proceed. He answered them he would command, if they would not forbear for entreaty. They replied, would he command ? Meantime, Sir Frederick comes into the room (who had, unknown to them, made much way for that business in these parts before they came), and, in great boldness and animosity, according to his manner, said to the Mayor, "Mr. Mayor, take heed what you do or speak to these gentlemen." Likewise a lieutenant present, and belonging to the town companies, did express his resolution to take the covenant in a daring way. So that the Mayor replied no more to the ministers, but that he would take it to advisement, and see them in the afternoon. However, the double guards which had been placed in the town were ordered as before, and

Colonel Mervyn's regiment, which was marching towards the town, did return to their quarters, and the gates which had been shut were opened again. In the afternoon the mayor sent Captain Hepburn to the ministers, to desire a conference with them in his own chamber—where they attended him. There he showed them a letter from the Parliament of England, recommending to them the taking of the covenant when it should come to the Scotch army—and withal, a proclamation by those who then ruled in Dublin, prohibiting the taking of it—and declared his great straits what to choose. Whereunto the ministers answered that he should lay the balance—on the one hand the gracious purpose of the Parliament of England for their true good, together with the hopes of support from them, and from Scotland, and their brotherly affection desiring to be in one league and covenant with them; and on the other hand the corrupt disposition of those who then ruled in Dublin, with the experience they had found of their small help, or what could be expected from them. And so the ministers left him, and received another discouraging letter from Sir Robert Stewart, sent by Major Galbraith. However, the ministers sent for the keys of the church against the next Sabbath. The mayor told them the sacrament was then to be administered in the great church, but they might have the little church that day, and should have the other the next. But the ministers, finding the little church not sufficient to contain the number of people there met, went to the market-place (where about two years before the mass had been publickly used by some Irish regiments, who were to be sent to Scotland against the covenant), and there preached on the subject of taking God's people into covenant, declaring the divine authority of it; whereunto was added the exemplary encouragement of two sister churches, England and Scotland, entering into it. They also spoke from 2 Chron. xv. 15; Jer. l. 5; and Neh. ix. 10: paralleling the cases then in hand, both as to the persons entering into the covenant, and the case of the time requiring reformation and preservation of religion, which was engaged into in the covenant, and explaining the covenant as it rendered secure both what was proper to them and what was due to God. They also laboured to make the people sensible of the sin of the Black Oath, showing that, by engaging to obey all the King's Royal commands (the contents of the oath), they had opened a door for the Prince to bring in whatever religion he pleased, if it were the Turk's religion; and had deprived themselves of the liberty of passive obedience, which they said was, *ipso facto*, a protestation against the iniquity of the command. For a Royal command is whatsoever the King commands, whether it be lawful or not, as appears in Daniel vi. 7. The ministers required that all who were thus sensible of this evil, and who now resolved to enter into covenant by lifting up their hands and countenances, should abjure the one and enter into the other, which was done with many tears by the multitude there. And thereafter prayer was performed with great solemnity and affection both in speaker and hearers, wherein they owned God as their God, and gave up themselves to Him. This was on the Lord's Day; and the Mayor and others coming from their Sacrament stood somewhat amazed, yet with reverence did behold what was a-doing in the market-place. The Lord's Day being thus spent, the ministers desired the keys of the church on Monday, which were sent them; the bells were rung, and the multitude, both from town and country, increased that day more than on the former, wherein the happy condition of a sanctified and true union was the subject insisted on. A great many more, and some persons of quality from the country, did embrace the covenant with much sign of affection, and thereafter, according to the usual way, much time was spent in subscribing it.

The ministers having been blessed in Derry against much discouragement and opposition in the beginning, went the next day to Raphoe, accompanied by Sir John Cunningham and Lieutenant-Colonel Saunderson (who had taken it in Derry), with many others. There the whole regiment of Sir Robert Stewart did meet them (except himself), and great multitudes from the parishes about. They followed the same way here, and had the same success which they had formerly in other places. The one was necessitated to preach without the church when the other was within, and receive the people to covenant with the same solemnity. There were two curates, Leslie and Watson, who did oppose and reason against the covenant before the people, especially as to the abjuring of Episcopacy, &c. But it was to the advantage of the cause, for the men's weakness did much appear before the people, and understanding gentlemen present said that the dispute appeared to them as an assize, wherein the bishops were, as by a jury found guilty, and cast.

From that they went to Letterkenny, where the most part of Sir William Stewart's regiment, and many others of that part entered. From that they went to Ray, where on the Lord's day the multitude was so great, that one of the ministers was forced to be without, when the other was within the church. Two ministers, among the other multitude, did abjure the Black Oath and conformity, and entered into the covenant before the people, the ministers keeping their former method in explaining, proving, and answering objections against the covenant. From thence on Monday they went to Taboin,* being in the centre of the country, where an

---

* St. Johnstone.

extraordinary number of people were met from all places, some fifteen miles off—some who had not taken the covenant in order to take it, and some had taken it, to be further confirmed—and the ministers here made it their work to do both. Here Sir Robert Stewart himself began to draw nearer and confer with the ministers about the covenant—his whole regiment having entered into it before—and some more ministers. There came a letter from Major-General Monroe to the ministers, and another to the Mayor of Derry, which, when he read, he said to some Covenanters with him :—" Now, I will be as arrant a Covenanter as any of you." They come next to Ramelton, where they received the rest of Sir William Stewart's regiment, and very many of Colonel Mervyn's, contrary to his threatenings. Also, one of those who opposed the covenant at Raphoe—Watson—being the most judicious, did now come in and confess his errors, and entered into it with apparent ingenuousness. From these places they returned to Derry, where Sir Robert Stewart, Colonel Mervyn, and Major James Galbraith came now to hear the ministers preach and explain the covenant; and the ministers, hearing of some of their scruples, answered them in public. Divers ministers also were present then, and publickly renounced their former errors, desiring to enter into the covenant. But, some of them speaking ambiguously anent church government and church's and magistrate's power to make laws, the ministers put them to explain themselves fully before they would admit them; and took occasion to clear before the people the limits of divine, and human, and church power, and things of that nature. And, withal, whenever they received ministers into the covenant, they declared to the people publickly that these ministers were not thereby properly made capable of exercising their ministry if there were other considerations to hinder their exercising it, as insufficiency, &c., and that, if judged competent, they might, and should, have their own way of admitting them to the exercise of the ministry, according to the church's order.

The garrison of British at Enniskillen had sent to the ministers, earnestly desiring they would come and administer the covenant to them. The ministers delaying to answer, the garrison sent again, and told them if they would not come to them, they (the garrison) would leave that and come to them to take the covenant—there being then a general inclination that way among the most part of people, even among those who were ignorant of religion, or unfriendly to it. Even some of the Irish, who had come in under protection, offered themselves partly through fear and terror, and considerations of that kind, though many did it with great affection and sincerity. And the ministers did caveate in administering that solemn oath as much as possible in receiving such a multitude in so short a time—who thought they were in that case over scrupulous. However, they were difficulted in this matter, for to go there wanted not hazard, many enemies being between them and that place. And for the garrison to come to them would be dangerous for it, the country about being full of the rebels not yet subdued, and they having daily skirmishes with them. However, the ministers, after calling on God for direction, did resolve to venture themselves, as they had done in other cases, and found much of the providence of God preserving them, and his assistance with them in helping them in their work, and much blessing following on their endeavours. Meantime the mayor of Derry, with some few who had waited on his motions, did desire them to stay a day or two till he could take the covenant. But they, not finding ground for the delay, went to take horse; which he hearing, came after them and entreated them before their departure, to go to church and administer the covenant to him and these few others—which they did. Sir Robert Stewart also declared his resolution to take the covenant, only he put it off upon some considerable reason, alleged by him for that time.

After this they went towards Enniskillen, and the first night to Clady, where the two troops belonging to Sir William and Sir Robert Stewart did meet them to convey them to Enniskillen without hazard. And the worthy gentleman, Colonel Saunderson, went along with them, as at that time the generality of the officers of these regiments were both most respectful to their persons and instrumental in promoting the work they were about. They came along to Enniskillen without sight of an enemy. For the Irish, who were protected, hearing the covenant was coming that way, fled, because they heard that the covenant was to extirpate all Papists,* and was against protecting them. And some so suddenly fled that they left their stolen goods, which they used to steal and send privately to the enemy, who then lay in the County of Cavan. Likewise, the enemy in these parts near about, hearing the covenant was coming, which, as they understood, was against the cessation of arms with them (then driving on), they did beat drums through their quarters, and marched, bag and baggage, thirty miles into the country.

However, the ministers were very kindly received by Lieutenant-Colonel Atcheson, of Sir William Cole's regiment, and all took the covenant, except one poor ignorant minister, and Sir William Cole himself, who said he would take it upon further consideration. However, his whole family took

---

* The Covenanters pledged themselves to "endeavour the extirpation of Popery," but they expected to accomplish this by other means than murdering its professors. They also pledged themselves to "endeavour the extirpation of profaneness," but they had no idea of putting all the wicked to death.

it. Besides, divers garrisons thereabout, as Beleek and Ballyshannon, took the covenant, which kept the ministers two days at their usual work. They then returned, accompanied by Sir William Cole and the strength of his own troop, together with the other two troops, toward Derry, wherein one of the ministers stayed "per vices," and the other in the country for a little time. Mr. Adair being in Derry, Colonel Mervyn came usually to hear, and thereafter propounded his scruples upon some evil considerations on the fourth article of the covenant, which were answered; yet he did not seem satisfied at that time. But within a few days he wrote to Mr. Adair to come to [Strabane?], where the rendezvous of his whole regiment was to be, and he with them would enter into covenant. This appointment Mr. Adair kept, where Colonel Mervyn, with the whole officers, solemnly declared their satisfaction in the covenant, and entered into it, and, while they were doing so, the soldiers who had taken it before, cried out—"Welcome, welcome. Colonel!" From this, Mr. Adair returned with Colonel Mervyn to Derry, being entertained with no small courtesy and protestations of forwardness for the covenant thereafter.*

The ministers, to close the work at Derry, did celebrate the Lord's Supper publicly in the great church, where the altar was removed, to give place to the Lord's Table, and God appeared most sensibly and comfortably in that administration, by the power of His Spirit on ministers and people. All things were done with as much order as was possible in such a case. No scandalous or unknown person was admitted, and the gravest gentlemen in the town and regi-

---

* There are good grounds for believing that the author of this narrative had the use of a journal kept by Mr. Adair at this time, and that he was nearly related to him. We may thus account for the minuteness of these details. The Rev. W. Adair, mentioned in the text, was the brother of Sir Robert Adair, of Ballymena.

ments attended the tables. After this work, the ministers, accompanied by special friends, came to the Water Side, to Captain Lawson's house, where, kneeling down, they commended the people to God. They came that night to Ballycastle [potius Ballykelly?] near Newtonlimavady, where were numbers of people waiting on them to take the covenant, which accordingly was administered to them. From that they came to Coleraine, where Sir Robert Stewart meeting them with Major-General Monroe, did the next day publickly enter into the covenant, together with some few others who had delayed it till that time. So also did Sir William Cole, at Carrickfergus, in his passage for England.

From this the ministers returned to the congregations of Antrim and Down, where the covenant had been before administered, partly confirming the people, who had entered into it already, and partly administering it to some who had not taken it before, among whom was the Lord of Ards. Thereafter they did administer the communion in Newtonards, Holywood, and Ballywalter, in which three places Mr. Adair, Mr. Weir, and Mr. Hamilton (who all this time had staid in these parts) did divide themselves for this work. Mr. M'Clelland, being then come to the country by commission, did also join in celebrating the communion, and those who were ministers in the country and army concurred.

After all this, the holy wise providence of God so ordered it that these worthy men immediately met with sad troubles, lest they should be exalted above measure upon this great work wherein God had assisted them so signally. Mr. Adair fell into a long and dangerous fever, and relapsed again at Newtonards, and thereafter in Stranraer, as he was going home. But Mr. Hamilton and Mr. Weir met with a sorer trouble. The occasion of which was, that at that time my Lord Argyle, being Chief Justice of the isles, had one Colonel

Kittoch in custody, who had been guilty of many enormous things. He had a son named the same way, who was prompted by Satan's instigation to meet the vessel wherein Mr. Hamilton and Mr. Weir were going to Scotland, and did take them prisoners to the Highlands, thinking thereby to get his father loosed by the Lord Argyle. But, upon some weighty considerations, it could not be granted. Whereupon these godly ministers were kept in great restraint and sad straits, without any accommodation or refreshment to their bodies till Mr. Weir died; and Mr. Hamilton, with much ado and great hazard of his life, was got delivered, and lived long, after that, useful to the church at Dumfries and Edinburgh.

CHAPTER VIII.

CASES OF DISCIPLINE—THE MOCK PRESBYTERY OF ROUTE—MINISTERS SETTLED AT BALLYMENA, ANTRIM, CAIRNCASTLE AND ELSEWHERE—THE PRESBYTERY AND THE COMMISSIONERS OF PARLIAMENT—MINISTERS SETTLED AT RAY, LETTERKENNY, AND OTHER PLACES—DR. COLVILLE OF GALGORM—DEFEAT OF THE SCOTCH ARMY AT BENBURB.

BOUT this time, upon a supplication from many in Belfast to the Presbytery for erecting a Session there, it was recommended to Mr. Adair to perform it—which was done, July, 1644. The Presbytery being informed of the scandalous lives of some who had been Conformist ministers, their drunkenness, and selling baptism in private, &c., did summon them, and they compearing and being convicted, were suspended from the exercise of the ministry—Mr. M'Clelland being at that time moderator. (Two of these were Mr. John Bell and Mr. H. Cunningham.) In the next Presbytery the suspension was taken off, upon their promise of amendment, where also Mr. M'Clelland was present. Likewise, upon the Presbytery's desire, Mr. M'Clelland spoke to the Major-General, entreating that the whole army might be subject to discipline, and the people within the bounds where the army lay—there being many scandals both in the army and country. This request, upon his application to the Major-General, was granted. And having this encouragement from those who in that confused time did rule in the country, the Presbytery did improve it to the best advantage, both against some sectaries appearing in some places, and scandalous Conformist ministers, as well as other scandalous persons, summoning them before the Presbytery, and according as they found ground, either censuring or relaxing them.

They had greatest trouble with Mr. Brice,* and with Mr. Hamilton of Dundonald, who obstinately adhered to their former courses, and denied the covenant and the authority of the Presbytery. Upon which these two hirelings were suspended, and thereafter restrained from the exercise of the ministry. The place where there was the greatest hazard of spreading the errors of Independency and Anabaptism, was Belfast—through one Matthews and one Lees being so industrious there—upon which the Presbytery recommended it to *Mr. Hugh M'Kail* and *Mr. William Cockburn* (now come commissioners from Scotland, and having directions from the commission of the church to have a special inspection on that place) that they would visit Belfast frequently for obviating this infection.

At this time, being in or about September, 1644, there was an erection of a new Presbytery in Route by divers ministers who had been Conformists, and had taken the covenant of late, who had no sessions nor commissions from any, but themselves concurring together. The Presbytery, hearing of this, did write a letter to them, by the Moderator, desiring them to send some of their number to the Presbytery to inform them of the grounds of so doing and the manner of their proceeding. Accordingly, they sent Mr. Donald M'Neill with a letter subscribed by their Moderator and Clerk to the next meeting of the Presbytery. But, this not being satisfying, the Presbytery summoned them all to the next meeting, upon which this new Presbytery sent a commission, with two other members, subscribed by all the rest. The Presbytery, hearing what their commissioners—Mr. Fenton and Mr. Donald M'Neill—said for them, did,

---

* This, as Dr. Reid remarks (I. 472, note,) is probably a mistake, for Price. Robert Price, Dean of Connor, and represented as "a great sufferer for the royal cause," was made Bishop of Ferns and Leighlin at the Restoration. —*Mant* I. 610-739.

upon serious consideration, declare that these ministers had erected a Presbytery without order, constituted of several corrupt men, and that they were endeavouring to bring others in daily; and, therefore, for preventing dangers which might come upon religion and the people of God by such disorderly actions and such dangerous proceedings, they did enact that it be suppressed as an unlawful pretended Presbytery, having no calling to meet together from the people, but usurped by themselves. And, whereas, one of their own number, Mr. John Lithgow, had joined with them, they discharged him, unto which he submitted, and the Presbytery ordered them to be summoned to the next meeting—viz. Mr. William Fenton, Mr. Donald M'Neill, Mr. William Fullerton, Mr. James Watson, named Doctor; James Graham, James Hamil, and Thomas Vesey. The most part appearing, and being interrogated if they would submit to the Presbytery, did refuse as members of the Church of Ireland, except the Presbytery could exhibit their commission from the Parliament of England, or Synod of Divines there. Unto which the Moderator assured them, and gave them under his hand, that the commissioners of the Parliament of England and of the Assembly of Divines, being sent to Scotland to the Assembly by commission, desired and entreated the Assembly of Scotland to send over ministers to Ireland for setting up the work of reformation there. After which these ministers did submit themselves to the Presbytery. Upon this, the Presbytery sent some of their number (to wit, Mr. James Baty and Mr. H. Cunningham, ministers, and Lieutenant Lindsay, elder), to Route to try their carriage there, and what calls they had to their parishes where they did now reside and preach. It was found by their commissioners first, and thereafter by supplications and complaints to the Presbytery by the most part of the people of these parishes, and all the sober, religious part of them, that these ministers had generally come in upon these parishes at their own hand, with the consent of a few not well inclined people. And, having been ministers of other places before the rebellion, they had no clear call to reside there till they would give satisfaction. And those who were not so were permitted to preach where they had a call, having before that publickly renounced the Black Oath and conformity, and taken the covenant when commissioners from Scotland did administer it in the country. However, those ministers who had been Conformists before, and of whom some now seemingly subjected themselves to the Presbytery, as to their carriage and preaching were not savoury to the people; and breaking out sometimes into drunkenness and quarrelling, they proved a great trouble to the Presbytery. Besides, others of them altogether refused subjection, though summoned to appear, and were public enemies to the work of reformation then growing up. The Presbytery at this time were frequent in keeping solemn days of publick humiliation for causes relating to the state of that time, as troubles in Scotland by Montrose, or the slow proceedings of reformation in England, both by Parliament and Assembly; the insolence of malignants in this country, especially ministers; sin abounding generally, notwithstanding of our troubles and late entering into covenant, &c. They also continued to send commissioners, consisting of a minister and ruling elder (on this occasion, Mr. John Drysdale, minister, and Captain Wallace, elder), to the Assembly of Scotland, partly for obtaining their opinion in some doubtful cases of discipline; partly to procure more ministers to be sent for visiting, which was procured.

About this time, April, 1645, Mr. David Buttle is called to Ballymena, and Mr. Archibald Ferguson to Antrim; and within a while after, the due order of trials past, were ordained and settled in these places.

About this time, too, the Presbytery finding the Irish Papists—partly who had not been in rebellion, partly who had come in under protection—to grow numerous in the country, and considering their numbers might thereafter prove dangerous to the Protestant religion, and that by the treaty between Scotland and England no toleration is to be given Papists,* and also pitying their souls in their ignorant and hardened condition, made an act that they should be dealt with by the several ministers, to convince them of their idolatry and errors, and bring them to own the truth; or otherwise to enter into process against them in order to excommunication. And they appoint some of their number to speak to the Major-General that he use that authority he hath for forcing them out of this part, and wholly out of the army, if they remain obstinate. The act of the Presbytery was publicly intimated in the several parish churches. The parishes of Newtonards and Killileagh supplicated the Presbytery to concur for a call to Mr. John Livingston (being then present at the Presbytery, and formerly a minister in Ireland), to their parishes, each of them endeavouring to have him. Mr. Livingston entered a protestation that these calls be not prejudicial to the interest of Stranraer, his parish and people in Scotland. This motion, however, had no success. For though the parish of Killinchy did many years after that —in the year 1655, or thereabout—call Mr. Livingston, and he came to Ireland then for a visit, upon their call, and Mr. Hamilton was also invited to Ballywalter; yet the motions

---

* Few at this time could well distinguish between the toleration and the establishment of a religion. Many thought that as the Israelites were forbidden to tolerate idolatry, Protestants were not at liberty to tolerate popery. Even Archbishop Ussher stoutly maintained that Romanists should be compelled by pains and penalties to attend Protestant worship, that they might receive instruction.

for bringing back these worthy men to Ireland did not succeed. They had been driven out of this country, and were necessitated and clearly called to settle in Scotland thereafter, and became singularly useful there, and subject to the Assembly of the Church of Scotland and other church-judicatories who would not part with them. However, about this time Providence supplied the defect, partly by sending over a new supply of able ministers from Scotland, one year after another by turns; and thereafter by sending over divers young men, near together about this time, in 1645 or '6. besides Mr. Ferguson and Mr. Buttle—viz. Mr. Antony Shaw to Belfast (where he was settled and staid for a time, but afterwards was driven away from it by the party then called the malignant party),* Mr. Patrick Adair to Carncastle. Mr. Antony Kennedy to Templepatrick, Mr. Thomas Hall to Larne, Mr. John Greg to Carrickfergus, Mr. James Ker to Ballymoney, Mr. Jeremiah O'Queen to Billy, Mr. Gilbert Ramsay to Bangor, Mr. Thomas Peebles to Dundonald, Mr. James Gordon to Comber, and Mr. Andrew Stewart to Donaghadee.

All these within a year or two were settled in these places, other congregations making way for others, and using the means for bringing them from Scotland. And here it were sinful to pass by and not to mark God's wonderful providence in ordering the beginning and foundation of a church here, raised out of the ruin and ashes into which it had been formerly brought, first through the persecution of prelates, and then by a bloody rebellion and massacre by the barbarous Irish Papists, by which it was brought very low, having before been but as an embryo. Then the first visible relief was by the army sent from Scotland against the Irish rebels; these generally consisting of officers who had no inclina-

---

* The malignants were those opposed to the Covenant, or the High Church party.

tion towards religion, except in so far as the times and State who employed them seemed to favour it; only their chief commander, Major-General Monroe, was not unfriendly, but a countenancer of these beginnings. However, the officers generally were profane, and the bulk of the soldiers haters of the purity and power of religion. There was no visible encouragement in the country for planting a ministry in congregations, for the inhabitants were but few, and much oppressed and burdened through the maintaining of the army, which was much neglected at this time in their pay, through mistakes between the Parliament of England and some officers of the army sent thither, or rather by the indiscreet management of the army's officers by their commissioner, George Monroe. Besides, there was a stock of old Conformist ministers in the country, who had for their own ends gone along with the covenant, and yet returned to their former disposition. They were labouring to carry a faction in the country and army for their way, and had many to abet them, especially men of most note, both in the army and country, and in whose eyes the little beginnings of a Presbytery were despicable, consisting at first only of a few in the army, and two newly planted in the country, insomuch that divers of them did refuse to appear before the Presbytery, and others who did appear denied their authority, having then no shadow of establishment by King or Parliament, and thereafter, when times seemed better, very little countenance from authority. It was also the wonderful hand of God to bring men from Scotland at this time (for from England none could be had of sound principles, having then some encouragement at home, and having antipathy to come to Ireland), considering that Scotland had then use for hopeful young men to plant among themselves. And almost none came hither who had not calls from congregations to stay in their own native country among their friends, having proportion of settled maintenance. Whereas, coming here, they came to a place unsettled, where was a mixture of three divers nations, their maintenance neither competent, nor what was promised secured to them; and coming, moreover, during the time of a bloody war, when nothing was settled in the country. That these few young men should have hazarded in such a case, was by the Lord's hand overruling them,* and it was more his hand that they were in any tolerable measure helped in their difficult and discouraging work, considering they were young, not attained to maturity of judgment, nor having had any experience in the government of the church, especially in the midst of difficulties, and none of the old stock who had been there before being settled among them. Yet God helped these young men into a diligent following of their duty, not only in their own congregations where they did reside, but in watering desolate congregations in the country, and keeping the presbyterial meetings, insomuch that sometimes they were necessitated to be as often abroad in other congregations in the country for supply, and stirring up the people for their own supply, as in their own, and this by the appointment of the presbyterial meetings upon petition from desolate places. These young men, then, minding their work, and delighting therein, mutually comforted themselves in the company of one another at their meetings in the Presbytery, and considered not their present toil, but with a kind of honest delight, not perceiving the hazard they were in, through the unsettledness of the times and many adversaries, which, also, they felt thereafter. And,

---

* The reader must recollect that the author of this narrative was himself one of the young men mentioned in the text. The modesty with which he here speaks of himself and his brethren is highly to his credit.

indeed, want of that sort of sagacity and anxiousness was their mercy; for had they foreseen but the half of what they often did meet with, their young raw spirits, not experienced in affliction, could not have digested it.

In the year 1645 the case of Scotland was very sad, through a flood and inundation of troubles brought on by the Earl of Montrose, who, against six divers armies carried all before him, having overcome them in six battles,* upon which many families fled from Scotland to Ireland for shelter, and these not of the worst affected. And though persons of quality returned to Scotland again, yet many of the more common sort of people staid in the country and added to the new plantation here.

About this time both British and Scotch in the country were in great straits for want of pay from the parliament in England. Upon which the British officers had a meeting at Antrim, in May, 1645, and did draw up a Bond of Union, as they called it, and a protestation to be sworn and signed by all the officers of the army, and the oath to be ministered to the soldiers also, who were bound thereby to go wheresoever they should be led. This some of the officers of the army did scruple at—as Captain Alexander Stewart and Captain Kennedy and others—and desired the mind of the Presbytery in it; to which the Presbytery gave an answer and declaration, which they ordered to be read in every regiment in the British army—which ought to be recorded to show the prudence and faithfulness of the Presbytery in that case.

Toward the end of this year (1645) the ministers of Route, formerly mentioned, and others, took hold of a seeming opportunity to interfere with the Presbytery. The Parliament of England, having, in October, 1645, sent over commissioners to Ulster to rule the affairs of this country—viz.

---

* Montrose was on the side of the King, and opposed to the Covenanters.

Mr. Annesley (afterwards the Earl of Anglesea), Sir Robert King, and Colonel Beal, these ministers applied to them— viz. Messrs. Fullerton, Watson, Vesey, and M'Neil, accusing the Presbytery of bringing a foreign jurisdiction against the laws of Ireland, and that the Presbytery took on them to exercise authority over them, &c. Of this the commissioners gave notice to the Presbytery, sending them a copy of the said libel. And they met with these commissioners at Belfast, by translating the Presbytery thither, where they sent some of their number to the commissioners to give them satisfaction as to these accusations and reflections—which they having done, the commissioners were satisfied. But, withal, the Presbytery told the commissioners they did not appear before them in answering the libel as their proper judges in matters ecclesiastical, but as persons in the quality and station they were now in—as they were bound to do to all men, and especially to those in civil authority. Here the commissioners sat in Presbytery; the Presbytery was encouraged and countenanced, and the others dismissed without satisfaction. The commissioners also did give order, at the Presbytery's desire, that the covenant should be tendered to such as had not taken it at Carrickfergus, Belfast, Lisnegarvy, &c., which was done accordingly. They also did give a right of the tythe of parishes to as many of the new entrants as did apply to them, and did add the civil sanction to the Presbytery, and gave commission to cognosce upon the lives and abilities of scandalous ministers in Lagan, encouraging the Presbytery if they found cause to pass censure on them, which accordingly was done. Some said this gratifying the Presbytery was a piece of emulation and State policy, they finding Major-General Monroe and the army had a great stroke in this country and in Ulster, partly through countenancing these courses. Therefore, they would not be behind with them in giving all countenance to the Presbytery. However, this did much daunt those sorts of ministers at that time, and did strengthen the hands of the few new beginners. For, at this time [in Down], there were none settled of the country ministers but two, and in Antrim but other two —Mr. Buttle and Mr. Ferguson—and the other party were many in all parts of the country. It is true some unfriends did reflect at this time as if the Presbytery had taken commission from the magistrate to exercise their authority, and some friends did scruple at the first offer made by the commissioners, because then the Erastian spirit much prevailed in the Parliament of England. But the commissioners at the very first assured them it was not to make the Presbytery or their discipline subordinate to the magistrate, but only an accumulative power which they intended, and accordingly did give them by their commission or warrant. Upon this, the appointed ministers and elders went to Lagan, preached daily, erected sessions, took depositions against scandalous ministers, and made way for calling ministers to congregations. And there, the people of the country did accuse divers of these ministers, and brought in witnesses, making evident their lewd lives and unministerial carriage—upon which they were first suspended by the commissioners, and then deposed by the Presbytery. And the people thereafter petitioned the Presbytery, by Captains Hamilton and Kennedy, for supply of ministers by turns, the whole country being then void of ministers, except one—Mr. Robert Cunningham—who had been a Conformist, and then seemed to be serious in the profession of the truth, and was then at Taboin (*alias* St. Johnstone). Upon which the Presbytery did send them ministers, the commissioners also concurring with the desire, by turns as they became able and in any measure furnished, and continued the supply till the Lagan got some stock of ministers amongst themselves—as Mr. Hugh Cunningham, at Rye; Mr. William Semple, at Letterkenny; Mr. Thomas Drummond, at Ramelton; Mr. David Gamble, at ——; Mr. James Wallace, at Urney, &c. —all settled in 1646 and '47.

At this time the Lord helped the very small number of ministers in the Presbytery to diligence in stirring up the parishes in the country that were then all generally desolate, to seek after ministers, and consider some way of maintaining them. For which end they appointed one minister and four or five of the most knowing elders, who had weight in these parts, to the principal parishes which wanted. And this was not without fruit; for the parishes set about means for that end as they had a capacity, which was the means of hastening divers young men out of Scotland, as was before related. The fewness and weakness of the Presbytery at this time was supported by God's special countenance, by the honesty of the men, and by the goodness of their cause and intentions; as well as by the commander of the Scotch army, who did, in his own person, usually sit with them at Carrickfergus—besides divers other officers, who were elders of other regiments. And thereafter it was a great encouragement that the commissioners of the Parliament of England did own the actings of the Presbytery. So that though God did not build His temple there by might nor by power (Zech. iv. 6), yet so much of the countenance of those in power and authority as was necessary for the day of small things, was not wanting in the beginning.

The Presbytery at this time, and a while before, did use great diligence to convince Dr. Colville* of divers unsuitable

---

* Dr. Colville, who was by birth a Scotchman, resided on his property at Galgorm —now the estate of John Young, Esq., J.P. He seems to have possessed in an eminent degree the art of money-gathering; and hence, probably, the traditions of his skill in witchcraft. In 1682, a female servant in Irvine, when committted to carriages, both in private discourse with some of their number, and by summoning him before the Presbytery, and had witnesses to prove the allegations against him. But he never appeared, except one time, before the commissioners at Belfast, when he would not direct his speech to the Moderator, but to the commissioners. He had also beforehand applied to the commissioners, vindicating himself and insinuating on them. Upon this, they desired the Presbytery to deal with him as favourably as they could, in regard they had use for the Doctor in reference to their affairs in the country, he being a man knowing that way. The Presbytery had gone so far before the commissioners came over that he was publickly prayed for, in order to excommunication. Yet, thereafter, they found it not convenient to proceed further. And some knowing friends thought it had been greater prudence to have let him alone, since he now owned subordination, and did not preach. However, his wife and son did take the covenant, administered to them by Mr. David Buttle, and that by order of the Presbytery in a publick way—for the Presbytery received none into the covenant but before the congregation—yea, when the commissioners from the Parliament began to receive some to the covenant privately, the Presbytery, hearing of it, sent to them and admonished them, —whereupon they promised to forbear that way of administering it, and allowed that those should take it again publickly.

The Presbytery at this time, when expectants were coming from Scotland, made an act that the young men who came over should have sufficient testimonials—should converse with the most judicious and godly in the places they were called unto, and entertain conference with them—should sometimes

---

prison on a charge of witchcraft, confessed the charge, stating that "she had learned the art from Dr. Colvine (or Colville), who used to practice it in Ireland."—*Statistical Account of Scotland*, V. 633. Colville was made D.D. in 1636. All his estates in the county of Antrim, which descended by the female line to the present Earl of Mountcashel, were recently sold in the Encumbered Estates Court.

preach in other parishes, and converse with good people there —and that private letters should be written by friends here to ministers and other godly persons in Scotland, concerning their conversation while they were there. Hitherto they had the assistance of worthy men from Scotland, and at this time of Mr. George Hutchinson, and thereafter of Mr. John Livingston—by whose assistance also, there was a letter written to the General Assembly of Scotland, from the Presbytery, together with a supplication from the country for new supplies of ministers—there being as yet but two in each county settled in parishes. And this letter and supplication were sent by a minister, Mr. Ferguson, and ruling elder, who were also appointed to enquire for qualified expectants, in order to a call from parishes in this country. They were also commissioned to deal with the Assembly for an act of transportability to the ministers who, before the rebellion had been settled in this country—and instruments in the planting of the Gospel in it—these being now in Scotland.

At this time, in the beginning of June, 1646, the Scotch army, under Major-General Monroe, together with the British, took the field to seek for the Irish army in Ulster, under the command of Owen M'Cart,* who had been bred a soldier in Spain, and came over and gathered together the scattered Irish forces into a body, and was marching toward Sir Phelim O'Neill to join with him against the Scotch and British forces in Ulster. But the British and Scotch armies received a sad blow at Benburb, near the Blackwater. They were wholly routed and many slain, and some taken prisoners, among whom was the Lord of Ards, then a youth. This rout sadly alarmed the country, as well as the army,

---

* Better known as Owen Roe (Eugenius Rufus) O'Neill. He is here called Owen M'Cart, because he was the son of Art, an illegitimate grandson of Feardoc or Matthew O'Neill, Baron of Dungannon.—Carte's *Life of Ormonde*, I. 349, London, 1736. Owen MacArt had held high military command in the Spanish service.

who were called together in divers companies (together with the scattered forces who had escaped the slaughter) to march to the borders of the country for defence of it against the enemy, if he should pursue his victory at the Blackwater. But the Lord restrained the remainder of the enemy's wrath. Their General, being a bred soldier and a wary man, imagined the army and country would be as bears robbed of their whelps, and in a readiness to fight; whereas, indeed, they were but faint-hearted, and in a very evil case to encounter an enemy. But God saw the affliction of his people in the country at that time, and would not destroy the new bud of his own work, which was but beginning to spring up; and, therefore, he did withhold the barbarous Irish from further pursuing, which they might easily have done. Yea, it is observable that, a while after this, when Sir Phelim O'Neill sent parties to prey upon the country and drive the cows of such as they could, the places where the Gospel was planted, though lying near the quarters where the rebels came, were preserved from plunder.

Yet, it is not to be forgotten that this stroke came by the righteous hand of God, especially upon the Scotch army, for many of the soldiers were prodigiously profane and wicked in their lives, and set themselves to prey upon the poor country scarce crept from under the ashes of a horrid rebellion. Being secure, and without any apprehension of fear from the enemy, they went to the fields for a prey, rather than expecting any encounter, only fearing not to see the enemy, being so full of confidence in their own valour and the enemy's cowardice. Therefore, Providence so ordered that they were not together in a body when they met the enemy. Colonel George Monroe, son-in-law to the Major-General, a proud, self-willed man, having divided a considerable number of the forces, led them another way from Coleraine, to meet the Major-General, before they should encounter the enemy. And the Major-General, on his march, finding the enemy almost between him and that party, did overmarch the body of the army that very day on purpose to meet with Colonel Monroe's party, and prevent the enemy meeting them alone; so that, when they came to the view of the enemy, the soldiers were tired and faint, as well as discouraged, to see a very considerable force, and they without their expected aid. Besides, it was said the Major-General at that time did not so manage the business as it might have been, and had not that spirit of command and conduct which usually he had, the Lord making all these things to concur for bringing a stroke upon a guilty, proud party. However, after this sad defeat of the Scotch forces in Ulster, and humbling of his people there, a merciful providence fell in shortly after in giving Colonel Jones and a considerable party of English under his command a victory over the Irish, at a place called Caronis, in the west of Ireland.

The Presbytery, after this blow and danger in the country, ordered a day of public humiliation for the sins procuring it, and in a great measure yet remaining. The commissioners formerly mentioned, from England, being troubled with this defeat of the Scotch and British army, and judging it came through bad management at this time, though both Scotch and British forces had always prevailed against the Irish before that time, and done notable services for the country under the King and Parliament of England, did represent the business so to the Parliament, that the next year they sent over Colonel George Monck to command the British forces in Ulster, and returned to England, having left the Presbytery a desire and allowance, by the authority of Parliament, to administer the covenant where and to whom it was not yet administered.

CHAPTER IX.

MINISTERS SETTLED AT BALLYMONEY AND BILLY—PRIVY CENSURES —COLONEL MONCK AND SIR CHARLES COOTE—THE ENGAGEMENT— MONCK SURPRISES CARRICKFERGUS—SIR ROBERT ADAIR.

DURING the year 1646, and thereafter, the new plantation in Down and Antrim did increase. The Presbytery were constantly employed in taking trials of the young men already mentioned (see page 124), according to the manner used in the Church of Scotland,* and thereafter settling them in their respective parishes. They were somewhat troubled in settling Mr. James Ker at Ballymoney, and Mr. Jeremiah O'Queen (a native Irishman, bred by Mr. Upton to be a scholar), at Billy. In these two parishes of Route, where they were called by the plurality of the people, but opposed by some disaffected persons, particularly by Mr. Stewart of Ballintoy, who had some interest in Ballymoney, and by Mr. Donald M'Neill in Billy, who, with their party did apply themselves to the commissioners from England yet in the country, and appealed to them from the Presbytery. They had given in divers things in a libel against these two expectants, anent the unsoundness of somewhat they had delivered in their doctrine. In answer to these, the Presbytery in the first place appointed two of their number to go to the commissioners, and inform them of the groundlessness and error of this appeal from a spiritual judicatory to the civil magistrate; and that they presumed

---

* The General Assembly of 1638 required the Old Scottish Confession of Faith to be subscribed "by all scholars at passing their degrees," and "by all ministers of the kirk." In 1647, when the Westminster Confession was adopted, the other Confession was laid aside. We see from the text that the Irish Church was guided by the example of the mother Church of Scotland.

the commissioners would not own such proceedings. Unto this the commissioners assented, yet sent this libel to the Presbytery to be examined. This the Presbytery did with all diligence, recommending the examination of it to those of their number who were going to Route to Mr. John Beard's ordination, where the other party might bring their witnesses. But, upon fair trial, they found nothing to obstruct the settling of these men.

In July, 1646, Mr. Archibald Ferguson, returning from the Assembly of Scotland, reported his diligence, and among other things given him in commission, stated, that the Assembly had declared four ministers transportable from the places they were then in into Ireland—viz. Messrs. Livingston, Hutcheson, Henderson, and Robert Hamilton, provided their own consent and that of their parishes could be had. Upon this the Presbytery, together with the parishes to which they were here respectively designed, to wit, Newtonards, Carrickfergus, Killileagh, and Islandmagee, did use all means in their power for obtaining them. But all came to nought. For those places and presbyteries would not want them; and the next Assembly, in 1647, seeing this country beginning to be so likely to be furnished, were not so forward to transport men, but promised the commissioners further supply and expectants. Besides this, the Assembly did recommend the Directory for Worship unto the practice of ministers in this country, which was accordingly by act of Presbytery begun.

Likewise, the commissioners of England at that time sent to the Presbytery some books declaring the way of the Parliament, in approving the exercise of Presbyterial Government in England, and desiring the Presbytery here to follow the same way. Unto this the Presbytery returned answer that they must have more copies, and have time to consider the same. This motion was not further followed by the said commissioners, and therefore did soon vanish. There were some restrictions by the Parliament of England put upon ministers in the exercise of government, which did much entrench upon the freedom and fulness of that government committed to the Lord's servants, and which the ministers here could not swallow.

Lagan all this while was without one settled minister, except Mr. Robert Cunningham, who preached in Taboin, yet not settled; and, in 1647, Mr. Hugh Cunningham was settled at Ray, being transported from the regiment to that place, upon which the special gentlemen and persons who were concerned for the gospel in the country wrote and sent commissioners from time to time to the Presbytery for supplies. Upon which they were sent, both in the years 1646 and 1647. And most of those who were settled, shortly after their settlement were sent once and again, staying four Sabbaths, and among other things pressed the people of the country to provide ministers for themselves—which, accordingly, they fell about, as they became in a capacity—the ministers and expectants being usually sent to congregations destitute of ministers.

The work of God did, this year, 1647, get good footing in the country, and was not retarded by the late stroke on the Irish and British forces. But thereby God's hand of mercy was seen in preserving His poor people and promoting His begun work, as well as his justice in punishing profane men and a secure country by barbarous enemies. Ministers continued to be planted, and, where these could not be had at first in congregations, sessions were erected by the Presbytery's concurrence, ministers and expectants being usually sent to congregations destitute of ministers to stir up and prepare congregations for planting ministers among them, whereby the young ministers were sent to other places frequently, besides having the constant charge of their own congregations. Where ministers were, communions continued to be observed, and the Lord was pleased to give his presence and help to young beginners. However, the Presbytery, according to the laudable custom of other Presbyteries, did make an act, that once or twice a year the members of the Presbytery undergo an admonition or censure of their brethren, if need require it, as to any part of their carriage, whether in the Presbytery or otherwise, or in the discharge of their ministry, known to any of their brethren; and for that end one or two at once were removed till the rest considered what grounds there were to admonish, censure, or encourage them;* and others by degrees were removed, and their carriage considered by the rest, till the whole members, especially the ministers, received the mind of the rest. This was thought a fit means for keeping the brethren more watchful in their conversing, both with their brethren and their congregations and otherwise, as well as for keeping up the authority of Presbytery over particular brethren.

At this time Colonel Monck, commander-in-chief of the British forces in Ulster, kept a fair correspondence with the Presbytery, assenting to what desires they proposed to him for keeping discipline in force over scandalous ministers and persons within his quarters. An instance of this appears in his first letter, directed to one of their members, who, by the Presbytery's appointment, had written to him to that effect, which letter was as follows:—"Sir,—Upon the receipt of your letter, I have inquired of the minister here whether any of these abuses were committed, and he certifieth to me that there hath not been any done these two years. I have laid an injunction upon him not to permit any such scan-

---

* These exercises have been known by the name of *Privy Censures*.

dalous actions for the future; and if any other ministers within my quarters shall either marry any scandalous persons, or christen children that are unlawfully begotten, I will render him up to the justice of the Presbytery to receive censure for his disobedience. This I desire you to acquaint the Presbytery with, there being nothing within my power which may be a means to suppress these scandals but shall be readily performed.—Your friend, to serve you, GEORGE MONCK, Lisnegarvy, 17th of December, 1647. For his respected friend, Mr. Archibald Ferguson, minister of Antrim." Upon this letter, the Presbytery appointed some of their number to go to Colonel Monck, and give him thanks for his professed zeal—who had these promises renewed to them. It is to be remembered that Major-General Monroe, with the Scotch army, had then a great command and interest in the country, and the said General Monroe had evidenced much friendship to the Presbytery for a long time. And it was believed that Colonel Monck, though otherwise principled and inclined, did profess favour to the Presbytery and their proceedings, from politic grounds, as appeared thereafter. The like course was also followed by Sir Charles Coote, President of Connaught and Commander of the British forces about Derry, who at this time wrote to the Presbytery desiring they would send commissioners of their number to these quarters to take courses with scandalous ministers, and other persons under scandals, unto whom he would give assistance.

Though the Presbytery were not ignorant of the ends and pretences of this politician, yet they made use of the opportunity Providence brought in their way, and did send some of their brethren—ministers and ruling elders, persons of knowledge and quality—to these parts, giving them commission to correct abuses there by censuring scandalous and intruding ministers, and to make way for planting the Gospel in these parts. Accordingly, these ministers and elders did in an orderly way call before them divers who had been received as ministers in these parts before, and, there being divers scandals proved before and upon them, they were deposed. These were:—Mr. Robert Barkley, for trading in a way inconsistent with the ministry, for cursing and swearing, profaning the Sabbath, intruding on a neighbouring parish, and for frequent drunkenness; Mr. ———, for drunkenness, swearing, and railing against authority; Mr. James Baxter, for drunkenness, swearing, baptizing, and marrying promiscuously, and for railing against the professors of godliness; Mr. Robert Young, for known debauchery; Mr. Archibald Glasgow,[*] for drunkenness, swearing, and railing against religion; Mr. George Hamilton, for tippling, and sometimes inveighing against professors of godliness; and Mr. Major, for profaning the Sabbath, and promiscuous baptizing, &c. In all which the President did confer with the Presbytery's commission, and a letter of thanks was returned to him for his zeal.

The Presbytery made an act, that there be no sudden vote about any matter, till the thing be first debated and disputed; and that after the voting be commenced there be no more disputing or debating on the subject in hand.

When matters were thus in a hopeful condition, and the Presbytery owned and assisted by persons of present authority in the country—both the English commanders of the army, with their commander-in-chief, striving who should most oblige the ministry—there fell in a new trouble in the year 1648, which did on a sudden, like a land-flood, overflow Scotland and the North of Ireland, and became a searching trouble to the truly godly, especially to officers and soldiers

---

[*] After the Restoration, Robert Young became Rector of Culdaff, and Archibald Glasgow, Rector of Clondevadock.

in the Scotch army here, and to the Presbytery. It was that Engagement undertaken by the Parliament of Scotland against England—for the occasion whereof we refer for full information to other histories, and shall give but only a short hint. The King and Parliament of England, having fallen into misunderstanding, and armies being raised on both sides, and divers battles fought, the Parliament was like to be worsted by the King's forces. Upon which they dealt with the states of Scotland—and the Assembly of Divines in England with the General Assembly in Scotland—by sending commissioners with many fair insinuations and great persuasions to raise an army in Scotland for their aid against a powerful faction of malignants, atheists, papists, &c., a rabble of the profanest in England, who, under pretence of the King's authority for defence of bishops and the present courses of the times, which then had been tending towards Popery, were in a fair probability to swallow up the sincerest Protestant party in England.

The Scotch Parliament and General Assembly considered that if profanity, persecution, Popery, &c., prevailed in England they could not be secure, having not only such a powerful enemy there, but a considerable faction of the like among themselves. Besides, they judged it a necessary duty to support a people who were, as they professed, aiming at the same reformation as themselves, and to rescue them from the barbarous cruelties which were then begun to be exercised, under the command of Prince Rupert, against any who had but the profession of godliness. Having these considerations and the like before them, they raised a considerable army, and sent it into England, under the command of General Leslie, Earl of Leven, having, by their commissioners in London, in the first place, entered into a Solemn League and Covenant with the Parliament and nation of England, generally sworn unto through England, Scotland, and Ireland, wherein safety was not only provided for religion, and for the subject's liberty, but also for the King's safety, honour, and prerogative, and large and plain agreements were made between the two kingdoms and their commissioners for mutual security.

It pleased God that, after the Scotch army went into England, the Parliament's forces, with their assistance, prevailed every day, so that, in the year 1646, the King, finding his forces broken that he could not longer hold out against the Parliament, and the Scotch army being then in England not disbanded, did privately convey himself in a disguise, and rendered himself up to the Scotch army—coming first to General Leslie's quarters, where he was entertained with great joy, the Scotch thinking he would now yield to those propositions which had been long offered to him by both kingdoms for settling the Government, &c. In order to this, they conveyed his Majesty to Newcastle, where the States of Scotland waited on him, together with some of the ablest of the ministry, to persuade him to offer to his subjects proposals which they judged neither derogatory to his honour and greatness nor to the interests of religion. They dealt with him, along with his chief noblemen and greatest courtiers, with tears, and on their knees beseeching him to discountenance the bishops, but all in vain. The King was inexorable; would not part with the bishops, &c.; but judged that, since he put such a great confidence and respect upon the Scotch, they should protest and defend him upon any terms—thereby designing to take them off from joining with England any further in that affair. By their assistance and his own party in England and Scotland (now, indeed, broken, but ready to appear on any occasion), he could soon have reduced the Parliament's forces. The Scotch were thus in a great perplexity. A Parliament was called in the year 1646, and the case stood so before them that they were in doubt what to resolve on. Not to own the King, having, by an unusual trust, put himself into their hands when in arms against him, seemed to be dishonourable, as well as disloyal. On the other hand, to adhere to what he expected from them was the highway to undo all that they had done, destroying the National and Solemn League and Covenant, and putting things in the old channel to Popery and slavery. Besides, the raising up of the wickedest in both nations to oppress those who had stuck fastest to the work of reformation was engaging in a present war against England. Being in this uncertainty what to do, it was resolved by the whole Parliament (five persons only excepted, whereof Duke Hamilton and his brother Lanark were two) that the King should be kept in safe custody in one of his houses in England, with that honour and respect that became him, till it pleased God to incline him to a further condescension to the joint proposals of the Parliaments of England and Scotland. And there were commissioners from both appointed to attend his Majesty, and further deal with him, if it were possible, that he might be brought to a good understanding with the Parliaments, and matters in debate settled upon the right basis of the interest of religion and the King's just authority. The Parliament of England alleged if the King at this juncture should be admitted to full liberty, or be publickly assisted by the Scotch army then in England, he might undo all they had done for vindicating the purity of religion against the corruptions tending to Popery that had crept into the church, and also their civil liberty, which had been much wronged and entrenched upon by the conduct of bad counsellors about the King, most part since the beginning of his reign. Therefore, they required the Parliament of Scotland to call back their forces from England, they having no more use for them, and proposed them the pay that was due. They proposed further, that if the Scotch would leave the King in England (as was said before) they would continue their former amity with Scotland, and concur by all lawful means for promoting the ends of the Covenant, and they would preserve the large treaty between the nations, and be tender of the King's honour and preservation, so far as by any means could consist with religion and liberty. But if the Scotch would needs adhere to the King in present circumstances, he being nothing diverted from his former principles and projects, then they would be necessitated to break with the Scotch and see to their own preservation. Upon these proposals the Parliament of Scotland, considering the King's adhering (as formerly to his former courses,) and being convinced of the justness of the Parliament's proposal, and withal, that their army were only auxiliaries to the Parliament of England, and called in by them and under their pay; and finding themselves unable to preserve the king against the power to which the English Parliament had attained, though in a great measure through their help, the English being in a very low and desperate-like condition when they engaged with them and sent in their army; and withal, as they had not only the power of England then to grapple with, but the power of the malignant party in Scotland (except they would join with them, and so desert the cause they had formerly undertaken, and at the cost and expense of so much blood and treasure, now, through God's mercy, advanced in a good measure)—therefore they were forced, much contrary to their desires, and with much sad reluctancy, seeing it was not possible to prevent it, to leave the King in England—but with such cautions and conditions from the Parliament as firmly did secure the King's person, honour, and interest.*

This is, in short, the true account of that transaction which thereafter was generally imputed to the Scotch, as a selling their King to the English. Whereas, if matters be impartially and without prejudice looked on, the King was neither sold nor bought. For the money the Scotch army had then was their pay, and but the one-half of their arrears, and they were forced to disband and return for Scotland, except they would immediately wage war against England to the apparent ruin of themselves and the cause. Neither was the King bought by the Parliament. For they performed only some part of justice to friends and auxiliaries, in giving them a part of their pay upon their disbanding upon the former grounds. Neither did they intend the King's prejudice in keeping him in England, but to bring him to better terms, in order to religion and liberty, as appeared by their treaties with him thereafter, and latterly by their voting his confessions satisfactory, and that he should be brought to London with honour, freedom, and safety—which vote passed by the plurality a few days before his death, and upon which vote the plurality of the Parliament were forcibly, by a sectarian party, thrust out of the house, and many of them imprisoned for owning the King's interest.

But that which marred the intentions of both Parliaments in reference to the King was the army in England, then under Fairfax as general, but most led by Oliver Cromwell. The King was by a party of this army taken from Holdenby House, and conveyed from place to place (the particulars whereof we leave to their proper histories), till at last he was placed in Newport, in the Isle of Wight, in the custody of the

---

* The true character of this transaction is here described by Adair with great perspicuity and propriety.

army—yet so as they always did further insinuate upon him, and made him believe they would restore him to liberty upon certain conditions proposed by them—as indemnity and liberty of conscience, and certain favors to some of their leaders. These, it is said, the King did for a time hearken unto, and intended to comply with, finding himself now in their power, and not having a right understanding with the Parliament, till he found himself but deluded by them. They only, and particularly Cromwell, kept him in some hopes, till he got his own ends better wrought. But, to come nearer our purpose. It fell out so that, while the King is thus kept prisoner by the sectarian party in the Isle of Wight, the States of Scotland sadly resented the case, and knowing what sad reflections it brought on them who left him in England, did entertain correspondence with his Majesty by some of their number, and declared themselves ready yet to appear for his Majesty upon the terms formerly proposed. But he so dealt with the person (the Earl of Loudon, then Chancellor of Scotland) who was with him from Scotland, that this lord yielded to such terms from the King as did not satisfy the party in Scotland (nor England) which had owned the work of reformation. Yet, a Parliament was called in Scotland to cognosce upon the business, and the commission of the church was then there sitting. The generality of the Parliament being sensible of the King's present case and of their own dishonour, resolved to enter a new war, and rescue the King's person from that captivity, to their utmost hazard, which the other party would willingly have complied with, and run the same hazard for the King's Majesty, if they had found religion secure upon his restoration; but that was not found to be sufficiently provided for. But they did foresee that if the King should be restored to honour, freedom, and safety (which was the resolution then owned) without security first had for religion, all things would be reduced to their former channel, religion overturned, the ends of the covenant frustrated, and the godly in the land exposed to greater hazard and persecution than ever before.

Wherefore, that party in the Parliament did protest against the proceedings of the rest, and withdrew. Likewise, the commissioners of the church, having had many debates with commissioners from the Parliament, did declare that the Engagement against England was unlawful, undertaken without the consent of the Covenanting party in England, or without any breach made by them against Scotland; and, withal, no security for their reformation being provided for, but the King left to his liberty, as to this matter, after his supposed restoration.

Notwithstanding, the Parliament raised a considerable army, and sent over commissioners to Ireland for auxiliary forces from their army in Ireland, who were under the pay of the Parliament of England. This army in Scotland being declared against by the ministers generally, and being levied out of the grossest sort of men, both officers and soldiers, who had least respect for the covenant and work of reformation—they, during the short time before they went to England, became very insolent, and, upon the matter, the enemies of both ministers and people who had any profession of godliness, not only threatening them, but committing outrageous actions upon them, even in publick congregations, and upon the soberest and most religious sort of people, who, they thought, did not approve their way. The same were the principles and practices of that part of the army here who were sent for to Scotland to join with them there, breathing threatenings against the Presbytery and all good people. The Presbytery, being assisted by the reverend and worthy Mr. Livingston, sent from the commission of the church in Scotland, emitted a warning or declaration against their proceedings; and the ministers having read it in their pulpits, and having before that kept publick humiliation for preventing that unlawful Engagement, used all other means in their power for that end, both in the counties of Down and of Antrim, as well as in the Lagan, by sending some of their number there to give warning to those of the British army who were inclinable to go to Scotland. This faithfulness and freedom of ministers enraged that party, and made them intolerable in their carriage, not only to ministers, but to the country that generally owned the ministers. But this was only a "nubecula." This party soon went on their way to Scotland to join with the Scotch army. Yet they came not the length to join. For before they could reach that army it was broken at Preston, in England, and they forced to return to Scotland, where, having bad reception—the Covenanting party, upon the defeat of the Engagers in England, having the command of the country—they were forced to disband, and much misery came upon both Scotch and Irish armies engaged in that design, the particulars whereof we refer to their proper histories.

The Presbytery having sent Mr. John Greg as their commissioner to the Assembly of Scotland this summer (July, 1648), the Assembly returned an answer by him, and appointed to supply in Ireland Messrs. Alexander Livingston, Henry Semple, Andrew Lauder, and John Dick. In these times there was frequent correspondence between Presbyteries in Scotland and the Presbytery in Ireland anent scandalous persons fled from Scotland hither. And, accordingly, the Presbytery here did prosecute them according to the desire of those Presbyteries, usually returning them back to Scotland to answer their scandals there. The Presbytery, also, upon every necessary occasion, did keep correspondence with Colonel Monck and Sir Charles Coote, and had their fair promises for concurring in settling presbyterial government in their quarters, and restraining irregular ministers of the old Conformists who acted without subordination to the Presbytery, and also some private men who were venting the errors of Independency and Anabaptism. Colonel Monck's professions may appear by the letter returned in answer to divers demands of the Presbytery, as well as those of Sir Charles Coote by his letter. The Presbytery appointed a committee to consider these letters, and what overtures they thought fit to propose to the Presbytery upon the same, with other particulars of moment. This committee consisted of three ministers—viz. Archibald Ferguson, Patrick Adair, and Anthony Shaw, with three elders—viz. Captains Wallace and Eccles, and Mr. James Shaw, of Ballygelly.* The committee overtured—first, that two brethren be sent to visit the Lagan; secondly, that these brethren declare publicly against Erastianism, then much followed by the Parliament of England. They also produced the draught of a letter to Sir Charles Coote, all of which the Presbytery approved. An act, too, was made by the Presbytery, that, where ministers are necessitated to be absent from the Presbytery at any time, and a process or any business be depending where they are concerned, then they give an account, by writing—that such process or business be not retarded by their absence.

After the defeat of the Scotch army at Preston, and the disbanding of the Irish party in Scotland, there fell out a great alteration in the government of these parts of Ireland upon this occasion. George Monroe, after his disbanding, intended to return to this country, together with a profane crew of officers who had followed him, and who had been professed enemies to the ministry and people of God at his

---

* The family of this gentleman retained possession of the estate of Ballygelly, near Larne, until about fifty years ago.

departure. The Major-General, Robert Monroe, his father-in-law, though from his first coming to Ireland he had countenanced the Presbytery, and been in his station very instrumental for promoting presbyterial government in the country, yet had been consenting to the Engagement against England, alleging that he was, by his commission from the Parliament of Scotland, bound to answer their demands in disposing of the army, or any part of it, according as he was required by their commissioners. Upon this, there was conceived a fear among good people that he would receive and entertain the said George's adherents in so far as he could advance them again; yet there was no desire in the country or by ministers to be rid of him who had been so much their friend. However, Colonel Monck then commanding the British forces, cunningly fomented jealousies of that nature; and, understanding that Major-General Monroe had disobliged one of the Scotch regiments (Glencairn's) by straitening their quarters, and also the gentlemen who then had considerable interest in these quarters, by forcing the soldiers to oppress the tenants, did secretly consult with some of the officers of that regiment, especially with Captain Brice Cochrane and Major Knox, together with those gentlemen that were concerned in the quarters, in what way the Major-General's garrison might be surprised and be removed—withal, promising great things to them if they would be instrumental in it. The gentlemen, having a grudge at the Major-General, and fearing his receiving of George Monroe, with his associates, and not discerning Monck's policy, and what he was driving at, nor foreseeing the prejudice that would thence follow upon the Scotch army in Ireland after their long service, and expense of so much blood against the Irish, resolved to hazard by coming into the garrison by night—knowing, as the gates were carelessly kept in his quarters at Carrickfergus, they might, by the help of an ambush without the wall, surprise the soldiers at the north gate, and leave the gate open to a great party, under Monck, immediately to enter the town—all which they did early in the morning of September 13, 1648, and surprised the Major-General in his bed. Colonel Monck immediately shipped him for England, where he was kept prisoner in the Tower of London for several—some say for five—years.

Thus the Major-General was discarded, and the interest of the Scotch army in Ireland easily broken by the inadvertancy of a very few Scotch men, gulled by Monck. There was another Scotch gentleman, Sir Robert Adair, not being upon the contrivance but upon this occasion. He then had his residence in Scotland, but having a considerable estate in this country, and withal, a troop of horse given him by the King at the rebellion, which was now under the command of Colonel Monck. He came upon his occasions to Ireland, and after he had ordered his affairs, was returning back as far as Belfast at that very time when these gentlemen were upon this project. He got strict orders from Colonel Monck to return to his troop for some special service; and so returning and consulting in a council of war, anent the business, though he declared his dislike of the design, especially carried on in that way; yet, the authority of his commander forced him to enter the town with the rest, and in person to go to the Major-General's lodging and apprehend him. This gentleman having been of unspotted carriage, and in great esteem in his station before this time, for candour, religion, and many singular qualities, this action did relish worse in his person, though his circumstances in it were not like others concerned.*

---

* Adair here evinces a very laudable anxiety to vindicate the reputation of his father-in-law.

The Presbytery, out of gratitude to the Major-General, their old friend, and good instrument for promoving of discipline in the country, did much resent this practice in these gentlemen, and particularly in Sir Robert; and did refuse to admit them as members of the Presbytery—though chosen as elders from their respective sessions. But, Sir Robert returning shortly after to Scotland, and declaring how he was engaged in that affair, and the grounds upon which he went, had the approbation both of the state of Scotland and commission of the church, which was certified to the Presbytery by a letter from the commission of the church. Meantime (as was before mentioned), Colonel Monck countenanced the Presbytery, and sat with it at Lisnegarvy, as their great friend and promoter of the work. But it was the first and last Presbytery which sat in that place.

CHAPTER X.

THE REPRESENTATION—RENEWAL OF THE COVENANT—COLONEL MONCK AND THE PRESBYTERY—SIR ALEXANDER STEWART BESIEGES DERRY—KER AND O'QUIN SUSPENDED AND RESTORED.

BUT after this, matters began to run in another channel, and the ministers, with the good people in the country, began to grapple with new difficulties upon this occasion. After the defeat of the Scotch army at Preston, and Cromwell's coming to Scotland—after he routed the remainder of those forces there and returned to England again triumphant with the army—that army of his, and especially himself, began to appear in their own colours; to leave the former road of reformation and covenant, preserving the King in his just power and greatness, and to carry on a course of lawless liberty of conscience, overturning the foundations of government in England. Upon this, February 15, 1649, the Presbytery in Ireland drew up a "Representation,"* by which may appear the condition of that time. And they appointed the renewing the covenant next Sabbath, save one, after the Presbytery, and a fast to be kept the week before. And withal, they appoint one of their number, Anthony Kennedy, to go to Dundalk to Colonel Monck, and show him a copy of the "Representation," and acquaint him with their intentions to renew the covenant; and withal, to show him their resentments against the multi-

---

* In this Representation the Presbytery charge "the Sectarian party in England and their abettors," as proceeding "without rule or example to the trial of the King," and as putting him to death with cruel hands. Milton was employed by the Council of State in England to answer this document. His reply may be found in his Prose Works.

tude of Irish papists protected in the exercise of their idolatry, who had been in the late horrid rebellion. He wrote back a letter by the commissioner, wherein he declared himself not satisfied with the resolution of the Presbytery, and desiring they would delay the things till he returned to Lisnegarvy, where he would call a council of war, and consult with them, which he accordingly did. But before this letter came to the hands of the Presbytery, the "Representation" was read in the whole congregations of the Presbytery, except by three ministers (of whom hereafter), and the covenant was renewed everywhere with great affection among the people; and so his desires could have no place. It may seem strange that a few young men, concerned with an inconsiderable people in two or three counties in the North of Ireland, who had neither power nor policy, nor were formed into any united way among themselves, should adventure upon a thing of this nature, publickly to declare their opposition to two great parties at that time:—the sectarian party, ruling in England, with some adherents here; and the remnant of the malignant party, who then had most of Ireland. But in this the Presbytery walked not upon principles of policy, nor did much consult natural prudence; but were led thereunto by the example of Scotland, which did at at that time renew the covenant, and did declare against the King's murder; not considering the vast difference between their state here and Scotland, an entire kingdom. None, however, from Scotland did advise them to it, nor did say it were wisdom in them to go about such things in their circumstances; yea, the most grave and wise, both of church and state, did rather dissuade from it at that time, apprehending it might be a means to crush the small hopeful bud of God's work in this country. Yet they, being informed by one of their number (Mr. Patrick Adair?) as well as by a zealous gentleman, Lieutenant-Colonel Wallace,* who had lately come from Scotland (1649), of the proceedings of that church and state; they judged themselves bound to follow so good example, not considering, as in duty they ought to have done, the difference between Scotland and them in many respects, they being but a small colony in Ireland, under the dominion and government of England, where now the sectarian party prevailed and ruled over all, and being also unable to make any resistance to an enemy; while, on the other hand, Scotland was a free kingdom, formed in a government subject to none, and entire among themselves as to this matter of declaring against the sectaries.

The Presbytery ordered all their number to perform this duty in their own congregations first, and thereafter each minister in the congregations next adjacent to his own. All this accordingly was performed in February, 1649. And it was observed that those who before had been no friends to the covenant upon the King's account, now became very zealous for it, and owned the " Representation," notwithstanding it declared against the malignants making new use of that opportunity for preserving the King's interest asserted by the covenant. But, when their other helps were gone, they were glad to take hold of it. Therefore, the Lords Claneboy and Ards, with their officers, did generally and with great alacrity renew the covenant. Yea, they made a show of some reformation for a time, restraining all drinking, swearing, and profane courses as had been usual among them. They entertained the ministers kindly, and did

---

* Shortly after this time Colonel Wallace resided at Red-hall, Ballycarry. He commanded the Covenanters at the battle of Pentland, in 1666, after which he fled to the Continent. He was married to the daughter of Mr. Edmonstone, of Ballycarry, and was brother-in-law to Sir Robert Adair.—*Reid*, II. 30.

much simulate strictness, but still with a secret intention to espouse the old quarrel in the person of the young King. Therefore, they found it their fittest course to deceive the well-meaning ministers and good people in the country with fair pretences till once they got themselves formed in power and some capacity to work their own ends, especially having the Marquis of Ormond there in Ireland with a very considerable body, and having some hopes that Monck would comply with him. In all this the Lord of Ards was the great contriver, director, and pattern, in his own carriage carrying himself so fair and so friendly with the Presbytery, and pretending concurrence in all the ends of the covenant, as that few doubted his integrity, even while, withal, he kept constant correspondence with Ormond, who then commanded the King's forces in Ireland. Notwithstanding, he, with his own hand, formed a Declaration for the Covenant, and against both malignants and sectaries, which was read and approved by the Presbytery, after some alterations and additions. Meantime, the commission of the church or General Assembly sent a letter to the Presbytery to this effect, not knowing their renewing of the covenant, and having heard a good account of Monck and Coote there concurring with the Presbytery. The Presbytery, having renewed the covenant in their own congregations and those about them who were willing, appointed some of their number to repair to General Monck and the Council of War of the British forces at Lisnegarvy, to desire an order to be given for renewing the covenant by the army and in their garrisons. The Presbytery made this proposal in an humble and respectful manner to the chief commander. The General and Council of War returned answer by their commissioners, Lieutenant-Colonel Trail and Major Ellis, that they thought it not expedient at this time, seeing it had been sworn before, and was now renewed by the most part of the congregations; and any who had not might do it if they pleased. But they judged it inconvenient to give an order for it—withal reading a protestation that they all resolved to adhere to the ends of the covenant against all enemies of it. But the Presbytery could not obtain a copy, neither was this protestation subscribed. The Presbytery ordained one of their number to repair to the Council of War, and from them to declare their dissatisfaction with the Council of War's answer, and that they ought to renew the covenant themselves in giving order for it. And, because Colonel Monck had promised a Council of War to consult of means for securing the country, consisting of some officers from each regiment and some country gentlemen of both counties, the Presbytery appointed their commissioner to remind the General of his promise; and, withal, they appointed a committee of their own ministers and elders to attend the said Council of War, and have their own meetings from time to time, in order to the preservation of religion—which accordingly they did.

Meantime, the Presbytery sent two of their number to Lagan to offer the covenant to congregations who would take it there, which they accordingly did, and found many very willing, and others not. The commissioners also (being appointed by the Presbytery so to do) proposed the same desires to Sir Charles Coote, at Derry, which had been made to Colonel Monck anent the covenant. But he refused. Seeing that the covenant did not now bear sway in England as formerly, and the prevailing party there slighting it, he turned his course another way, and all along complied with them. Notwithstanding the Presbytery from time to time sent down brethren to water these parts, there being few ministers yet planted there. The Presbytery ordered, too, that where any persons had at first spoken against the covenant, or refused it, before they be admitted to it they be convinced of their scandal, and publickly acknowledge it, and that this be publickly intimated in congregations.

Lieutenant-Colonel Cunningham, in subscribing the covenant, had this singular condition in Latin:—"Ego G. C. subscribo tantum morali parti hujus fœderis." The Presbytery being informed of this limitation, judged it scandalous, and ordered the said Lieutenant-Colonel Cunningham to acknowledge his sin and offence publickly before the congregation of Carrickfergus, and that he tear the subscription out of the paper, and subscribe as usually—which accordingly he did. On this, the Presbytery ordained that those who refused to take the covenant in a due manner, should be declared enemies to it publickly before the congregations where they dwelt. The Presbytery having commissioners in the Lagan, gave a commission to them, with the few ministers settled there, to meet in a committee with proportionable ruling elders, to consult of the affairs relating to the church and covenant there, and return their diligence to the Presbytery. This was the origin of the Presbytery of Lagan. Withal, they direct divers letters to considerable gentlemen in the country, whom they found in any measure favourable to the covenant and work of God, to encourage and thank them, particularly to Sir Alexander Stewart,* a gentleman of great integrity, and fervent in propagating the gospel interest in these parts. They also wrote to Colonel Saunderson,† a sober gentleman, and to others. Meantime, the Presbytery renewed the commission to their committee, to attend the

---

* Sir Alexander Stewart was a decided Presbyterian. He was killed the following year at the battle of Dunbar, in Scotland. His only son, born six weeks after his father's death, became the first Baron Stewart of Ramelton, and Viscount Mountjoy. —*Reid*, II. 95, note.

† Of Castle-Saunderson, Co. Cavan.

council of war, to give them advice in point of conscience in order to the securing of the country, and of religion therein. And the Presbytery, being asked by their brethren of the committee, what might be the least they would accept from Colonel Monck and the Council of War for security of religion; resolved upon these four heads—1st. That the General and Council of War subscribe the covenant, and give orders for the same to those under their command; 2nd. That Colonel Monck take no orders from the prevalent party in England, which may not be consistent with the covenant; 3rd. That he act nothing of publick concernment without a council of war, till there be a free parliament in England; 4th. That he give a proportionable quantity of arms and ammunition to every regiment, for the defence of religion and the country.

These four proposals the committee afterwards made to Colonel Monck, and withal at this time most of the congregations of the country sent some of the most discreet and knowing persons of their number with petitions to Colonel Monck and the Council of War to Lisnegarvy, much to the same purpose, declaring their sense of God's mercy in their quiet enjoying the Gospel* at present, and withal their hazard through enemies on all hands—Irish (many whereof were lately protected and armed)—malignants, and sectaries, and desiring that the General, the Council of War, and the army would engage in the covenant, and put the country in a posture of defence against the enemies of it. Unto these petitions from the country, and humble desires from the Presbytery, there were some specious arguments given by Monck to comply with the times and the circumstances he was in, but so as not to disown the prevailing party in England, nor to secure the ends of the covenant, although the most part of the Council of War would have concurred with these desires as reasonable and religious. Upon this there were divers messages between the Presbytery and him, and debates in writing, in all which the Presbytery always discovered and showed that in his answers and seeming concessions to their demands he reserved a latitude and evasions to himself, never closely nor cordially complying with the ends at which they were driving, but always keeping himself free to join with whatever party would most prevail.

It was not only the Presbytery and their committee who dealt with Colonel Monck in those affairs; but also the officers of the army. He thought to have trepanned officers to a Declaration on a sudden, in a council of war, which (many of them under his command being men of good principles), did refuse till further consideration and advising with the regiments. Upon this they appointed a meeting of the most considerable officers, by which meeting this Declaration was refused, and another drawn up, which, after being seen by the Presbytery, and some amendments to it made, was approved. The reasons for rejecting the Declaration framed by Monck were—1st. Because he shifted the renewing of the covenant, and proposed persecuting the rebels as the only present duty; 2nd. He mentioned rebels in general terms, not Irish rebels, according to the usual designation, by which term he might mean those who rebel against the present pretended Parliament in England, called the Rump; 3rd. Because he mentioned nothing of the sectaries in it; 4th, Because he required in it absolute obedience to himself against all such as he should require; and though he added this condition—"According to the ends of the covenant," yet that binds not him who answers the ends of the covenant in so lax a sense as to allege that the party in England break it not. The other declaration was framed by the Lord of Ards and the army, and was afterwards somewhat refined and approved by the Presbytery.

Colonel Monck dealt subtilely to endeavour to engage the officers to his Declaration under fair pretences before the other came to their hand. The committee of the Presbytery being then at Belfast, where Colonel Monck had met with the Council of War, dealt with the officers in a meeting with them to subscribe, first, their own Declaration, before they take into consideration the other proposed by Monck, and give in the reasons in writing—1st. Because the subscribing this Declaration unites the army unto the ends formerly proposed against temptation to the contrary, which is now carrying on; 2nd. Every day's delay in declaring against the sectarian party gives advantage to the adversary to work their own designs; 3rd. Delay to subscribe will give further ground of jealousy conceived by many in the country that they are but gaining time, and not single in their first profession; 4th. They have already consulted the committee and the Presbytery in that "Declaration" as to points in conscience and duty, and now to waive it were to declare they have been but mocking; 5th. If this be waived, no ground can be given for securing religion, &c. It may be observed that about this time there was an act passed by the Presbytery that no particular minister should give testimonials to any to beg without their own parishes.

After the officers had subscribed this "Declaration," and had rejected his own, Colonel Monck proceeded in his concessions; and these not satisfying the Council of War or committee of Presbytery, he gave more ample concessions; but still, as before, with a latent reservation of a back door to himself, which not satisfying, he desired a delay for a week, and, meantime, consulted with Colonel Jones, who commanded in Leinster, under the Parliament of England, and who had refused to join in this undertaking of the Council of War here. Thereafter he obtains a delay for a month; but after that, Colonel Monck perceiving the British army

L

under his command to be upon designs wherein he would not concur, and that the Lord of Ards drew to the field upon pretence of the ends of the Declaration, but rather to surprise him in his garrison of Lisnegarvy, he (Colonel Monck) broke off further treaty with him, and went to England. Upon this occasion the Lord of Ards, and those of his officers who had formerly been no good friends to the work of reformation, and now of late had, in appearance, joined heartily in the covenant, and emitted the former Declaration for the ends of it, got more room and opportunity to work their designs, which were to bring the army and country here under subjection to the Marquis of Ormond, who was Lord Lieutenant in Ireland under the young King,* and was carrying on the old design in this country which Montrose was intending and engaged to do in Scotland—all at this same time by the King's commission. However, as yet their designs did not appear to be against the covenant. They were only proposing to the Presbytery to send one of their number to the King, as they were about to send one from themselves to his Majesty, that both may go together to propose the covenant, and espouse the work of reformation to his Majesty, according as the Church and State of Scotland, by sending commissioners to him, were about doing. But the Presbytery, as to their part, thought it not expedient to send any from them to the King.

During this time of treaty with Monck, the Presbytery had sent some of their number to Lagan, to join with the few ministers there in renewing the covenant; and withal, to make the same proposals to Sir Charles Coote, who commanded those parts, which they had already made to Monck

---

* Charles II. Charles I. was put to death on the 30th of January, 1649. About this time there were, in addition to the Romanists, who were also divided, three other parties in Ireland—viz. the High Church Royalists, at the head of whom was Ormonde, the Republican Independents and Sectaries, supported by Coote and Monck, and the Covenanters, or Presbyterians.

here. The Council of War also sent commissioners to those who had renewed the covenant—viz. Cunningham, Maxwell, and Moore, advising them to draw their forces to the fields for the ends of the covenant—as they of Down and Antrim had done before. But Sir Charles, notwithstanding he had been seemingly forward before for the Presbytery, and had concurred with them and was sworn a ruling elder in Derry, now finding things going in another channel in England, altogether refused to declare against the party in England, or to give order for renewing the covenant. Upon this, animosities arose between him and those of the army and country there who had renewed the covenant, and had subscribed the same Declaration which was subscribed in Down and Antrim by the Council of War. And on this occasion, the officers who had taken the covenant and declaration, had drawn together some other forces to the fields, according as they were advised by them. But Sir Charles sent out a party from Derry and Coleraine, and fell upon a considerable number of persons at the rendezvous near Derry. Upon which Sir Alexander Stewart marched toward Derry with his regiment, and sat down before it. Others really affected, joined with him, so that Derry was surprised and brought to straits.

When they were thus besieging Derry for a considerable time, the old malignant party in the country pretended great affection to the cause, and, submitting to the covenant and declaration, mixed with them in the league, and become a stronger party there than the other commanded by Sir Alexander Stewart. As the Presbytery all these times had supplied the Lagan by commissioners of their own number, upon their own charges, one or two at a time; so the ministers, who had, upon Sir Alexander's desire, been sent from the Presbytery to join with the few ministers of Lagan, in order to further the renewing of the covenant, and entering into the "Declaration" in that country, being invited to preach in the league, did comply with the desire for a time—the rather to know how things were going on, and to understand the designs of that party. But a few days discovered to them that the malignant party carried all before them, and that they were generally profane and unconcerned for religion and the ends of the covenant. The ministers could not in duty but testify this in their preaching; whereupon, though for a little time they were seemingly entertained and consulted with, as the circumstances of that party called for in that juncture; yet within a very little time they were slighted and mocked by the new party who had joined. But Sir Alexander Stewart, with his party, still persisting in his respect for the ministers, put it to them for their advice what was best to be done. The ministers saw no grounds for him and his party to continue the league, and so declared, not from respect to Coote's party, but that they saw the the old malignant interest carrying on. At this they were yet more discountenanced by the other party, upon which they left off frequenting the league, and employed themselves in such places of the country as were destitute of ministers. Thereafter, divisions grew between the two parties in the league; and, honest men being put on the hardest pieces of service, divers were killed, and all of them found it hard to continue the siege. Therefore, they acquaint the Lord of Ards with their condition, who, with his attendants, went to Derry, pretending to bring about a right understanding between Coote and them. He was received into the town with civility and compliments, and had communion with Coote, but no agreement followed. Therefore, he returned that night to the league, where, being at supper, and having drunk largely in the city, he became more free in his discourse in the audience of one of the ministers of

Down, who came thither to take leave with some friends, saying, "If Coote would engage for monarchical government in the person of the present King, the devil take him that meddles with religion; let God fight for his own religion himself." And, indeed, thereafter, returning homeward, he, in his actings, proved the same man he then professed himself to be.

At this time George Monroe was fast hastening from Ormond with a band of Irish Papists who had lately been in rebellion to join in this siege of Derry. He brought a letter to Sir Robert Stewart, one of that party and an old malignant, who then used the ministers civilly, desiring him to lay hold on the persons of the ministers as the greatest enemies to their design. This letter being intercepted and presented to a meeting of the ministers, they found it their duty to be on their guard. Those of the Lagan lurked in the country, and those of the Claneboys returned home.

But before we go on, it is fit to remember a troublesome passage the Presbytery had with two of their brethren, lately admitted to the ministry, though not young in years, for whose settling in opposition to the malignant party the Presbytery had had great difficulty. These were James Ker and Jeremiah O'Queen (by birth an Irishman), both of them men of great reputation for honesty and zeal, though of little learning and no great judgment. When the Presbytery appointed renewing the covenant and reading the "Representation," in February before, these brethren, not being then present at the Presbytery, did decline to concur in the Representation. The next Presbytery, hearing this, questioned the brethren; and they, pretending some reasons for not reading the Representation, the other brethren did divers times, and at the meetings of several Presbyteries, use all means to satisfy their scruples. But they still persisted in their opinion, and refused to concur in a duty so necessary at that time; and in discourse, finding they did not absolutely condemn the murder of the King, nor the courses of the sectarian party in England, but rather mitigated their practices and put a good construction upon them after they had overturned the foundations of government, both in church and state, the brethren, having waited long on them, at last passed upon them a sentence of suspension, and appointed a brother to intimate it in their churches. But they despised the sentence, and justified themselves to the people they conversed with; and therein by many they were believed, and the Presbytery were condemned and reflected on for severity and rashness. Upon this consideration, and also to inform the commission of the church in Scotland of the proceedings of the Presbytery in their late actings, the Presbytery sent over Mr. Thomas Hall, to the Commission of the church. The suspended brethren after this made divers applications to the Presbytery for opening their mouths, but having no sense of their wrong, they were rejected. Yet, when these men had run their course for a time, and concurred a while with the sectaries after their brethren were lying under their persecution; they at length discovered the course that party followed, and that they aimed at temporal dominion rather than religion, and that when they came to the country the greatest malignants were greatest with them, because they could flatter and comply; and that the truly godly, who could not justify their proceedings, were exposed to their hatred, contempt, and persecution. These brethren did return to the rest, and acknowledge their errors both before the brethren, and as they had occasion, also before the officers or governors of the sectarian party in this country. Upon this, they were received into their former fellowship, and their suspension taken off. The Presbytery also put forth a vindication of their proceedings in this case.

CHAPTER XI.

SCHEMING OF THE LORD OF ARDS—HIS DISPUTES WITH THE PRESBYTERY—ARRIVAL OF CROMWELL IN IRELAND—SIR JAMES MONTGOMERY OF GREYABBEY — DEATH OF OWEN O'CONNOLLY — MINISTERS PRAYING FOR CHARLES II. ARE APPREHENDED — CONFERENCE BETWEEN THEM AND COLONEL VENABLES—THEIR HARDSHIPS.

BUT to return to the account of the party now carrying on their designs. George Monroe, leaving the siege of Derry, advanced and surprised Coleraine with his band of Irish. Meantime, the Lord of Ards, having from the beginning of this late rebellion, had intercourse with Ormond, and having received a commission from him by order of the King to command-in-chief the forces in Ulster, carried on his correspondence with George Monroe in private, and endeavoured to engage the Lord Conway to his party, assuring him he would in due time suppress the ministers and discard such officers as were not fit for their purpose. This was made known to the Presbytery, and my lord questioned on it; but he denied it all. At this time, also, when the country was alarmed by George Monroe and his Irishmen coming over the River Bann, and he making open profession of his intentions, some gentlemen in the country, with the advice of ministers in the County of Antrim, resolved to meet him, with the assistance of some soldiers, under the command of Major Clotworthy and Major Ellis, and some of Glencairn's regiment, not thinking all this time of his correspondence with the Lord of Ards and his faction. They went as far as Clough, near Ballymena; but the soldiers were few, and the country utterly unarmed and untrained, and divers gentlemen there were altogether unwilling to engage. Besides that, some in the company were set on to weaken the hands of the rest from engaging. And so, the wiser sort seeing nothing but confusion likely to ensue upon this business, some of their number were sent to Monroe to know what he would be at. He told them he designed nothing but the restoring of lawful authority and the opposing of sectaries, and that he would molest none who opposed not him, or were known enemies to authority, or friends to the sectaries. Upon the confidence of this, it was resolved by the officers and country gentlemen to return home, which they did.

The Presbytery now began to be more jealous of the late reformers, and particularly of the Lord of Ards. Therefore, they appointed a committee to meet frequently at Belfast to observe their motions, that being the place where country gentlemen and officers then most haunted. The Lord of Ards not finding it convenient as yet to discover himself, proposed to the committee that the country should subscribe the former Declaration. The committee being jealous of his sinistrous designs, waived it at that time, and in the meantime desired a further explication of the clause in it concerning their declining Ormond. To this they had words given them which might have been sufficient from men resolved to stand by their professions. But while this is doing, Monroe was secretly commanded to come to Belfast, and threaten to take it, the design of the Lord of Ards being to have Colonel Wallace* out of it, who had been appointed governor of Belfast by the Council of War to please the Presbytery.

---

* Colonel Wallace was an earnest Presbyterian. Steven, in his *History of the Scottish Church*, Rotterdam, gives an interesting account of his death there in 1678. The writer says—" He had lived abroad such an ornament to his profession as he was not more lamented by us (the Scotch ministers) than by all the serious English and Dutch of his acquaintance. . . . I must say he was the most faithful, feckful, compassionate, diligent, and indefatigable elder in the work of the Lord that ever I knew at home or abroad."—Pp. 68, 69.

Monroe accordingly hastened to Belfast and threatened to fire it. It was found not well enough manned and furnished to resist, upon which the Lord of Ards, with common advice, sent for a considerable party from his own regiment to assist Belfast garrison against Monroe, and the gentlemen and ministers were ordered to go home from the hazard of the enemy. Thus, Ard's men entered publickly the town, where, having secured himself, he then declared indeed what he was, produced his commission from the King, and discharged Wallace of his trust.

This treachery of the Lord of Ards was an astonishing surprisal to the ministers and country who formerly had concurred with him. They knew not where they were, nor what cause to take. Mr. Antony Shaw, then minister of Belfast,[*] did, with great zeal and ministerial authority, upbraid the Lord Ards before his officers, for his strange dealing, showed how inconsistent he was with his former professions, and that ere long the righteous God, who hates falsehood of any kind, and in a special manner, betraying the truth and cause of God, would be avenged of him and his house. But my lord put all off by smooth pretences, and told them he intended no hurt to the ministry or good people; if they would comply with the government they should find him a friend. But the ministers then, though young in years, had so much experience of men's falsehoods, that they knew it was folly to lean to fair words.

Monroe came with his forces near Belfast, and his soldiers being forbidden to enter, the new General gave orders to return to Carrickfergus and demand entry or besiege it, being now in the custody of persons who resolved to stand to their former engagements, especially Major Ellis, a worthy and religious gentleman. My Lord Ards followed shortly after;

---

[*] Mr. Shaw soon after retired to Scotland.

where, after a short siege, the officers of that garrison, not finding themselves in a capacity to hold out, gave up the town upon terms. The town was given to the government of Colonel Dalzell, who had been an officer in the Major-General's regiment before, and a great promoter of that party in Ireland, to concur with the engagement the year before. He continued there, with a crew who followed him, by the Lord of Ards' command, for a short time, being a terror to the country about, and exacting from them what he thought meet. Yea, this party under Ormond did at that time possess all the garrisons in Ireland, except Dublin and Derry—both of which were besieged by them—Sir Alexander Stewart having left the siege of Derry to be managed by that party; and they were in this juncture encouraged by Montrose's return to Scotland, by commission from the young King, hoping to follow forth his former victory there. But the triumphing of the wicked sometimes is but short; for that invasion of Montrose, as well as their power in Ireland, soon failed.

Meantime, the Presbytery met in other places of the country, and considered what was to be done, finding the Lord of Ards and Colonel George Monroe were endeavouring to bring in the remainder of the army under their control, and were for that end proposing a treaty to the Committee of War to join with them and come under the Lord of Ards' command. The Presbytery used all means with the Committee of War not to enter into any treaty with the said Lord and George Monroe, in regard they now acted on the old malignant quarrel by the King's commission, and thereby owned the King to be in the full exercise of his power, without giving any security for religion, and because they were now promoting the very design carried on the year before in the "Engagement" against England, which was so much opposed by the reforming party in the three kingdoms.

Besides, the Lord of Ards and his party were now associated and embodied with the party under Ormond, which consisted only of enemies to the work of reformation—not only haters of the covenant, but entertainers of Papists and rebels. They, therefore, besought the committee to keep themselves free from such unlawful treaties and associations. In the meantime, however, while the country and Presbytery were in confusion, they go on with the admission of Mr. Henry Maine and Mr. William Richardson in a more private way, as the times would admit—the former to Islandmagee, and the latter to Killyleagh.

The Lord of Ards, knowing how much need he had of the favour of the country, and how the country was generally affected toward the covenant and work of reformation, and adhered to the Presbytery, procured a letter from the Lord Inchiquin, commander of the army under Ormond, to the Presbytery, and wrote another letter with it himself. Withal he gave forth a "Declaration" to satisfy the country as to his present actings, which Declaration the Presbytery did answer at large, and which was ordered to be read in the several congregations by the ministers. This accordingly was done, though with some opposition, in congregations where malignant officers were present, yet no violence was done to the ministers.

There was also a letter returned to the Lord Inchiquin, giving his Lordship a reason for the Presbytery's present actings. The Presbytery, after they had been accused by the Lord Ards in a message sent by one of his officers—viz. Hugh Montgomery—of mutiny, treason, and sedition, in face of the Presbytery; and after they had sent some of their number to discourse with him of his proceedings, who received no satisfaction, but were partly mocked and partly threatened (though not without some exhortations of peace and promises to give the civil sanction to the Presbytery by virtue of his commission from the King, if they would not oppose the present course), ordered the Lord Ards to be summoned to the Presbytery as one who had owned himself of their number and under their jurisdiction, and had now fallen from his former professions and become guilty of a fearful breach of covenant. This summons they knew he would undervalue, and accordingly he enquired of the person summoning him by what authority he did so. Yet the Presbytery judged it their duty in this case to own the authority Christ had put into their hands. And indeed, the Lord so ordered matters, that for a little time they were not troubled; the Lord Ards not judging it fit for his design at this time. Meantime they received an encouraging letter from the ministers in Edinburgh.

The Lord Ards, seeing he could not prevail with ministers to be silent from testifying against his course, or from the exercise of jurisdiction, summoned the ruling elders to appear before him that he might threaten them from joining with the ministers; but the elders, by advice, withdrew themselves. And George Monroe, as then commissioned by the Lord Lieutenant Ormond, directed a letter by way of summons to several of the brethren to compear before him at Coleraine, with certification that, if they did not, he would pursue them; telling them that he was informed their preaching tended to the prejudice of the King's interest; and that if they would undertake not to meddle in State affairs, nor to encroach on the magistrates' power, they should have countenance from him. Upon consideration of the threatenings of a prevailing party now become enemies in the country, and assisted with Irish rebels, and of some ministers being violently hindered from preaching in their own pulpits, and there being an information gone up to Ormond against the ministers, desiring he would use some violent course with them for restraining them; and furthermore, because ministers could not preach freely against the present enemies without apparent violence, they resolved unanimously that brethren finding themselves in apparent hazard, and not in a capacity to exercise their ministry, may withdraw for a time till God give an open door again. Meantime, they had a letter from the General Assembly of Scotland, by their commissioner, Mr. Ferguson. But the storm growing more violent, some of the ministers— partly to shun present hazard, partly from other causes— retired a little to Scotland; but having discoursed with worthy and experienced ministers there, and being advised by them, did presently return. Others, however, stayed in the country at that time. And indeed the Lord of Ards' government in the North lasted not long. For, being called to join Ormond with what forces he had, with the Lord Claneboy and his followers, they left that part of the country and were broken at Dundalk. For though they had then the power of the whole kingdom, except Derry and Dublin, yet Ormond's whole party, and a great army lying about Dublin, and minding their drinking, cards, and dice, more than their work, were surprised by a party out of the city by Colonel Jones, and scattered; and the country gentlemen and malignant faction about Derry (after Sir Alexander Stewart and his party had left them), were broken by Coote, with the help of one Owen Macart. This was the beginning of the breach of that party in Ireland, by which the ministers and those who owned the reformation, being the generality of the Scotch in Ulster, had a little respite for a time.

But shortly after they entered upon new troubles and more lasting, which, that we may understand, it is to be remembered that, after the King was murdered by the sectarian party in England, and Oliver Cromwell, the chief instrument and promoter of this practice, had moulded and settled the army there, so as to be subservient to his designs (not without difficulty, however, from the party of levellers in the army, as well as from some remainder of the King's friends), and finding the States of Scotland in terms with the King, then at Breda, for restoring him to his just rights, and, withal, knowing Ireland was yet in the power of the King's party, all the garrisons being so, save Dublin and Derry, he was sent over to Ireland as General of the army, and Commander-in-Chief of Ireland. He arrived at Dublin on the 15th of August, 1649, with 9,000 foot and 4,000 horse. Shortly after (August 30), he marched to Drogheda, where was a strong garrison kept for the King of 2,500 foot and 300 horse, under the command of Sir Arthur Aston, a Papist, who had served the King in England as Governor of Oxford. The town was thrice stormed with resolution enough, and as resolutely defended. But in the third assault it was taken, and all in arms put to the sword, to the number of 3,000, being the most resolute soldiers in the kingdom, but consisting of profane Protestants and Irish Papists, who, in the righteous judgment of God, met with a scourge from unjust hands. From Drogheda he marched to Wexford, and, there having been repulsed at first, he got entry (October 4), and destroyed 2,000 men more of the like sort. And so he went to other chief garrisons, who, being terrified by these first attempts, surrendered upon easy terms to him, and thereafter he had not occasion to use the like severity. Thus, having in a very short time broken the forces in Ireland that adhered to the King's interest, and settled garrisons in all parts of the kingdom, he sent down to the northern parts Colonel Venables to command where Monck had done before; and gave commission to Sir

Charles Coote to command the forces in and about Derry and Connaught, and both to join together, as necessity called for.

Upon Venables coming down to the North, the garrisons easily yielded to him, and Sir Charles Coote took Coleraine; while their forces in other parts of the kingdom, under command of Ireton, had the same success. Venables at this time did emit declarations to encourage ministers of the country, giving all encouragement to the well-affected, and those who had been in opposition to the malignant party before, and declaring it was for their preservation he was sent to Ireland, and, in order to that, for reducing the malignants. This Declaration was sent out in September, 1649. Meantime, the remaining forces who had formerly appeared for the King, as well as those in the other parts of the kingdom, melted away and took what conditions they could get. It is observable that Sir James Montgomery, of Greyabbey, who a little time before was a chief instrument to corrupt his nephew, the Lord of Ards, teaching him, then but young, subtilly to deceive the ministers by his feigned pretences and declarations, though a man of great parts, is now put to his wits' end what course to take. He knew no better way than to apply to the ministers of the County of Down for recommendation to Scotland (then preparing to receive the King), which the ministers, upon his declaration of repentance and changing his principles under his hand, did give him, directed to Argyle and Robt. Douglass.* Yet, going there, he only obtained liberty to go to Holland, the states not thinking fit to own or trust him among them. Thereafter, returning from Holland when things had been overturned in Scotland, and going to England in a ship to

---

* Robert Douglass was a very distinguished Scottish minister. He was appointed one of the Commissioners from the Church of Scotland to the Westminster Assembly.

make his peace with the new commonwealth, he was shot to death by a cannon bullet from a pirate pursuing the vessel he was in. All his life-time he followed worldly policy, yet it failed him. There was also an observable passage concerning a person mentioned before as a great instrument for good to the city of Dublin, and to all Ireland—viz. Major O'Connolly. He had fallen in with the sectarian party, got the command of the regiment in Antrim, which formerly belonged to his old master, Sir John Clotworthy (now a sufferer and prisoner under the sectaries, for declining their courses and adhering to the King's just right and interest.) This O'Connolly and some few English met accidentally with a party under the command of—as well as the company—of Colonel John Hamilton (who at that time was subject to Colonel George Monroe, then in the country) at Dunadry, near Antrim, where there was a sharp debate. O'Connolly was mortally wounded, and carried with no more respect than a dead ox behind a man to Connor, where he immediately died. This man, from what could be observed, was of an ingenious nature, and truly sincere, yet he was then deceived by the pretences of that party, and seemed violent that way. Therefore, though God had brought him to great respect and a considerable estate* upon occasion of his former faithfulness at the breaking out of the rebellion; yet falling from his first principles, and going along with the declining party, the Lord would punish him with this temporal stroke of being thus cut off for a warning to others to beware of such courses. His wife died shortly after, and left a son and daughter — his son a very idiot unto the greatest height, and the daughter,

---

* When he saved the Castle of Dublin in 1641, he obtained a reward of £500 in hand, and a pension of £200 per annum "until provision would be made for an inheritance of greater value."—*A Sample of Jet Black Prelatic Calumny*, p. 174.

though thereafter married to a worthy gentleman (Mr. Hugh Rowley), yet proved but more than half a fool, and a burden to her husband for many years, and without posterity.

George Monroe, having a party with him, mostly of Irish, who had been rebels, and concluded in the peace, about this time coming along toward Antrim, and alleging that he was fired against from the Mount, set fire to the town and burnt it all, except some few houses, and also Lisnegarvy. The one had been long famous as a place where the Gospel flourished, and godliness was countenanced both by landlord and inhabitants—the other, as a place where neither landlord nor people (a very few excepted) did give countenance or entrance to the Gospel—which teaches us not to judge by events as to these common calamities. However, George Monroe, with his party, soon vanished. He, with Dalzell, Hamilton, and others, who a little before commanded the country with great absoluteness, are now forced to submit, and beg license to go to Scotland, where, also, they had no assurance of any comfortable reception. Before they could find opportunity to get over, they walked on foot from some places to others, few giving them any respect. This was observable, considering what a terror they had been to the country but a little before, to be now brought so low.

At this time the ministers preached publickly in their congregations, and continued to pray for the new King, and declare against the sectarian party. This did endanger divers of the brethren in those places where any of the army heard them preach. The officers threatened them with severity, and the rude soldiers also. However, the governor, Colonel Venables, though he was informed of these prayers and preachings, was not sudden to call ministers to question. Having had occasion to discourse with some of them in places where he sometimes travelled, he found them sober and religious, and in everything was pleased with them, except in that particular. He studied much to insinuate upon them as he met with them—but especially he forbore in regard he was not yet fixed in the country, and the enemies remaining therein. They, however, continued in their own way (though with as much prudence as sense of duty permitted) till about the Spring, when he went to the fields. He sent a message to them, met at Bangor (1650) at a Presbytery,* by way of summons, to appear before him at Dromore, only insinuating that he was informed of their opposing the present government in England, and that if they would live peaceably and engage not to disturb the government, nor speak against the party under it, he would encourage them. Otherwise, if they did not agree to that, they should have liberty to go to Scotland. However, the brethren met together. After consultation, they found it not safe to go to Colonel Venables upon the summons without a safe conduct, but resolved for a time to return to their several homes. Only, in the meantime, they wrote back a letter, partly to give him civil respect, partly to vindicate themselves from those foul aspersions put on them, as if they were the troublers of the country. This Colonel Venables had not only insinuated to themselves in his letter, but the officers and soldiers had

---

* The following remarkable story is related on the authority of the Rev. J. Boyse, of Dublin, a distinguished Presbyterian minister, who flourished in the reign of William III. :—"I heard both Dr. Gilbert Rule (Principal of Edinburgh College) and Mr. Archibald Hamilton (an ancient Presbyterian minister in the north of Ireland) relate the following passage in the time of King Charles the Second's reign—viz. that in the year 1650, there was a Meeting or Synod of Presbyterian ministers in the north of Ireland—among whom, one ancient minister sat seemingly drowsy, while the rest were debating some matters before them. Upon which, being asked if he were taking a nap, he replied, No, his soul had been ravished with the prospect of the happy days the Church of God in these kingdoms should enjoy under a Prince of Orange. That this passage was by the same reverend persons related to me some time before King Charles the Second's death, I do freely attest.—J. BOYSE."—See *Calamy's Life and Times*, ii. 515.

laboured to persuade the country, both gentlemen and others, that the ministers were the persons who kept up a distance between them and the country, and occasioned more burden and oppression on them. However, the next week after that, instead of a safe conduct, parties were, by his command, sent in one night about the same time to the several ministers' houses in the country to apprehend them and bring them to Carrickfergus. This was on June the 11th, 1650. Divers were apprehended—others, and the most part, did at that time escape their hands, some of whom went privately to Scotland, but most part stayed. And some who were apprehended, not having been at the Presbytery the week before, and so not receiving the summons, wrote to Colonel Venables that they had had no intimation to wait on him, he being then at Dundalk. Unto which, hearing that ministers had been rudely handled the week before by soldiers, and that others had fled to Scotland, and others had hid themselves, he gave a discreet reply by a letter under his own hand, yet promising to encourage them if they would not meddle with State affairs, and oppose the power under which they now were; and declaring that, in the meantime, they should not be farther proceeded against till he returned from the fields, and so gave orders to dismiss them for that time. They, therefore, continued preaching as before for a considerable time. Others who had escaped apprehension, but had not gone to Scotland, also began again to preach in their several congregations, but with great wariness, having no protection. But, in the meantime, there were divers ministers in the County of Down kept prisoners for a while at Belfast, and afterwards brought to Carrickfergus to Colonel Venables, where he and they thus reasoned about the present quarrel—1st. He could not charge them with anything they had done, but put them to it, what they would do hereafter; 2nd. Whereas, he urged they were under the Parliament of England, and now the Parliament had put down King and Lords. To this they answered—*First.* That though Ireland was subject to the King of England, yet they had a Parliament of their own, by which the subjects of Ireland were governed, and Ireland's Parliament had made no such acts against King and Lords. It was further urged that now they were a conquered people under England and this party. It was answered, a conquest might draw from them passive obedience out of necessity, but no acknowledgment of their lawful power. And though they had all these times owned lawful Parliaments of England (this kingdom not being in a capacity to have one), yet the present Parliament was not a lawful one; for, if it were, they could not but obey it, and have always done so, and the commissioners from it concurred with them; *Second.* They had not yet declared the laws of the conqueror in this country, nor was it declared to the subject; *Third.* His own declaration at his first coming to the country said he was come only against the malignants, and for the support of godly ministers and others, and now things were quite contrary. There was thus a long reasoning between those ministers and Colonel Venables about this breach of covenant and obligation to the King and Government. Yet, the result of it was, that since they would not carry themselves submissively to the present Government, they must be gone, and that they could expect no favour. This order for their removing was signed by Charles Coote, Robert Venables, Chidley Coot, and Robert Barrow. However, those that stayed in the country, though they could not exercise their ministry orderly as formerly, and though their stipends were sequestered, yet changing their apparel to the habit of countrymen, they frequently travelled in their own parishes, and sometimes in other places, taking what opportunities they could to preach in the fields, or in barns and glens, and were seldom in their own houses. They persuaded the people to constancy in the received doctrine in opposition to the wild heresies that were then spreading, and reminded them of their duty to their lawful magistrates, the King, and Parliament, in opposition to the usurpation of the times—in their prayers always mentioning the lawful magistrate.

CHAPTER XII.

CONTINUED TRIALS OF THE MINISTERS—THEIR DISCUSSION AT ANTRIM WITH TAYLOR AND WEEKS—CONFERENCE AT BELFAST WITH COMMISSIONERS OF THE REVENUE—MESSRS. FERGUSON AND ADAIR GO TO DUBLIN AND CONFER WITH FLEETWOOD AND OTHERS—MR. ADAIR'S PAPERS SEIZED AND RECOVERED—MINISTERS AND PEOPLE REFUSE THE ENGAGEMENT TENDERED BY THE COMMISSIONERS OF THE REVENUE—MINISTERS ENJOY GREATER LIBERTY—A PROPOSAL TO TRANSPLANT THE SCOTTISH SETTLERS TO TIPPERARY MISCARRIES.

THIS continued till the next summer, 1651, at which time diligent search was made anew for them. Some were again taken and others fled; and those taken were imprisoned, first for a time in Carrickfergus in lodgings, where they quartered; and thereafter, Colonel Venables not gaining any ground upon them, they were sent to Scotland, where all of them were invited to parishes, and exercised their ministry for about three years in divers places of Scotland. They were admitted as members of the Presbyteries where their congregations were; but withal, they reserved liberty to return to their places in Ireland, if ever God should open a door. Those remaining in the country and not apprehended, being only about six or seven—viz. Messrs. Thomas Peebles, James Gordon, and Gilbert Ramsay, in the County of Down; and Messrs. Anthony Kennedy,* Robert Cunningham,† and Patrick Adair, in the County of Antrim,

---

* Anthony Kennedy was ordained at Templepatrick on the 30th of October, 1646, and died minister of that congregation on the 11th of December, 1697. His tombstone may still be seen in the graveyard of that place.

† Mr. Robert Cunningham was minister of Broadisland, or Ballycarry, upwards of fifty years.

were now put to greater difficulties than before, being more earnestly searched after than in their houses. Yet they continued preaching in remote or private places, where the people willingly met them. They had frequent meetings amongst themselves in order to strengthen one another, and consult about their present carriage; and they drew up causes of fasts and humiliations to be kept among the people in a private way in several little societies, as the times permitted. Sometime the minister would, in his parish, call them all together a part of the day, and preach and pray with them; and thereafter, the people would repair to their several societies for prayer the rest of the day, the minister always joining with one of these little societies after another. This continued for another year, during 1652, at which time the people were discouraged through want of the public ordinances. The ministers also wearied, and ceased this manner of living and preaching; yet indeed it appeared that these small endeavours of an oppressed people, and remnant of the ministry, were not in vain; for after this, matters began to grow more encouraging.

For it was an Holy Providence thus ordered it. It was before recorded that two of the Presbytery had been suspended, about three or four years before, for their declining to declare against the sectarian party. And, they continuing obstinate in their opinion during the government of the Presbytery, when the sectarian party commanded in the country, these brethren were much encouraged by them, and not only had the liberty of their ministry, but considerable salaries. They met along with some ministers belonging to the army, whereof Timothy Taylor,* an Indepen-

---

* Mr. Taylor was originally a Presbyterian, but, when the influence of that party began to decline, he turned Independent. At Carrickfergus he had an endowment of £200 per annum, and a free house.—*Reid* II., 138, note.

dent, was the chief, both for power, parts, learning, and gravity. They had also meeting with them some old curates, who now had fallen in with Mr. Taylor, and others who were rather of Anabaptistical principles. These two brethren, together with Mr. (Hugh) Vesey, who now followed their way, and was minister of Coleraine, remembering the sweet society they sometimes had had with their former brethren of their principles, and now beginning to discern that party better, and having compassion on their brethren, whose bodies and spirits were much spent with tossings in the country, made a motion to Mr. Taylor to desire a conference with these few brethren in the country, in order to a right understanding between him and them, which he and the rest with him accorded unto. They therefore wrote a letter, in which, after fair and brotherly language, they invited the brethren to appoint a time and place of meeting with them, when they should spend one day in fasting and prayer, in order to a right understanding among them in matters of controversy, both relating to the Commonwealth and other matters; and, thereafter, that they should immediately fall upon an amicable, brotherly conference upon these subjects to give or receive satisfaction. The Commissioners of the Revenue, who then governed the country, whereof Colonel Venables was one, being made acquainted with this proposal, promised a safe conduct, that, if there were no agreement, these ministers should be *in statu quo prius*. This letter was sent by Mr. Jeremiah O'Queen to be delivered to Mr. Anthony Kennedy, of Templepatrick, and he was commissioned to confer with him anent the time and place of their meeting. But Mr. Jeremy could not find any in Templepatrick (though the place where he was bred, where he before had been in great reputation, and where he had much acquaintance) to tell him where he might find Mr. Kennedy. He was, therefore, forced to leave the letter to its venture. It came, however, to the brethrens' hands, upon which they met together, and, after consultation with prayer to God, they resolved they would not, nor could not, meet these brethren, *primo instante*, in the exercise of fasting and prayer till they knew them better. Some of them they had never seen and were of principles professedly contrary; others of them being under a censure of the Presbytery, yet untaken off, they would not countenance at all. However, they wrote a letter back, declaring they were willing to meet with Mr. Taylor and Mr. Weeks, two ministers of the army, and confer with them. They named the day and place, at Antrim, in March, 1652, which was near four months after the date of their letter.

These ministers having received the letter which intimated the day and place, gathered together all they could persuade, who were inclining toward their way of Independency or Anabaptism, in the whole County of Antrim; and the brethren who had fallen from the Presbytery came along with them. Though Thursday was the day appointed, they met on Tuesday, and kept Wednesday wholly in public preaching in the church. On Thursday morning there was preaching also, and a very throng congregation. The seven brethren, being near Antrim on Wednesday at night, came into the town on Thursday morning; and finding there was preaching in the church, they also went in among the crowd. It was Mr. Weeks that was preaching. This gentleman perceiving the ministers coming in—immediately in discourse to the people—did indirectly reflect on them as troublers of the country, and dividers of God's people; but there, he did profess, they would be forced to stop, alleging to the people, Rev. iii. 9. This was the first entertainment these ministers got, instead of their brotherly conference. But immediately after ending the sermon and prayer, they had another "salve," which was somewhat affronting, and very surprising to them. The people were warned by the same Mr. Weeks to be present in the hall of the castle, immediately after dinner, to hear a dispute between these gentlemen (as he called the ministers present and now in the eye of the people), and us, meaning Mr. Taylor and himself. At this time neither himself nor Mr. Taylor had ever seen the ministers, nor they them; nor had they ever any intercourse but by the one letter before mentioned. But Mr. Taylor—hearing they were young men, and knowing himself to be of a considerable stand and not unlearned, and long before this having put forth a book in print, in vindication of Independency—thought to surprise the country young men, and affront them before the people as not able to defend their cause; and thus bring the Independent way into credit in the country, in opposition to Presbytery. Mr. Weeks concurred with him thus far; but being an Anabaptist, had a further design than Mr. Taylor, but was much more unable to follow it, being void of human learning, never educated that way, but a tradesman, and imprudent.

After the summons to a public dispute, unexpected by the ministers, coming out of church, they met Mr. Taylor and Mr. Weeks at the door, and saluted each other without more words ; but they refused to take by the hand those brethren who had fallen from the Presbytery, and were now joined with the sectaries. Instead of going to dinner, however, they went together to a room in a private house, with some few friends who had been present at the sermon, to consider what to do, and they resolved not to dispute. After the two brethren had dined in the Castle, they sent to the ministers to desire them to come to the dispute. The people were now gathered, and, indeed, the people, having such public warning upon such an unusual occasion, did readily throng into the place. The brethren returned answer they could not dispute, but were willing to discourse, in private, with Mr. Taylor and Mr. Weeks, according to their own proposal. They replied there must be a dispute since the people were advertised, otherwise they would publickly declare to the people that the ministers would not defend their own cause. However, the ministers went down to the Castle, and had first a meeting with the brethren in a chamber, and discoursed with them of the unreasonableness and unfairness of their carriage, thus to take advantage and bring men to a dispute not only without any previous warning of any such thing, but who knew not so much as what should be the subject-matter of their dispute. They desired only that they might agree upon the points in debate, and let them be now formed into theses, and they were willing to debate with them to-morrow morning. But nothing would do save a present dispute, as the people were gathered, and would without that be disappointed. They would dispute on nothing but what they commonly taught and owned. And so they went down-stairs to the common-hall, where the people were gathered very strong, and where were a long table and forms set for the ministers, and a chair at the upper end of it. There Masters Taylor and Weeks sat down and cheerfully looked to one another. They spake to the people, saying—" It seems these gentlemen will not come to dispute and defend their cause." Meantime, the brethren stayed in the chamber, and those who had joined with the sectaries stayed with them, persuading them to the dispute, and telling them there was no fear. Yea, Mr. Jeremy O'Queen offered himself to undertake it, if the brethren would allow him. In the meantime, one of their friends came up, and besought them, as they regarded the credit of the profession, to go down and answer those men, for they were triumphing. Upon this message the brethren, without any further deliberation or discourse, hastened to the place. And one of them (Mr. Patrick Adair), whom the rest had been speaking of among themselves to entertain this debate, and who had entertained most of the discourse in the chamber, did, with a kind of animosity and resolution unusual to him, step into the chair, and set himself down there—Messrs. Taylor and Weeks sitting below upon a form. On this Mr. Taylor made a motion to Mr. Weeks that a brother should pray before the dispute begun, which Mr. W. mentioned to the brother in the chair. Mr. Adair readily yielded to the motion and prayed, and then sat himself down in the chair, waiting what further step the brethren would make toward the dispute. Mr. Taylor then rose up, and delivered before the people a discourse elaborate enough, and cunningly contrived to commend Independency, and disgrace Presbyterian government. In this he stated the question between the one and the other, made the Independent opinions more plausible to the common people, as to the constitution of their church-members; their tenderness in their walk; the freedom of God's people in that way, without anything like tyranny over their consciences; not measuring their congregations by mearings of land, but by godliness; not taking in all the promiscuous multitude to be partakers of all ordinances, &c.

After Mr. Taylor had thus discoursed near to an hour, he sat himself down and said no more. Upon this, the brother who was in the chair rose up, and first spoke to the people, declaring the occasion of their coming there—that it was upon a brotherly letter from those gentlemen (pointing at Messrs. Taylor and Weeks), to a private and amicable conference, which now, they of themselves—without their consent—had turned to a public dispute; that they knew not what should be the matter of their debate till now; and that therefore, they were not fitted to dispute upon such weighty matters off hand, especially with such a grave man as Mr. Taylor. But, as Providence seemed to call them to say something for Presbyterial government and the constitution of our churches in opposition to the Independent way, they would now, as they could, answer what Mr. Taylor had said. And they besought the people, if their cause were not well managed by them, not to attribute it to the weakness of the cause, but to them, and partly also to that indirect way which had been taken with them to come to a public dispute. Upon which, this brother (Mr. P. Adair) then turned to Mr. Taylor, and told him that not having known what should be the ground of his discourse before he heard it, and having no theses from him to found a debate on, he could not so exactly mention all that Mr. Taylor had said, only some few heads he observed, and mentioned. The first, and principal, was anent the constituent members of their and our churches. They were for visible saints, or such as in ground of charity had positive holiness. We took in all those who were willing to profess the truth, and be subject to Christ's ordinances. And thus Mr. Adair laboured to overthrow Mr. Taylor's pious-like opinion; and evidenced the way of constituting the visible church, not only by the constant practice of all the churches of Christ since the Apostles' times, except Donatists, Anabaptists, &c., but also by the way of constituting churches, both under the Old and New Testaments, wherein Mr. Adair instanced the first church formed by Moses, and thereafter in the times of David and the Prophets. Mr. Taylor gave some answer to these instances, which were readily replied unto. The truth is, Mr. Taylor did not speak much after his elaborate discourse. Mr. Adair, who most spoke to him, being irritated by his unfair carriage, and his drawing them to a dispute under so much disadvantage, spoke with a piece of confidence and animosity, which Mr. Taylor expected not from a youth, otherwise not much endued with that gift.* But it was owned by Mr. Adair to be more God's special hand at that time giving light and courage, than any personal ability in himself. Thereafter, another brother began to debate the business with Mr. Taylor a little between themselves, more quietly. And, in the meantime, Mr. Weeks proponed an argument to him who sustained the debate, in a direct syllogism, which was easily answered by a distinction, to which Mr. Weeks had no reply, nor did he propose another argument, for he had not been taught syllogisms. When he became mute, Mr. Taylor turned from the other brother, with whom he had been conversing, and openly said to Weeks, "What is become of your argument, brother." At this Mr. Weeks looked angry and bashful, but gave no answer. After this Mr. Taylor again proposed that one should pray. He himself, being desired to do so by the brother who had prayed before, prayed, and therein gave thanks to God for the moderation that had appeared in that debate. He seemed to take the brethrens' carriage well, and so they parted.

But those who favoured that way, who had been brought there of purpose to hear the brethren affronted and disputed out of their principles, declared much dissatisfaction with Mr. Taylor's management, and said, "He but lost his cause." The people who favoured the poor ministers returned much confirmed, and rejoicing. One of them, a very pious gentleman, said to Mr. Adair, that when he heard Mr. Taylor's first discourse, wherein he set forth the Independent way

---

* The manner in which Mr. Adair speaks of himself here and elsewhere supplies evidence of his humility and good sense.

with all its advantages, he was like to be taken, till he heard those pious-like pretences answered from Scripture, and the constitution of God's church opened, both under the Old and New Testaments.

The brethren having a safe conduct, sent them in order to this meeting with the other ministers, parted fairly with them. They ventured to return to their congregations more confidently and openly than before ; and thus they continued half-a-year in greater freedom than before, no man forbidding them for a little time. This little respite, as a fruit of God's special providence, and the news of this dispute went to Scotland, and reached the brethren there. Shortly after, there came over Mr. Archibald Ferguson, minister of Antrim, who had a letter from Venables, upon a request by my Lady Clotworthy, mother to Sir John Clotworthy—a worthy matron, and who, with her whole family, had been of a long time not only favourers, but avowed friends of the way of God. Mr. Andrew Stewart,* minister of Donaghadee, being then in Galloway, judged it also his duty to venture to give his congregation here a visit, and came over when he heard that Mr. Ferguson had been sent for. Immediately after Mr. Stewart's coming over, which was in summer, 1652, there were letters sent to the several brethren, and to him also, from those who then governed the country at that time, called the Commissioners of the Revenue, showing that, in pursuance of orders from the commissioners from the Parliament (whose chief end it was to advance the Gospel), they desired a meeting and conference with them on the 21st of October, at Belfast, to advise how the Gospel may be preached without disturbing the peace of the Commonwealth, which, they were informed, some ministers still con-

---

* Mr. Stewart, who died in 1671, left behind a fragment of the history of the Irish Church, part of which is appended to this narrative.

tinued to do, as well as for begetting a greater unity and better understanding. This was subscribed by Colonel Venables, —— Rawdon, and Tobias Norrice, at Belfast, Oct. 16, 1652. The brethren, on receipt of these letters, immediately acquainted one another, and appointed a meeting amongst themselves, at Comber, the day before their appearance at Belfast, when they easily supposed a new trouble was coming their way, in order to consider their carriage to the present Government. Therefore, they seriously advised and debated what length they ought to go in pleasing their governors, in order for liberty for preaching the Gospel, and drew up in a paper, somewhat to that purpose, declaring that, though they could not own the Government as lawful, nor bind themselves by any oath or subscription to it, yet their only calling and aim was to preach the Gospel to their congregations; and, for their part, they were upon no intention of insurrection or disturbing the peace, and they were confident the rulers had no ground to apprehend any such thing of them.

After they had agreed among themselves what to stick to, they came next day to Belfast, and were immediately sent for (Mr. Taylor, &c. being messengers) by the commissioners, before whom they appeared, October 21st, 1652. After the commissioners had discoursed a little to them, according to the contents of their letter, the brethren being demanded what they would do, gave in the paper they had drawn up. This being immediately before dinner, they again appeared before the commissioners after dinner; and having appointed one of their number to speak the mind of the rest to the commissioners, they fell upon the debate of that paper they had given in—viz. whether they would take the "Engagement,"* or at least the negative part of it, which was to act

---

* The following is a copy of the Engagement :—" I, ——, do hereby declare that I do renounce the pretended title of Charles Stewart, and the whole line of the late

nothing against the Commonwealth of England, as now established, without King or House of Lords. Upon this they debated for five or six hours without intermission. The Commissioners received no satisfaction from what the ministers could condescend unto; and next morning, appearing again, they could do no further. At this the Commissioners were much offended, and some of them spoke bitterly to the brethren, and particularly to the brother who had been mouth for the rest. Yet, at that time they thought it not fit to use severity, and therefore they dismissed them to their places, with a command to appear again within six weeks, and in the meantime to make no insurrection in the country. The brethren waived this, but promised the former. They also delivered to them a draft, differing in words from the "Engagement," which they desired the brethren to advise upon—but it was found ensnaring. They were thus let go. On Monday, the 25th, they appointed a private meeting in a barn, and there Mr. Andrew Stewart was appointed by the brethren to return to Scotland, and inform their brethren, with the reverend and experienced ministers there, how it stood with them in Ireland, and to require their advice how to carry themselves. They also sent over a copy of the paper they had given in to the Commissioners, with a relation of their carriage—in all which they were approven by all the worthy and reverend brethren that Mr. Stewart spoke with, such as Messrs. Blair, Dickson, Wood, &c. They did not choose to give a draft, but rather thought the ministers might profess to them that they did not purpose to raise people in

---

King James, and every other person, as a single person, pretending to the government of these nations of England, Scotland, and Ireland, and the dominions and territories thereunto belonging, and that I will, by the grace of the Almighty God, be true, faithful, and constant to this Commonwealth, against any King, single person, or House of Peers, and every of them, and hereunto I subscribe my name." This test, called the *Tender*, or *Engagement*, was taken by many of the Episcopal clergy in Ireland. It appears from the text that Bishop Jones was one of the Commissioners for pressing it. Not one Irish Presbyterian minister could be induced to subscribe it.

arms, but to live as a godly people, and to inform and prepare the people for suffering in the maintenance of the Gospel, if God called them to it. At this time also Mr. James Ker, who had formerly fallen off from the Presbytery, and had continued in great charity toward the sectarian party for a considerable time, desired to be re-admitted to his former society with his brethren, and gave great testimonies of his ingenuously loathing his former course. The brethren at this time gave him a favourable hearing, yet delayed his full reception until they acquainted their brethren (being the greatest number of the Presbytery) now in Scotland. For that purpose they gave commission to Mr. Stewart to acquaint them, and have their mind on it. Unto this the brethren in Scotland did readily assent; and so Mr. Ker was received into the fellowship of his brethren upon his declared repentance, as thereafter also were Mr. O'Queen and Mr. Vesey.

While Mr. Stewart was in Scotland, the winds continuing contrary, so that he could not return before the prescribed six weeks were completed, the brethren were again necessitated to appear before the Commissioners—but still remained the same. So at length the Commissioners, being weary of them (and they still more weary), proposed to the brethren that they should send one or two of their number to Dublin to see if they could satisfy the Lord-General Fleetwood and the council of officers there, wherewith they should be satisfied. The brethren, though they expected not much good from this essay, yet saw not how they could shun it, being thus proposed to them. They, therefore, chose Mr. Archibald Ferguson and Mr. Patrick Adair for this purpose. They gave them injunctions to make their application to Fleetwood, yet restricted them from giving him any titles, which seemed to approve his present power. They were also instructed to declare that they had no mind of insurrection, but

only desired to preach the Gospel to a poor afflicted people—
themselves being also in poverty, having their maintenance
sequestered, and that they only desired liberty to preach
without impositions. These two brethren having a pass
from Venables, with a letter in their favour, as to their persons, to Fleetwood, went, and met with much civility from
him, and from divers of the officers, especially Colonel
Zanchy and Colonel Huston, being men of good tempers,
and lovers of good men. They also met with much bitterness
from others. However, they obtained nothing to their purpose. Fleetwood, though in great power, took little upon him.
The Anabaptist faction carried most sway, and Fleetwood,
after divers applications to him, referred the brethren to a
meeting of officers, who met in the Castle of Dublin, of all
sorts and sizes. The brethren appearing before them, were
questioned why they and their brethren would not take the
"Engagement," nor give security to live quietly. Mr. Ferguson answered, as he was enjoined, that they intended not
insurrections, &c. It was aggredged, with many absurdities,
that the ministers should expect protection within the Commonwealth, and not promise fidelity. Mr. Ferguson replied
it might be dangerous to permit men in the Commonwealth
in such a case, who, upon worldly and political considerations, refused; but that they were to be looked upon as
refusing upon no such grounds, but merely in conscience,
and that withal they were men insignificant for insurrections,
and not dangerous. One Allen, an Anabaptist, replied—
" Papists would and might say as much for themselves, and
pretend conscience as well as they." Mr. Adair answered—
" Sir, under favour, it's a mistake to compare our consciences
with those of Papists, for Papists' consciences could digest to
kill Protestant Kings, but so would not ours, to which our
principles are contrary." This harsh expression, reflecting on

many there who had a hand in the King's murder, procured a great silence, some drawing their hats down on their faces, who were in heart haters of that wickedness, and others were angry. So there was no more discourse at that time, neither were the brethren called again. But within a day or two they went to Fleetwood, who fairly dismissed them, and so they returned home with no more security than they went.

Though the Commissioners of the Revenue did not own them, yet the brethren continued as formerly for the matter of six weeks more, at which time there were Commissioners sent from Dublin to offer the " Engagement" to the whole country. These were Dr. Henry Jones,* afterwards Bishop of Meath — Colonel Hill, Colonel Venables, and Major Morgan, afterwards Sir Anthony Morgan. They remained at Carrickfergus. They first sent parties of soldiers to each minister's house, there being but seven in the country then, as already mentioned—all at the one time—who were to search all papers and letters in their houses, and bring them along from the ministers. They were suspicious that these few ministers, who so boldly owned the King's interest upon divers occasions before themselves, must have some secret

---

* The history of Henry Jones is remarkable. He was nephew to Archbishop Ussher. Through the interest of the Marquis of Ormonde, he was made Bishop of Clogher in 1645; but, as it soon afterwards became apparent that the church was not the way to promotion, Jones turned Republican, and joined the regicides. We here find him pressing the Engagement; and, during the Protectorate, he was appointed one of the Trustees for the Schools of Erasmus Smith. The Protector saw that he possessed ability and energy, and furnished him with employment. The Bishop accordingly laid aside his clerical character, arrayed himself in regimentals, and became Scout-Master-General in Cromwell's army (Carte's *Life of the Duke of Ormonde*, ii. 498). He is reported to have been an intrepid soldier, and to have signalised himself by his bloody achievements (Nalson's *Collections*, ii. 535). On the death of Cromwell, he anticipated coming changes—again turned Royalist, and exerted himself in promoting the Restoration. He was, in consequence, permitted to retain the See of Clogher, and was subsequently made Bishop of Meath; but in 1661, when a fresh batch of Irish Prelates was consecrated in Dublin, Jones was not permitted to join in the imposition of hands (Harris' *Ware's Bishops of Meath*).

correspondence with the King's party in Scotland, though now subdued, and under that party of the Commonwealth. The soldiers narrowly searched all, but found papers with none but Mr. Adair. They took from him every paper, though to never so little purpose—for they could not distinguish papers, there being none, among sixteen soldiers and a sergeant who took the papers, that could read. Among the papers they took there was one bundle which contained the Presbytery's Representation against the sectaries and that party, and another declaring the horridness of their murdering the King, with other papers much reflecting on their party. This bundle they took away with them in a cloak bag among others, though Mr. Adair had used all means to preserve it, knowing they might take much occasion against the brethren upon the sight of these papers. However, they took it along in one of the cloak bags which were full of papers. That night the sergeant kept one of the cloak bags in the chamber where he lay, about two miles from Mr. Adair's house, and in this was that bundle. The maid of the house, hearing a report that these were Mr. Adair's papers, resolved to restore some of them to him again. And so she went in the night when the sergeant and soldiers were asleep, and quietly brought a bundle of papers out of the cloak bag, not knowing what papers they were. This bundle was that which Mr. Adair only cared for, and she sent it to him next morning.

Next week after this, the commissioners gave summons to the whole country of both counties to appear at Carrickfergus, and assigned every barony or great parish their day of appearance; in each of which they pitched on certain persons to return all the names of masters of families in a list to the commissioners, to be called in order. Accordingly, the whole country generally appeared on their days assigned;

and their names being returned, they put the names of the ministers first on the roll, purposely that each of them might have occasion to debate the "Engagement," being first called; and the people, where each minister dwelt, being present, this gave occasion to most of them to debate the Engagement with the Commissioners. This was to the minister's hazard, yet, a special means to confirm the people in their duty to the King and covenant, and guard them against it. For it fell so out, that the people who came along with the ministers, and were present at their disputing with the Commissioners, wholly refused the "Engagement." This did much irritate the Commissioners against the ministers. However, they dismissed them for that week, and commanded them to return the next. Accordingly, the ministers came; and the Commissioners gave order that they should not go out of town without their liberty—this being about the middle of May, 1653. The guards at the ports were charged to watch to that purpose. The ministers were dealt with to give some security for their peaceable carriage in the country, and never to own any other power, or oppose this. They would, however, make no promises to this purpose. They were kept till Saturday, in the evening, attending the Commissioners' pleasure; and they were informed by some who were their friends, and yet who kept intercourse with the Commissioners, that there was a frigate ready to receive them to be transported to England. It is certain there was a frigate then attending for some service known to none but themselves. Notwithstanding this, they stood constant; and being called unto the Commissioners, they thought to receive a sad sentence, considering what had been their bitter expressions to them before, and considering what they had heard of the Commissioners' design and resolution that day. But, unexpectedly, they were entertained with much seeming favour and respect. The Commissioners did a little resent their so plain disputing against their power. They especially declared their dissatisfaction with Mr. Ker, who had been, as they thought, their own so long; and now, having been called to take the "Engagement" with the people of that country, did not enter fairly to debate the business, but fell down right upon them, declaring how he had been deceived with the pretences of that party at first—for which he justly had been suspended by his brethren—and now, whereas he thought they would favour the people of God, he saw the greatest malignants in the country were most in their favour, because they could turn any way for their own ends. This they did resent in Mr. James Ker, more than the carriage of any of the rest. However, they did much insinuate on the ministers, and desired they would yet resolve to live peaceably and preach the Gospel to the people without reflecting on their powers—and so desired them to go to their charges.

The brethren being surprised with this kind entertainment, did very joyfully accept of it, and the more cheerfully that no engagement was sought from them, as always before. And now, wondering at God's merciful providence unto them after so long tossing, they hasted home that night, though very late, and kept the next day—the Sabbath—with their congregations, in more than ordinary zeal; blessing God for that unexpected deliverence from their straits and troubles. Yet they knew not what was the particular occasion which moved these Commissioners to such a change in their carriage to them. But this, very shortly after they had notice of. It came not from any good-will in them to the ministers; but there was a sovereign Ruler ordering all things even in that confused and reeling time. We heard before, that the prevailing party in the army in England had taken away the life of their sovereign, and driven away by force, and imprisoned the far greater part of the Parliament (called then the Long Parliament), because they had voted the King's concessions satisfactory; and had resolved, upon the concessions he had given—he being then prisoner in the Isle of Wight—to bring him to the throne. This, that party could not endure. Therefore, they forcibly excluded the major part, and kept only a small number of their own friends, who had not concurred with the rest in that work and vote. This was called the "Rump," because it was only a small party of the Parliament, and the most despicable part of it. This "Rump" voted down the King and House of Lords, and called themselves the Commonwealth of England. They framed an "Engagement" to be pressed in England and Ireland, and they called it a "Tender" in reference to Scotland. By this they required every person to be true and faithful to the commonwealth of England as now established, without King and House of Lords. From this "Rump" Parliament came all the troubles of the Engagement—for refusing of which, and adhering to their loyalty to the King, the ministers of this country, as well as many in England of the same persuasion, endured long sufferings.

But, Oliver Cromwell having other designs—and being now Captain-General of all the forces of this Commonwealth in the three nations—did, partly by policy and partly by power now in his hands, so strengthen himself in that army, that he got the most considerable officers of the army with himself, to set themselves in opposition to it; picking quarrels with their government, alleging they did not follow the ends for which the war was first undertaken, and that the good cause was perishing in their hands, they only minding to perpetuate themselves in the government. Therefore, he, with his special officers, went in unto the House, April 20th,

1653, and after some upbraiding language, did violently dismiss them. Thus the government devolved upon himself and the council of officers, who thereafter changed from one thing to another till he was made Protector; the particular passages of which we leave to other histories.

The news of this raising the Parliament, which was the fountain of their power for the time, came to the Commissioners that Saturday in the afternoon, being about the midst of May; and so they knew not how to dispose of these ministers, their supreme masters being driven from authority, and they having no commission from any other power. However, that they might some way express their indignation against the country for disgusting their new Government, they did, by advice from Dublin, contrive a way to prevent hazard from this country to the Government. They fell about a way of transplanting the special persons whether for estate or parts, not principled their way, both ministers and others, unto the County of Tipperary, where they promised to give them who had estate here a proportionable value in lands there, and that others should be safely transported with their goods, and have protection in that part of the country where there was no hazard of their insurrection against the Government. They made a list of the persons to be transplanted, ministers and others, and caused divers gentlemen of the State to go to Tipperary and view it, in order to this design, among whom were Sir Robert Adair, Mr. Shaw, of Ballygelly—and others in the County of Down. But, matters in England being in a continual unsettledness through Cromwell's driving on his design for his own advancement to the supreme Government, and the opposition of many in the army wholly against the Government's being settled in any single person, this motion of the governors here in Ireland had no bottom to rest upon, and, therefore, their project of transplanting the Scotch to Tipperary did evanish within a little time ; and the ministers and people in this country began to have a great calm after all the former storms which they had endured. For Oliver, coming to the supreme ordering of affairs, used other methods, and took other measures than the rabble rump Parliament. He did not force any engagement or promise upon people contrary to their consciences, knowing that forced obligations of that kind will bind no man. For men who are not ruled by conscience can easily break them, and shake off these obligations whenever opportunity offers; and men of conscience, if they should be constrained and tempted to them, will find themselves under a necessity to repent. Thus, ministers in the country began to enjoy great liberty, and their brethren in Scotland began to return in peace to their parishes without molestation.

But it is fit that we here remember these brethren, not only as to the occasion of their being all this while in Scotland, but also their entertainment there, and their return again. They were thrust away from their congregations in Ireland, and sent over to Scotland by Colonel Venables, then governor of the English forces in these parts, because they had refused to acknowledge the then Government, and disown the King's right. Some of them were, by Venables' order, surprised with parties of soldiers, and kept a while at Carrickfergus in restraint, and thereafter sent to Scotland ; others had gone to Scotland before upon their apparent hazard in the country. Thus, all the ministers then settled in Ireland removed to Scotland, except seven who escaped the soldiers when they were sent to apprehend them, and had stayed in the country under disguise, and with great difficulty and danger all this while. After they were thus driven to Scotland, they had invitations from divers Presbyteries and parishes to exercise their ministry, which they undertook only on condition that they might have free liberty to return when they should have access to their own congregations in Ireland. They thus continued, in divers parts of the kingdom, joining with these Presbyteries in the inspection of their respective congregations.

CHAPTER XIII.

THE RESOLUTIONERS AND PROTESTORS—THE CHURCH RECOVERS HER LIBERTY—THE ACT OF BANGOR—SUPERVISION OF CANDIDATES FOR THE MINISTRY—THE MEETINGS OF DOWN, ANTRIM, AND ROUTE, WITH LAGAN—EXPANSION OF THE CHURCH—MINISTERIAL MAINTENANCE—CHARACTER OF SIR JOHN CLOTWORTHY.

MEANTIME, there fell out that division of the Church of Scotland between those called Remonstrators, or Protestors, on the one hand, and those who adhered to the public Resolutions of the Church and State on the other hand. The occasion and ground of this division among men eminent for godliness, learning, and usefulness in the work of God, we leave to those of that church and nation whose work it may be to record it.* I only mention it here with sad regret, as the beginning of the woeful breach in that church not yet repaired, tending to the reproach of the Church of Scotland, alienating the hearts of the godly one from another, and marring the work of God in it. The Irish ministers, being settled in divers Presbyteries of divers judgments as to this controversy, most part did incline to those opinions of which their respective Presbyteries were; and thus they became divided among themselves, insomuch that those of the protesting opinions joined with the Presbytery where they were, in emitting protestations and testimonies against the public actings of the com-

---

* In 1650, the Commission of the Scottish Assembly adopted two Resolutions, sanctioning the admission into the army of all persons except those who laboured under certain ecclesiastical disabilities. On this the Scottish Parliament passed an Act, throwing open all places of power and trust to those who had opposed the Covenant, on their professing regret for past misconduct. The Resolutions of the Commission were passed at a thin meeting. Those who favoured them were called Resolutioners, and those who opposed, Remonstrators, or Protestors.

mission, and other judicatories of the Church in Scotland. Upon this, the Commission of the Church did, in their public papers, reflect on the whole exiled ministers of Ireland as meddling with things which did not belong to them. These public reflections on the ministers from Ireland by the standing judicatories of the Church of Scotland did put these brethren upon unanimous thoughts of meeting amongst themselves from the divers places where they were, that after mutual conferring they might, if possible, agree among themselves, and walk orderly and harmoniously as became strangers in a divided church. They first met at Ayr, where the former acquaintance and heart-warming they had in Ireland did revive. After long and serious communication, they found the hazard of the present divisions among themselves, not only as rendering them more obnoxious to exceptions and reflections where they at present were, but being also hazardous, as if, through God's mercy, they should return to their charges in Ireland, they might carry as much of a strange fire in their skirts as might kindle division in that little church, and make irreparable rents among themselves. Whereupon, they entered upon a conclusion which had afterwards good influence on their appearance after their return to Ireland, that, whatever were their different apprehensions as to these differences in Scotland, yet all of them should forbear practically engaging in these divisions, but keep themselves free from divisive fasts, paper subscriptions of either party, and from Synods or Presbyteries which divided amongst themselves, and had gone to different parties, as was the immediate consequence of these sad differences at that time. After this conclusion thus unanimously adopted among themselves, they kept correspondence thereafter; and, for keeping it up, they resolved to meet once a month at Maybole, that they might have a good understanding of one another, and confer not only of their own carriage in their exiled condition, but in order to the case of Ireland, and their own return, as God should offer opportunity. These meetings of the brethren at Maybole did continue till their return to Ireland, not without mutual refreshment and good fruit; while their few brethren left in Ireland were conflicting with difficulties on all hands, whereof we have some account before.

The first beginning and day-break of liberty to this poor church of Ireland, seemed to be the dispute at Antrim, already mentioned. After this the few ministers were not prohibited preaching, though vexed with their appearances for a while before the Commissioners of Revenue. Thereafter, the Lady Clotworthy, a noble and religious matron, interceded with Colonel Venables, for liberty for her minister, Mr. Ferguson, to return to his church; which being granted, Mr. Andrew Stewart, at Donaghadee, did also hazard a visit to his congregation, though without license, and upon that account was not checked by the Commissioners. He returned after a while, and stayed till the rest of the brethren came over, having a commission from his brethren in Ireland to consult with the gravest ministers in Scotland anent their present case, and have their judgments upon divers questions as to their carriage under present circumstances; especially as to their carriage towards usurping powers. Unto all this, after a time, they had satisfying answers, very little different from the way they had been led in before.

After this the rest of the brethren returned from Scotland with papers from the English Government there, and, when they returned, presented themselves to Venables. Some of them also going up to Dublin procured a present maintenance to themselves, without any conditions asked or given, and they had the free exercise of their ministry. For Cromwell, being then at the helm, and his son Fleetwood being Deputy of Ireland, did labour to make friends of all sorts of persons and parties. Besides, Fleetwood, though inclining to Anabaptist courses, was no enemy to the Presbyterian party, and a man of much charity to all who had profession of godliness. Upon this favourable reception by those in power for the time, the brethren thought it their duty to fall about meeting together presbyterially, as they had formerly done, which they did publickly and frequently, without any restraint from the powers—sometimes in one place and sometimes in another, and for a while only in the houses of one another, where all the rest met, and brought their elders, who were fit and willing, always along with them. They met at Templepatrick, Cairncastle, Comber, Bangor, &c., for a while, till at last they settled their meetings as before. This was in the year 1654, when this poor church had a new sunshine of liberty of all ordinances, and much of the blessing and countenance of God concurring therewith in those congregations where ministers had been planted.

Yet, as it is usual in like cases, that God's goodness to his people generally enrages his enemies on all hands; there was in the country not only a standing power of the sectarian party, Anabaptists, &c., but the old episcopal party, who, now when the power was out of their own hands, to afflict the Presbytery, did insinuate on those who had power, as they did now with the sectaries, to incense them against the liberty the ministers had, and against their discipline and public solemnities at communions, &c.; besides, suggesting that these their meetings were dangerous to the state, and that they had therein consultations for strengthening their own faction. This so wrought with an Anabaptist governor, Colonel Barrow—then in the County of Down—that he became highly incensed, and jealous of these meetings, and resolved to use his endeavours to obtain an order for suppressing them. It fell out, that at a communion in Portaferry, there was an English gentleman from King's County —an Independent in his opinions—waiting for a passage to England, and though it was not his principle to join with Presbyterians in their public worship, yet being there, he wished to see the fashion. Being present at the whole work, he was so taken with it, and saw so much of the power and presence of God with his servants and people, that on his return to Colonel Barrow, his acquaintance, he professed he never saw more of God in an assembly of people; yea, he questioned if God was so much among any people as among these Presbyterians in this country. Colonel Barrow, being a man pretending to much piety, and though of Anabaptist principles, yet not of a malicious disposition, from this time had more respect to the ministers, and used not his interest to suppress their liberty in the country. Besides, he thereby got a better [more correct] character of the malignant informers.

Thus, this poor church being in a great measure restored to former freedom, and enjoying their ministers who had been banished, the Lord so countenanced their labours that many other congregations, in places of the country that had not been planted before, began to seek for ministers to be settled among them. In general, these motions from new places were well accepted by the Presbytery, who resolved to concur with the people. But in the entrance there fell in some difficulties upon occasion of the different opinions in Scotland, before mentioned, most young men there siding with the one party or the other. And some brethren who had lately come over, being of the dis-assenters' opinion, had invited one or two young men of the same opinion also to come over, and had employed them in preaching without acquainting the brethren of the Presbytery. The most of the brethren here, not being of these opinions, and hearing of this, did resent the practice as disorderly and dangerous—especially there being the whole country of the Lagan to be planted, having only two ministers, Mr. Hugh Cunningham and Mr. William Semple, who had been in Scotland, and favoured the Protestors, and other two who had lurked in the country, and were easily drawn to their opinion. The Presbytery apprehended they might plant that country and Route with persons so fixed in the protesting way as to found a division between ministers of that part of the country and the rest of the brethren, and to provoke ministers who were of the other opinion to deal as vigorously for men of their own views. Upon these considerations, the body of the Presbytery declared to those brethren their disorderliness, and told them that such practices could not be borne with.

However, another meeting was appointed at Bangor, where all the brethren met; and before their sitting down some jealousies and animosities began to appear between these two parties of brethren who came from Scotland; notwithstanding that before their coming over, they had come to a good understanding one with another, and had resolved to continue so. The few who had been left in Ireland were unconcerned in the difference; therefore, the brethren coming together to the place of meeting (the church of Bangor), one of these brethren whom neither party did mistrust, was by common consent chosen Moderator. Immediately, he, having been made acquainted with the present case by some of the brethren of both parties, proposed a committee to be chosen of more experienced brethren, to bring in overtures to the Presbytery, in order to establish unity among themselves, and for planting new congregations. This being assented to, the Moderator, according to custom, made a list equally of both parties—viz. Mr. Drysdale, Mr. Cunningham, and Mr. Semple, who were all of the protesting opinions; and Mr. Greg, Mr. Stewart, and another of the other side, who were also approven by the rest. They, together with the Moderator, were to meet for preparing these overtures. This accordingly they did; the rest of the brethren going through other business in the Presbytery in the meantime. The brethren did calmly consult of their present case, and hazard of division among themselves, and what mischievous consequences it might bring to this church; as well as of the dangerous consequences of bringing over young men from Scotland and settling them ministers, who were fixed on contrary parties and factions, which might lay the foundation of a constant rupture in this church, which the Lord in mercy had hitherto kept entire and in great unity and uniformity, in affection, principles, and practices. They, therefore, concluded upon some overtures to be presented to the rest of the brethren, which were readily assented to, and Presbyterially concluded by them.

The first overture, called the Act of Bangor, was, that as to the brethren present, though some differed in opinion from the rest, yet there should be no mutual contestings about the differences in Scotland, nor any owning of them on either side in public preaching or prayer, nor in conference among the people as siding with one party more than another. But whatever mention might indirectly be made of these divisions, it should be in order to healing them in Scotland, and praying for that end; and for preventing them among us, where there was not even an imaginary ground for such divisions.

The second related to the planting of the church with men from Scotland. On this subject the Presbytery resolved—1st. To endeavour for men of abilities for gifts of learning and prudence, knowing that there are many enemies and observers of ministers of our persuasion in this country, so that men need abilities to answer enemies on all hands, and a walk so as to convince gainsayers, and bring a good report from those who live without; 2nd. That they should be pious, knowing that other qualifications without this are not usually blessed in the ministry, and that men living in this country among so many troubles, and where there is no discipline, had need to be fixed on godliness, and have some savouriness in their carriage, in order to a bond on people's consciences, though they have no external power; 3rd. That they should be peaceable—*i.e.*, not violent in either of those ways now debated in Scotland; but, whatever were their private thoughts, they should be of that temper as to be submissive to their brethren, and not trouble this church with their opinions.

The third related to the sending and applying for such learned and godly men to Scotland. In order to this, the Presbytery arranged—1st. That no congregation should send to Scotland for a minister without acquainting them; 2nd. That the Presbytery should appoint some brethren to write to the gravest ministers of both judgments that they would give the persons commissioned from their respective parishes their advice, in order to obtaining pious and peaceable young men; 3rd. That none should be received here but such as had the recommendation of worthy ministers of both sides; 4th. And that, thereafter, none should be admitted but such as after trial and approbation otherwise, should engage and subscribe to the peaceable deportment inculated in the Act called the "Act of Bangor."

The Presbytery also determined that not only the young men from Scotland should have sufficient testimonials from learned and godly men there, but they resolved to take special trial of them themselves before they allowed any parish to give them a call—first by private conference with some brethren appointed for that purpose to know what they had read and what stock of learning they had, not only in those points taught in the philosophy colleges in Scotland, but also how they had improved their time after that, whether in colleges of divinity, or, if they had not that opportunity, how they otherwise improved their time as to grounding themselves in positive divinity, and studying common places in controversial divinity and church history, and what acquaintance they had with the Bible. They were, furthermore, appointed to preach not only in that congregation which might have an eye to them, but in congregations near its bounds, in order that both ministers and the more knowing of the people might have some taste of their gifts. This narrow scrutiny seemed then necessary, considering so many congregations were now calling for ministers, and that some young men came over of their own accord, though not without some testimonials and recommendations from worthy ministers in whose bounds they had resided, yet not altogether in the order the Presbytery appointed. Besides, the more that were to be admitted, there was the greater need of narrow searching, lest new places should be planted with insufficient men, whereby people who were but coming into the Gospel and not confirmed in it might have been at first entry stumbled, and the Lord's work in these places hazarded. It is true some did come over according to the order, and yet proved not sound hereafter, as appeared when the troubles came. When young men had thus come over and passed these private sorts of trials, then the brethren, being satisfied with them, did concur with the parishes who called them and put them upon ordinary public trials, in order to ordination, and settling them in that particular place, according to the common method and order—unto which was usually added at the time of their ordination, and before imposition of hands, that they declared their adhering to the Solemn League and Covenant; and they were put to subscribe the Act of Bangor, which was kept on record.

The Lord blessed these endeavours of the Presbytery very signally. For many young men were brought from Scotland by degrees; all of them with the testimonials required, and professing their willingness to live peaceably, without owning the differences in Scotland. Yea, both the brethren who had been here before, and those coming over of late, had a merciful harmony in everything, and no noise among the people of any differences which so divided the church of Scotland, but to regret them. And it is observable, that the most grave, experienced, and godly ministers in Scotland, of both sides, did much approve this way that the Presbytery took to prevent divisions, as all of them testified to the brethren of Ireland, who occasionally went to Scotland about these times, not one of them disapproving of their prudent measures.

The number of ministers in planted congregations, growing and considerably spreading unto all parts of the North of Ireland, it was found that the Presbytery could not all meet together in one place, as formerly they had done from the first beginning of church discipline in these parts. Therefore, the Presbytery found it necessary that there should be three different meetings in different parts of the country, for the better and more speedy carrying on the work of God in divers counties; taking order with scandals; and concurring in matters of discipline as particular congregations should require their help. And withal, that these distinct meetings should take trials of entrance within their particular bounds, upon their finding the calls clear to congregations. These meetings were not constituted into Presbyteries, strictly so called, as acting by power in themselves; but they acted by commission of the whole Presbytery met together—their commission being drawn and subscribed by the clerk of the Presbytery for what they did. These committee meetings had power only to visit empty congregations; to dissuade people from hearing hirelings; to erect and give advice to sessions anent scandalous persons and their repentance; to try what duties ministers and elders performed in their charges; to see what care congregations took to maintain ministers; to inspect expectants' testimonials coming from Scotland, and if approven to license them to preach till the Presbytery [met], but not in relation to trial; to preach and censure doctrine at their meetings; to take account of one another's diligence; and to divide the controversies of the times among themselves. But, on the other hand, they were not to enter expectants upon trial in reference to congregations, till the Presbytery was satisfied with their testimonials. Nor were these young men to be ordained till the Presbytery should have report and satisfaction concerning their abilities after trials were passed.

Thus the work of the Presbytery was facilitated by these meetings commissioned by them. They were then called the Meetings of Down, Antrim, and Route, with Lagan. Besides, the gospel spread into divers counties and places of the North of Ireland, where the purity and power of ordinances had never been known before—such as Armagh, Fermanagh, Tyrone, Monaghan, Cavan;* besides a further enlargement of the gospel in Londonderry. Though there were not above twenty-four ministers planted belonging to the Presbytery in the year 1653, yet they had multiplied to near

---

* Presbyterianism has never been adopted by so large a proportion of the Protestant population in these counties as in Down and Antrim.

eighty within a few years thereafter, even in the sight and to the angering of their adversaries on all hands—viz. the old Episcopal party, who then complied with the Government, and the Anabaptists and other sectaries, who then had special influence upon all affairs. This was the hand of God covering a table to His people in the sight of their enemies, and making His wonderful work to appear and prosper in the hands of a few despised and hated men; even under the eye of those who lately before had been their persecutors, driving the most of them out of the country, and the few that were left, into corners. And it ought never to be forgotten how in this poor church, from the beginning of planting the Gospel in it, though the sovereign-wise God thought fit to let loose the enemies of the power and purity of the Gospel so far against its servants and people, as to persecute and drive them out of the country for a testimony and sealing of the truth with their sufferings; yet the same faithful and wise God did shortly after take up the possession of the land with great advantage. Thus it was in the prelates' times. Thus it was in the sectaries' time, as appears by this narrative: all which we are only to ascribe to God's goodness and tenderness to his work, and people, and poor servants; though it be true that the Lord made use of the policy of Oliver Cromwell—at this time advanced to the helm of power and rule in these nations, who saw it for his interest to engage all sorts of persons, so far as might stand with his present peaceable possession. And because he had always a profession of religion, he pretended greatest favour to godly men and faithful ministers; thus walking in a course much different from the way of the Rump Parliament that he had destroyed, and with more policy. Beside, his son-in-law Fleetwood,' being [in the beginning of this time yet in government in this nation, was not only of a sober temper and gentle disposition naturally, but had a piece of tenderness to all whom he apprehended to be godly, being of himself inclinable to the Anabaptists. This in him, together with the politic designs of his father-in-law, gave a latitude and ease to the ministers in this country, so that it might in some measure be said of this church, as in Acts ix. 3, " Suddenly there shined round about it a light from heaven."

Meantime, the ministers had no settled maintenance. Those who after a while's suffering and want here had been banished to Scotland, were, during their abode there, provided for with the legal maintenance of the parishes which they supplied. Those few who were left in Ireland, beside their hazard from their persecutors, and many other inconveniences, had nothing allowed them for full five years (from 1649 till 1654), except what the people, under the burdens and oppressions of strangers, could, out of their poverty, spare them. And though for new entrants the Presbytery obtained some better conditions from the parishes that called them, than they got for themselves who had been called before, yet the conditions were but small, and in most places scarcely able to afford any comfortable subsistence. In this case, Providence ordered that Sir John Clotworthy came from England into these parts to visit his mother, and to order the estate and things for the family, whom he was to bring over shortly after. Mr. Adair having occasion to discourse with him in order to providing a minister for Antrim, Mr. Ferguson being now dead,* Sir John inquired how the ministers in this country were maintained in this juncture of affairs. Mr. Adair, in reply, gave the account just related. Upon which, that worthy gentleman did much regret the case of the ministers, and proposed to Mr. Adair that if the brethren would send one or two of their number

---

* Mr. Ferguson died in the end of the year 1654.

to Dublin along with him, whither he was shortly to return on his way to London, together with some from the country, to represent the case of ministers to Fleetwood and the Council there, he would use his endeavours to obtain maintenance for ministers who were known to be worthy. Upon Mr. Adair's acquainting his own meeting and that of Down with this motion, Down chose Mr. Stewart from the ministers, and Captain James Moor from the country, to repair to Dublin for this end. And Antrim chose Mr. Adair from the ministers, and desired Captain Langford from the country, that they might attend Sir John Clotworthy, and be advised by him.

Accordingly they all went except Captain Langford. In this negotiation, Sir John first applied to Fleetwood without their counsel, and to some other members of his acquaintance—from whom he had fair promises of their concurrence with his desires. The motion was from the country, and not from the ministers themselves, and the only desire was to take off the sequestration, that now had been, of ministers' maintenance for these last five years. Thereafter the motion was brought before the Council. In it there were men of divers complexions—some of Anabaptist opinions—who carried much at that time, and were no good friends to Presbyterians. Others were politicians, designing to bring ministers under an undue dependency on the state for their livelihood. They therefore proposed to give the ministers a competent maintenance out of the treasury, and that quarterly. This being considered by the ministers, who did not appear before the Council, but waited for what might concern them in this affair, they declined such a way of maintenance, but desired they might have their legal maintenance belonging to their respective parishes, though almost none of these maintenances were of nearly equal value to what the Council proposed. They gave into the Council's hands the reason of their so pleading, which some of their number having first seen in private, did much approve of. They were not, however, sustained by Fleetwood and the Council. Sir John being present before the Council, pleaded for the ministers' paper, and conducted it with much affection to the ministers, and magnanimous zeal, to have them provided for, with some express reflections on the present course of that time, where unlettered mechanics, inferior officers of the army, being Anabaptists, were largely provided out of the public treasury for their ignorant preaching and seducing of the people. But they had such a reverence for him that they overlooked what he said, and yet stuck to their own point. They returned the ministers this answer, that they would not allow them any other way of maintenance than by salary, according as some of their profession in the Lagan and Route had already. For these brethren, having been of the opinion of the Protestors in Scotland, had obtained this way of maintenance, previous to the motion of Sir John Clotworthy, and before the brethren of Down and Antrim had moved for themselves.

But before we close this passage, we owe it as a duty to the memory of this excellent person, then Sir John Clotworthy, to shew the cause why he, being such a stated enemy to the course then followed, had yet so much respect with the Council, and could prevail much with them. A long time before this, even before the rebellion, he had been forced to move with his family from his own habitation at Antrim. Being a Nonconformist, and Lord-Deputy Wentworth growing very imperious at that time, along with the bishop, he saw things growing to that height in this country, where he was more eminent and noticed, that he thought it safest to repair to London, where he—together with his truly noble and excellent lady, who in all these things went on in an equal pace with him as a fit and comfortable yoke-fellow —might live more privately and obscurely, and enjoy his conscience. Here he lived privately, till the sitting down of the Long Parliament, whereof he was chosen a member. There he proved eminent among those worthy patriots, steering a right course, opposing the high royalists on the one extreme, and the sectaries on the other; insomuch, that he was one of those eleven members whom the sectarian party, coming to a height, did for a time seclude from the House. For this interval he repaired to Holland; yet, thereafter he, with the rest, was admitted to his place, where he concurred with the Parliament in their vote for owning the king's concessions, given to the Commissioners of Parliament in the Isle of Wight, to be satisfactory, and that the king should presently be brought into London, and upon confirming his concessions in Parliament, be settled on his throne. But this vote not pleasing the sectarian party, he was thereafter, by Cromwell, violently thrust out of the House, together with the rest of the worthy members in it who adhered to the King—only the "Rump" remaining. He was for the most part of three years kept prisoner by that party, being a person of so much worth and weight, and so contrary to these illegal and treacherous proceedings. However, after that long imprisonment, he was released about this time. But these new upstart politicians then ruling in this country knew him to be more able than themselves, and fitter to govern than indeed almost all of those who sat together in the council in Dublin. And they being professors of religion, and many of them sometime Nonconformists, knew him to be more a religious man than most of themselves. Beside, Cromwell had a great respect for him, not only on account of his parts and noble qualities, but also for particular obligations. For, before Cromwell came to the preferment to be a captain of horse, being a man of parts and great profession of religion, and a gentleman by birth, Sir John had been instrumental in his advancement and command in the army; not presaging that thereafter he would come to that height as to detain him his prisoner for adhering to the cause which they at first undertook. However, we owe that respect to him, to look on him in his way with that party as a person of great magnanimity and honesty, not stooping to them; and yet of such prudence as to improve the respect they had for him towards promoting the good of the church and people of God where he was.*

But to return to our ministers, and the answers they had from Fleetwood. After they had waited a considerable time, and were wearied with attendance, not only on him but on others in power, yet whom they could not own as lawful powers, and in pursuit of a desire so contrary to the designs of those in power, they returned and communicated their endeavours and answers to their brethren, who—though they saw it inconvenient to pass from their legal way of maintenance, and much contrary to their inclination to have any dependence on an usurping power, yet considered it necessary that ministers be maintained. Their legal maintenance had been taken into the treasury, the tithes being then farmed by commissioners for that purpose, and had been thus violently sequestered by powers then uncontrollable. They considered, too, that what they got from the treasury was but getting their own again, and that it was still a maintenance out of the tithes that were due to ministers. The people, too,

---

* Sir John Clotworthy was one of the lay assessors in the Westminster Assembly. In 1660, he became the first Lord Massareene. He had only one child, his daughter Mary, who was married to Sir John Sheffington. In 1665, on the death of his father-in-law, Sir John Sheffington became the second Lord Massareene.

under so much oppression, were not able to bear further burdens, both lying under the weight of an army, and paying tithes to the Commissioners—to which was added this inducement, that there was no proposal of any terms or conditions made to them upon which they should have this maintenance, being a free gift without any shadow of a snare in the manner of receiving it. Upon all these considerations, they concluded to accept of that proposal, and were accordingly paid for two years by the treasury at Carrickfergus, and none excluded who sued for it. There were still a considerable number who received not this salary, because being then but newly come into the country and entered upon their trials, this way of maintenance was changed before they were settled.

CHAPTER XIV.

HENRY CROMWELL SUCCEEDS FLEETWOOD IN IRELAND—MINISTERS TO RECEIVE EACH £100 PER ANNUM—SYNOD AT BALLYMENA—DANGERS OF THE MINISTERS—DEATH OF OLIVER CROMWELL—PROCEEDINGS OF MONCK — PRESBYTERIANS ANXIOUS FOR THE KING'S RESTORATION—MEETING OF THE CONVENTION IN DUBLIN—PATRICK ADAIR CALLED THERE—ARRANGEMENTS RESPECTING MINISTERS—POLITICAL MANŒUVERING.

ABOUT the year 1655, Fleetwood was called over to London, and Oliver Cromwell's second son, Henry, sent over in his place. Fleetwood was too much an Anabaptist to carry on Cromwell's designs—now when he was aspiring to settle the supreme government in himself and his posterity after him. For the Anabaptist principle was against a single person, and Fleetwood, being more addicted to his [religious] opinions than to his politics, could not homologate with his father-in-law in these designs—on which Cromwell called him a milk-sop. The truth is, that except his delusion with the Anabaptist principles, which then bore sway in the army, he seemed to be a person of great candour, and of good inclinations in the main. He was much given to secret prayer, and was of a meek, condescending disposition, especially to those who were supposed to be godly, and had so much of a seeming self-deniedness, that he appeared not fit for government, especially of an army so difficult to rule, and of a whole kingdom in such reeling times. These his good qualities I have borne witness to from some experience of them; and besides, I have the same from the testimony of other judicious persons who knew him better. And it is not to be forgotten that when

Cromwell invaded Scotland, he utterly refused to go in that service.

But to return to Henry Cromwell. He came over with his father's instructions for moderation to all who professed the Protestant religion. He had a chaplain in his company who was then a Presbyterian, one Francis Roberts, who stayed not long here, and thereafter changed with the time in England. He acted more the governor and politician than Fleetwood had done, not only in civil and military affairs, but in reference to the Presbytery in the North. He not only, upon occasion, declared a good respect and affection for them, but fell on a way of restoring ministers to their legal maintenance. For this end he issued forth commissions to gentlemen in divers counties in Ireland, so to mould parishes that there might be a competent maintenance for each minister, not within £100, if possible.* This was done in many places, and their diligence returned to Dublin and approved, and where the £100 fell short in any particular parish, it was to be made up out of the treasury of tithes, by special command to the treasurer. But this, through the uncertainty of these times, came to nought before it could be well effected. It may be here remarked that in 1657, a further sub-division of the Presbytery took place. The meeting of Route supplicated the Presbytery to be disjoined from Lagan. This was, for the sake of convenience, accordingly done; so that from this period there were four meetings—viz. Down, Antrim, Route, and Lagan.

Some time after this, Henry Cromwell endeavoured to have the Church of Ireland, and all ministers who were of a moderate temper, though otherwise of different persuasions as to Episcopacy, Presbytery, or Independency, to come to a right understanding with one another, and so compose

---

* This sum was equal to from £300 to £400 of our present money, if not more.

matters among themselves as to live peaceably together, though his main end was supposed to be that he might feel their pulse and temper as to the government of himself and his father. In order to this design, he called for a considerable number of ministers, by missive letters, from divers parts of the kingdom, and particularly from the North, directing his letters from himself to those particular ministers that he desired. Yet, the ministers, who were sent for, having acquainted their several Presbyteries with these letters, were sent by commission from their brethren, and obliged to give account of their actings in that meeting upon their return. However, the design came to nought.

Soon after, there was a Presbytery at Ballymena, where all the four meetings were present, on April 8, 1659. Some called it the General Presbytery, and some called it a Synod. Here Lieutenant-Colonel William Cunningham, of whom we have spoken before, being then tenant to Henry Cromwell in Portumny, in the west of Ireland,* came with a letter and message from Henry Cromwell, desiring Mr. John Greg should be sent to that country, in order to planting the Gospel in those bounds, where at present were only Papists and a few High Prelatists and Anabaptists. He promised in his letter to give them all the encouragement in his power for this end, that the purity of religion and good principles might be settled among the people there. This motion was thought to come especially from Cunningham, who, at that time, had a considerable interest in those parts under Henry, as also divers others had, who wished their lands planted with British and sober persons, which they saw they could not so well do except ministers were settled there.

---

* Portumna is in the County Galway, near the River Shannon, the seat of the Marquis of Clanrickarde. Mr. John Greg, mentioned in the text, was minister of Newtonards. He had before been settled at Carrickfergus.

Beside, where they were to have their own residences, they loved to enjoy Gospel ordinances under faithful ministers.

The Presbytery, in compliance with this motion and desire of the then Chief Governor, did name some of their number—viz. Mr. Greg, Mr. Shaw, Mr. Cornwall, and Mr. Wallace,* to visit that country for three months, to see if there appeared any hope of doing good, but only on the condition that they be provided for and conducted to those places where they might be useful. But the motion was thereafter forgotten, and did evanish, Henry being taken up with grand affairs, and not being confident of our brethren that they would be for his purpose—*i.e.*, instruments to engage people to his Government—and the ministers who were named having no forwardness for that undertaking.

After this the Presbytery in these parts were hardly put to it by Henry and his Council, to observe their public fasts and thanksgivings, on account of the losses or victories of that party. The brethren, never judging themselves incorporated with them, durst not espouse their course, especially as to these solemn appearances before God; knowing that this government, though now flourishing and pretending some owning of religion, yet was iniquity at the bottom. The brethren, not joining in these days of theirs, were narrowly observed by the friends of that party in the country, and account transmitted to Dublin. Whereupon, threatening letters full of animosity were written to the Presbytery by Henry himself, and some particular brethren were charged, by letters from the Council, to appear before them at Dublin—which they did. Others were partly threatened ; partly insinuated upon at home. The Presbytery sent up two—Mr. Hart†

---

* Mr. Gabriel Cornwall was settled at Ballywillan, near Coleraine, and Mr. George Wallace at Holywood.

† Mr. Hart was minister of Taughboyne, or St. Johnstone, near Derry.

P

and Mr. Greg—on purpose, to endeavour to allay the present fury of the governors, especially of Henry, who at first so much professed to be our friend. There, after long discourse from Henry upbraiding their ingratitude, and showing the reasonableness of the demand, Mr. Greg did plainly tell them, that we could not in conscience join with them in these fasts and thanksgivings, and that it was no wordly consideration but conscience that kept them at that distance. However, this did not satisfy Henry, but rather increased his choler, and brought from him harsh and threatening expressions against the whole brethren. With this, these two brethren were at that time dismissed, and returned home with no account of the Governor's satisfaction. Yet, after that, came divers orders for keeping their days upon emergent occasions, which the brethren still waived. And, being again put to it, the brethren of Down particularly did give the reasons why they could not observe their days, partly considering that the causes thereof were matters which concerned that party and the carrying on their own designs, in which others beside themselves were not concerned, and partly because they were imposed by persons not having lawful power. Besides that, they were not lawful magistrates who in some cases enjoined fasts. There was in these parts a church, representative and constituted, whose duty it was to consider the causes of these public solemnities, and accordingly to call the people together to exercises of that nature. This plainness did so startle the Council that it was feared he who once had professed so much friendship should turn an enemy. This was the special difficulty that the brethren then met with from the ruling powers.

But the foundation of a great alteration of affairs was laid in the year 1658, by the death of Oliver Cromwell, who died the 3rd of September, in that year—a day wherein he had gotten two great victories, which tended most to his advancement—one at Dunbar and the other at Worcester, where the blood of many godly worthy men was spilled in defence of that cause wherein once he professed to be embarked with them. This day, too, it is said, he had begun to idolize, insomuch that he would have one of his Parliaments to sit down on that day, though it was the Sabbath.* What remark may be put on the sovereign hand and providence of God in removing him out of this world, on that same day, we leave to the prudence of others to judge.† However, it is certain that day was the beginning of the overturning of his family as to the government of these nations, and a putting an end to all his former designs, and the designs of that whole party whereof he was the head. For after his death, though his son Richard was proclaimed Protector, and entered upon the government and called a Parliament who much complimented him; yet, the army became so wild and unsettled in their principles, and did so much counteract the Parliament, that many reelings and alterations of government appeared through their giddiness, and the inability of Richard and his brother-in-law Fleetwood, to manage such unruly spirits now formed into a puissant army. It might have been said of them in that time, till a little before the King's restoration, that the Lord had mingled a perverse spirit in the midst of them; they erred in every work of their hands, as a drunken man staggereth in his vomit.

---

* " September 3rd, 1654, the Lord's Day, yet the day of the Parliament's meeting. The members met in the afternoon at sermon in the Abbey church at Westminster. After sermon they attended the Protector in the Painted Chamber, who made a speech to them of the cause of their summons, 'speech unreported;' after which they went to the House and adjourned to the next morning."—*Carlyle's Oliver Cromwell's Letters and Speeches*, III., 17.

† Though so much has lately been written in favour of Oliver Cromwell, it cannot be forgotten that some of his contemporaries who knew him well—including such men as Baxter, Howe, and Blair—never could place confidence in him.

But the particular narration of these events I refer to other histories. Meantime, the church of Christ, with its ministers in this country, being settled on its former basis, remained in peace and liberty as much as ever, beholding their late oppressors a reeling and mouldering away, and in that fury destroying one another, and their own hands bringing to ruin that which they had for a while been building on iniquity. In the meantime, congregations were planting, and the interest of Christ spreading very remarkably in these parts, by the settling of ministers in congregations not before planted.

Things remained thus in these parts, where the Presbyteries were settled, till a little before the King's return. As the sectarian party were so staggering and reeling among themselves, it must be presumed that there were not wanting in any of the three kingdoms, persons of all sorts who watched for their halting and studied to take advantage of their present condition. Among these the Presbyterian party were the most considerable; not only because those who then professed that way were most considerable for number—many moderate episcopal persons then owning their way, and being willing to have closed with it after the King's return, if he himself had owned it—but also, because true Presbyterians were fixed upon grounds of conscience and obligation, by covenant and other engagements, to oppose that wild party of the sectaries and own the just rights and government of the King, as appeared in their carriage and sufferings under that party during the usurpation. Thus the motion of bringing home the King began first among the most grave and wise ministers in the church of Scotland—who communicated it to some principal noblemen—and thereafter, under secrecy, General Monck was communed with in it—who accorded to the proposals made, and had then support from Scotland for the same undertaking, and the promise of more if there were need thereof. The same spirit did, after Monck's entering into England, actuate that party there. For all along in his march to London, they encouraged him and owned him. And being there, it was the Presbyterian covenanted party who brought him into credit; and therefore, he openly conversed with them, and their ministers brought the whole city to own him. In compliance with them, he so ordered matters that the first old Parliament was at length called. Meantime, the sectarian party under Lambert* mouldered away—many cities, and even London itself, calling for a free Parliament. The Parliament met in order to bringing home the King, as not only the undoubted lawful magistrate and sovereign of these nations, but then, considered as a Presbyterian, having entered most solemnly into the covenant when he was in Scotland, both at his closing the treaty with the States there for his return in the year 1649, and thereafter in the year 1650 at his coronation. This encouraged the Presbyterians the more, and though they never doubted his right to the crown, yet it made them with joy and acclamation endeavour his return to it.

In Ireland, though the Presbyterians had not men of note and quality to be leaders in these affairs, yet their prayers were not wanting for the King's happy restoration. And in this juncture of affairs the ministers encouraged the people, that in their station they would be ready and assisting in their duty. Meantime, some special officers in the army in Ireland, at consultation among themselves, resolved on a concurrence with other loyal persons in England and Scotland; and in order to this, the castle of Dublin was surprised and taken out of the hands of those that were then of greatest authority, and of the sectarian party, and divers

---

* Lambert was one of the officers of the army. He greatly offended Cromwell by opposing his acceptance of the crown.

other places were thus taken. In several places some regiments of common soldiers, and the inferior officers, did surprise and lay hold on their chief officers, and delivered them up to those honourable persons in Dublin who had undertaken this business. Thus, in a few days, not only the country generally, but the army were brought to declare for a free Parliament; and the principal persons who had been the heads of the sectaries in Ireland were secured and sent to London, where those of them who had been chief actors in the late King's death were thereafter executed as traitors. The true Presbyterians in the meantime were heartily acting and concurring in all these passages, in order to the King's restoration, and with a view to a happy settling of religion according to the first undertaking in Scotland. Others pretending the same end at that time concurred with them; and no doubt would have so continued if the King had stood to his solemn engagements, and countenanced religion accordingly. Particularly the Lord Orrery and Sir Charles Coote, then president of Connaught, and with his brethren and friends commanding a good part of the army, were special actors in the affairs of Ireland at this time. They, with other persons of quality and interest in the nation, resolved to call a General Convention from the several parts of the kingdom, chosen after the manner of members elected for Parliament—a regular Parliament being impossible in this juncture in Ireland as it was in England—her Parliament being the same which had long before that been legally chosen and confirmed by Charles I. to sit during pleasure, and having been only interrupted for a time through the prevailing of the sectarian party, did only then reassume its own power. But Ireland's Parliament had been legally dissolved. Therefore, to supply this defect, it was agreed there should be a

Convention called, which was accordingly chosen in the several counties of Protestants, and met in Dublin about the beginning of February, 1660, where it consulted how to order and settle affairs in the nation as the present circumstances of the times would permit; and particularly [manage] the army, which before this had been wholly under the command of the prevailing party, and opposite to the King and free Parliament. This Convention consisted of persons of divers principles, though most part prelatical, and such as always had adhered to the King against the Parliament of England. Yet a few were otherwise principled, and intended the Solemn League and Covenant; and all at first seemed to favour Presbyterians, even the enemies of that way now apprehending that possibly the King would own that side. They began to conciliate the army by proposing ways how to pay them their arrears; and pretended, not at first, a reformation of the church nor called upon ministers, as hereafter will be narrated. They chose for their chaplain to prayer, each time they had their meeting, a minister from Dublin, who was counted the surest Presbyterian,* and did everything that was popular till they had intelligence of the King's resolutions as to religion. Then they began to entertain those few bishops that were in the country, and to give all respect to them; and they voted considerable salaries to them till things should be otherwise ordered. Yet a due testimony is not to be denied Henry Cromwell, though the son of the usurper Oliver; who, when he perceived matters go to confusion in England after his father's death, and the Anabaptists carry all along both in England and Ireland, had a desire and resolution to be instrumental in bringing home the King to his just right, though upon terms by which religion and property might be

---

* The Rev. Samuel Cox, who officiated in St. Catherine's Church, Dublin.

secured. This he did communicate to some of the soberest of the officers of the army, who he thought would be most ready to concur, and particularly to the Lord President and to Lord Orrery. But the motion from him was crushed by those whom he looked on as his and the King's friends. And some of them seeing things go as they did, resolved to take the glory of the King's restoration to themselves.

Upon this, Sir Arthur Forbes, a gallant gentleman, who had been a great sufferer for the King, both in his blood and estate, was sent over to the King, then at Breda, with a tender of their service to his Majesty, and intimation how far Ireland was at his disposal, without any terms or conditions, for religion. Yea, these two lords in Dublin growing emulous of one another, and both being afraid of the King's displeasure on his return, having been great compliers with the times before, studied to ingratiate themselves with the King, and resolved to anticipate one another by offering the King, though then abroad, all conditions on his return that he could require. This they thought would be acceptable to the King, the rather because it was expected that England would not receive him without conditions somewhat equivalent to those upon which he was first received in Scotland—for the Parliament then sitting in England owned the covenant and work of reformation. But that truly worthy person, Sir John Clotworthy, a member of the Convention, being then in Dublin, and finding out these designs of the lords, so wrought with them that they concurred to send one from them both to the King, with conditions for Ireland as well as for England on his restoration. And they both pitched upon Sir John to go on this negotiation. He accordingly went as far as London on his way to Holland. But Monck's actings prevented his further journey, as we shall touch upon hereafter.

But to return to the convention of Ireland, at this time sitting in Dublin. I shall not, however, touch any of their actings, save wherein religion may be concerned. First, they chose for their chaplain a man reputed the soundest Presbyterian in Dublin, one Mr. Cocks, calling him to their prayers every morning when they began their business. Immediately they called eight ministers, two from each province in Ireland, all reputed learned and sober and prudent men, that they might give their advice to the Convention in order to settling the Church in Ireland, both in approving fit ministers, and ordering colleges * and schools, till a Parliament thereafter should be duly called. Next, the Convention appointed a general fast through Ireland, and, with the proclamation for keeping the fast, were inserted the causes thereof, among which, breach of covenant was one. This fast was kept universally where orthodox ministers were settled, and very solemnly in Christ Church in Dublin, where the whole members of the Convention were present, and in which was kept somewhat of the order used in these times, even by sober persons—viz. one minister to pray first and preach, and another to pray after sermon a considerable length, in which prayer the whole state of the times was mentioned, and both confessions and petitions at length insisted on : and thus four ministers carried on the work of the day. Those ministers that were called to the Convention did all appear in Dublin a little after, and had their commission given them, and ordered to consult among themselves anent what overtures might tend to the good of the church in the meantime; or to acquaint a committee appointed to consider of matters of religion, with their overtures ; and withal to give their advice to that committee anent such offers as they should be

---

* Even at this time the insufficiency of one college for all Ireland was acknowledged, and yet a second university has been only very recently established.

asked of by it. There was only called from the North, Mr. Patrick Adair, by an order of the Convention sent him. Upon which, he acquainted his brethren, and desired a meeting of them at Belfast from both counties, where they gave him instructions how to carry; mainly to endeavour the promoving the work of reformation, and to set on foot overtures for that end in the present juncture, when there seemed to be opportunity; and also to guard against episcopal courses on the one hand and sectarian on the other. He was obliged to acquaint his brethren in the North with what passages were necessary to be communicated to them. This he accordingly did during his abode there; and, agreeably to his instructions, endeavoured, with the rest of the ministers, that they should propose to the Convention the recommending of the covenant, and the owning of it, and thereafter the renewing of it. Unto this, most of them consented. But there being one (Mr. Vesey of Coleraine)* highly prelatical in his heart, and not sound in his principles (not so well known to the rest), he did from time to time make some of the high prelatical faction in the Convention acquainted with this private consultation about promoving the covenant. They, consulting among themselves how to obviate its being publicly proposed, resolved that the chairman, Sir James [Barry, should openly declare against such proceedings of the ministers. And indeed he did openly declare that if the covenant came in before the Convention

---

* In the Adair MS. the name is blank, but it is inserted in the text on the authority of a note in the margin, in another hand, to the following effect :—" This was, I suppose, Mr. Vesey of Coleraine, a very shifty, supple man, and never liked by Mr. Adair to be sound in principles, as he oft told me, for the Presbytery books are full of his tricks and disorderly walk."—V. F. These two letters are, I believe, the initials of Doctor Victor Ferguson, a well-known Belfast physician, who flourished in the beginning of the last century, and from whom, it is said, John F. Ferguson, Esq., J.P. and D.L., Belfast, is lineally descended. It would appear from this, that the Adair MS. was at one time in Dr. Ferguson's possession.

to be taken into consideration, and any votings passed about it, he would leave the chair and protest against it. Whereupon the rest of his party did applaud him; and those of the Convention who favoured it were of the fewest number, others were indifferent, and so that design was crushed in the bud.

However, these ministers had power to recommend all honest able men to the Convention, that such only should be capable of maintenance; and were charged to recommend none who were of Anabaptistical principles, who refused ordination by orthodox ministers, or were scandalous in their lives. Accordingly, they drew up a list of the ministers then in Ireland, who were judged sober orthodox men, to the number of near an hundred, besides those belonging to the presbytery in the North, upwards of sixty. They declared those who, to their knowledge or information, were scandalous in life, or Anabaptistical, or not orthodox in their principles; all whom they approved were allowed of the Convention to receive a legal right to the tithe of the parishes where they severally were; and, in order to that, they were to receive inductions into the churches by such neighbouring ministers as were appointed for that effect. And, withal, they inquired after, and gave in a list of those now enjoying salary, who were Anabaptists, whereof there was a large number in considerable salaries in Ireland, and divers of them members of the army, and some who refused ordination. These were degraded from their preaching, and deprived of their salaries, who a little before had ruled all. Besides, these ministers gave in their advice anent the more comfortable settling of ministers in their maintenance, in which most of them would needs have some helps added to the ministers' maintenance—against which Mr. Adair was necessitated to enter his dissent from the rest.

Thereupon, besides the Convention, another judicatory more seemingly legal (as that time could bear) sat in Dublin, constituted of three men who were Commissioners from a Council of State in England a little before this, and had power and injunctions from the said Council to endeavour the propagating of the Gospel in Ireland in opposition to atheism, idolatry, popery, superstition, and profaneness; but they had no commission then to suppress heresy. These Commissioners were Broghill and Coote, of whom before, and Sir William Bury, a religious, prudent gentleman. These, having some kind of authority from England, did act as they saw the time permitting; and, though they sat in the Convention, and were chief instruments for gathering it, yet they ordinarily sat and acted by themselves. It was by their authority properly that ministers were settled and had maintenance; and this authority they owned, as derived from the Council of State, which had been appointed by authority of a Parliament in England a little before this.

Thus, at present, things were not unhopeful in Ireland; and at this time, too, they looked well in England. For, after General Monck went to London, and the Rump Parliament being then called again, some years after its dissolution by Oliver, and after the dissolution of one called by Richard, things began to grow to confusion among them; and, they having given a distate to Monck, through the instigation of the best principled and Presbyterians, he required the Rump to call the remanent members of the first Parliament, called the "Long Parliament," which the army had, at the King's death, excluded from the House—unto which proposal, though against their will, they were forced to assent. Thus, the members of the Long Parliament were called, and met with the Rump after ten years' suspension from their trust. They began by rescinding two Acts which had militated against monarchy and the King's just interest; and the covenant was openly owned among them, and consultations held how to promote it, insomuch that it began to be hung up in houses and in some churches. Thus, for a moment, things wore a comfortable aspect with a Parliament such as formerly had been the instrument of reformation; and the King, then at Breda, was looked on as a covenanted King who would not resile from the solemn engagements that he was under. Withal, the King at that time before his arrival gave very fair words to those who were sent to him. But, within a very short time, the face of affairs changed; for Monck, having then great power, and the sole command of the army, and also being in considerable trust, carrying himself cunningly and closely as might serve his own ends, especially pretending to favour the Presbyterians and covenant, yet underhand, kept intercourse with the King. Whereby, after great assurances and promises to himself (which afterward the King nobly performed, and, withal, called him always father), he was induced first to dissolve the Long Parliament, and then brought home the King without any condition for religion or covenant.

CHAPTER XV.

RESTORATION OF CHARLES II.—MR. ADAIR'S EXPERIENCE IN DUBLIN—SYNOD AT BALLYMENA—ADDRESS TO THE KING—EPISCOPACY RE-ESTABLISHED — BRAMHALL, JEREMY TAYLOR, AND LESLIE—A PARTY OF HORSE SENT TO DISPERSE A SYNOD AT BALLYMENA—DEPUTATION OF MINISTERS TO DUBLIN—JEREMY TAYLOR'S VISITATION—THIRTY SIX CHURCHES DECLARED VACANT—HARDSHIPS OF MINISTERS.

KING CHARLES the Second, upon his restoration, was received with extraordinary applause and joy by all. Yet, a secret fear in the midst of this universal joy began to possess the hearts of godly people, lest religion should suffer, and matters prove as indeed they soon thereafter did. The King, immediately on his coming to the palace at Whitehall, owned the Common Prayer as a model of his worship. He was accompanied by the old clergy who had either been abroad in his company, or, upon account of their obstinacy against reformation, had left their country or lurked in England. These men, together with those of old called Cavaliers or Malignants, appeared in triumph, as if all were their own, boasting over and threatening the godly, and reviling the work of reformation as if all had been rebellion. Withal, immediately an inundation of profaneness broke in, which formerly had not appeared. Whereas, the Sabbath, in and about London, was formerly kept very orderly; now a present change appeared even in the streets and taverns on the Lord's day. In a word, profaneness became open and avowed; the godly were trampled on—who looked pale, fearing what was coming. Though they had the sense of duty to lawful authority engraven on their consciences, and had suffered for their adherence to it in the

Usurper's time; yet they could not but be grieved to see it again introduced with such a license. This was the first step and appearance of a sad change after the restoration of lawful Government. It is true the King issued forth some proclamations to restrain these exorbitances; but no restraint followed, and it was said they began at Whitehall.

A little after bishops were named for all the vacant dioceses in England and Ireland, for the king did not proceed so suddenly with Scotland.* A new Parliament was called in England, and means used for the return of such members as might be subservient for the ends intended—viz. to overturn the work of reformation, declare it all rebellion, and re-establish episcopacy and the liturgy. Such members were easily chosen at that time, because the treachery and disloyalty of the sectarian party, who had generally been professors of religion, had brought a general odium on professors, and to be loyal at that time was the greatest interest. Yea, where a man was sober and godly, his loyalty was by the common sort of people more suspected. So to be sure of loyalty, the country easily chose men who were unquestionable on that account. Thus a Parliament was framed which carried all things as the Court pleased; and, particularly, they burned the covenant. Their actings, however, I shall leave to others to narrate at greater length.

But to return to the Convention of Ireland: it was related before, that, when things were in doubt and suspense before the King's return, the Convention seemed to favour the covenant and the Presbyterian party, and matters seemed to be in a hopeful course. But when our grandees had intelligence of the pulse of the court at Breda, and especially of

---

* The Scottish ministers were not ejected until nearly the end of 1662. But bishops were appointed before that time.

the King's arrival in London, they altered their course. Then they began to court the few old bishops who were in Ireland, and who then had repaired to Dublin. They allowed them considerable salaries in the meantime, and began to give them their titles. I was then at most three months in Dublin. Some bishops who, at my arrival there, had very hardly access to the Commissioners upon any business, nor one seeming to own them in the streets, and who had been content with the countenance of any private person, before I left had become high, and much courted, and their titles given them. All things then turned just as the King's inclination was observed to be. Thus, when before those eight ministers (already mentioned) had denied recommendation to divers old prelatical men who were corrupt in their doctrine and immoral in their lives, and were generally known to be unworthy of all place in the church of God; now, at the present time, the committee of religion appointed by the Convention, began to plead for them, and said, that if the eight ministers would not give such men their recommendation, they themselves would recommend them to the commissioners for parishes and tithes. Yea, the greatest number of the eight ministers were drawn to be lax in these things, and would give recommendations to men with whom the fewest number would not join. But a little after the King's restoration, there was no more use for these ministers; therefore, they were dismissed, and the Convention sent commissioners to England to the King, desiring the restoring of the former laws, and church government, and worship. In the meantime, May 28, they adjourned till the 1st of November, 1660, a standing committee being settled for the interval. The king, by letters in December following, approved of this committee. It met again in January, 1661, and continued till the May following. But things were turned into another channel as to what concerned religion. They only defended the English interest against the Irish who, by virtue of the peace made in 1646 and 1648, pleaded for some special favour from the King. It was made known how they had neglected it, and had disobeyed the King's Lieutenant, and broken his interest ; upon which the King, immediately after his return, sent forth a " Declaration" against the Irish rebels, not only resenting the horrid rebellion, but requiring that all the rebels who could be found in England or Ireland should be followed in course of law; besides many other matters not proper for me to meddle in.

After Mr. Adair's return home from Dublin, there was held a Synod at Ballymena, where all the brethren in the North were present. He gave them such an account of his keeping their instructions and of the state of the times as he could. He also brought every one of them a warrant for the tithes of their respective parishes, so far as was in the power of the Commissioners in Dublin. This, however, lasted but for that year and the next, till the bishops were established. The brethren, considering what might be their duty in this juncture, resolved to send two of their number to the King with an address. In this address they humbly reminded his Majesty of God's wonderful dealing with him in his preservation and restoration, on which they heartily congratulated him ; but, withal, they humbly petitioned the settling of religion according to the rule of reformation against popery, prelacy, heresy, &c., according to the covenant. With this address, subscribed by all their hands, they sent Mr. William Keyes, an Englishman, lately settled among them, and principally sent because he was an Englishman, and Mr. William Richardson.* These brethren began their journey in May,

---

* Mr. Keyes was settled at Belfast, and Mr. Richardson at Killileagh.

Q

1660, and went to England. But, the nearer they came to the Court, they had intelligence of less ground of hope of any success to their desires. When they came to London, they applied themselves first to Sir John Clotworthy, their acquaintance and true friend. He went along with them to the special ministers of the city of their own persuasion—such as Mr. Calamy, Mr. Ash, Dr. Manton,* &c.—who, when they saw the address, told the brethren they thought the plainness of it, for the covenant and against prelates, would make it unacceptable to the Court. However, they applied to others, who, they thought, might prove their friends, and obtain access to the King—such as Lord Manchester, and Mr. Annesley—and Sir John went along with them. These promised what assistance they could, but, at the same time, told the brethren that the mentioning the covenant and writing against prelacy in the address would give offence to the King. For, by this time, the King had not only declared for prelacy and disowned the covenant, but had named bishops for all the dioceses in Ireland who were making ready to go to their bishopricks. They also went, not without difficulty of access, to Monck, now Duke of Albemarle, and General of all the army, being accompanied by the Lord Broghill, Annesley, and Sir John. But he disgusted their address, and would not concern himself in it as it was drawn up, but told them, if they would petition his Majesty, he would assist them. The honest brethren were thus put to great straits what to do, having instructions from their brethren to offer nothing else but that address; and all their friends, on the other hand, telling them it would not be acceptable; neither would the great persons who otherwise

---

* Calamy and Ashe were both members of the Westminster Assembly, and Dr. Manton the author of "The Epistle to the Reader," prefixed to the Westminster Confession of Faith.

owned them procure them access to his Majesty, except they would alter some expressions in it. They were, therefore, at last, prevailed with to expunge the mentioning the covenant and prelacy. On this they were introduced to the King by Mr. Annesley, then a professed friend to Presbyterians, though, thereafter, being made Earl of Anglesey, and advanced to high places of profit and honour about Court, he disowned Presbyterian principles, and in other things proved not so sound, as was expected.

When the brethren had access to his Majesty, he was pleased to hear the address, as then framed, read by Mr. Annesley. He looked with an awful, majestical countenance on them ; yet he gave them good words, owning the ministers of Ireland's loyalty in the time of the usurpers, and promising his Royal protection for the time to come. He bid them not fear, for he had appointed a Deputy for Ireland, who would prove their friend (this was the Lord Robarts, though another was appointed afterwards) ; and concluded by promising to give Lord Robarts his commands concerning them.

The brethren upon this returned home. At their arrival there was a meeting appointed at Ballymena, where they were joyfully received by the rest. They owned the providence of God toward them in giving them access to the King, as other addresses, sent from the ministers of their persuasion in other parts of Ireland by a very grave, learned, and bold man, could have no access ; but he was obliged to return home without doing anything. And they were thanked by the rest for their diligence. Yet, the brethren did signify their dislike of that alteration of the address ; that being more displeasing to them than all they had done was pleasing. They saw a change and overturning drawing near. The bishops would take no notice of words spoken in private by the King, and they were grieved that the testimony they had given against that sad defection and for the covenant should have been smothered, and yet they nothing the better dealt with. This did a little after appear. For the bishops hasted over to take possession of their dioceses, and were assisted therein by those who ruled for the time in Ireland. And immediately they set up their public liturgy, altars, bishop's-courts, &c. A little after, instead of a Lord Lieutenant, three Justices were appointed to govern Ireland—Lord Broghill, then Earl of Orrery; Sir Charles Coote, then Earl of Mountrath; and Sir Maurice Eustace, who was also Chancellor. Under their government, the bishops, after their consecration and instalment in their own mode, fell with all haste and diligence upon their work —*i.e.*, to crush faithful ministers and plant the churches with what others they could get, and to extinguish the remainder of Presbyterian government where it was. Three of them concerned in the North (where the Presbytery had been) were singularly fitted for that design. The first was old Bramhall, now made Bishop of Armagh and Primate of Ireland,* who, though formerly only Bishop of Derry, had been the principal persecutor of Nonconformists before the rebellion; but his power now reached not only over his own diocese where divers godly ministers had been planted, but over all Ireland besides, that other bishops must be directed by him. Secondly, there was set in the Bishoprick of Down and Connor, one Dr. Taylor, a man pretending civility and some courteous carriage, especially before his advancement, but whose principles were contrary to Presbyterians—not

---

* Bramhall was now about 68 years of age. He so much resembled Laud in his spirit and character that Oliver Cromwell used to call him "The Canterbury of Ireland." His life has been written by a very fitting biographer, Vesey, Archbishop of Tuam, the son of Vesey of Coleraine.

only in the matter of government, modes of worship and discipline, but also in doctrine. He had sucked in the dregs of much of Popery, Socinianism, and Arminianism, and was a heart enemy not only to Nonconformists, but to the Orthodox.* Thirdly, there was set first over Dromore, then over Raphoe, one Leslie, the son of old Leslie, of Down, who had deposed divers worthy ministers before the rebellion. This man was nothing short of his father in cruelty to Nonconformists, but rather exceeded him.† There were not three such bishops in Ireland,‡ the rest generally labouring to engage and forbear ministers in their dioceses.

Thus were the poor ministers in the North, who had met with many tempests before, and been under divers kinds of oppressors, given up to the power of men, of all others most fitted and disposed for their ruin. The first step the bishops took was to procure the Justices to issue forth a proclamation, discharging all Presbyterian meetings. Then, every one of them repairing to their charges, kept their visitations. But, in the meantime, when the bishops were making ready for their work, and previous to their visitations, the brethren (though by proclamation discharged from any presbyterial meetings) met first in a Synod at Ballymena, to consult and take a common course anent their carriage. This being known to some governors in the country, especially Sir George Rawdon, who had also been their opposer

---

* Jeremy Taylor was first brought into notice by Laud. His genius was great and his learning extensive ; but his writings testify that his views of the Gospel were confused and unsatisfactory. He died in 1667, in the fifty-fifth year of his age.

† In 1662, Leslie was transferred from Dromore to Raphoe. Dromore, in addition to Down and Connor, was then placed under the care of Jeremy Taylor. During the Protectorate, the Leslies of Raphoe and Down accepted pensions of £120 per annum each from Cromwell.—*Reid* II., 200. Archbishop Ussher had a pension of £400 per annum. He died in 1656.

‡ Here a contemporary, who knew him well, places Taylor on a level, in point of intolerance, with Bramhall and Leslie.

according as the times were, there was a party of horse sent by him to scatter the brethren; but Providence so ordered it, that they were dissolved before the troopers came. Here they met in a more private way than usually, and sent four of their number from their several Presbyteries to Dublin, to put the Justices in mind of the King's gracious-like promises to their brethren at London upon delivery of their Address. They, therefore, sent one of the brethren along, as one of the four, to bear witness to that circumstance. They went to Dublin and gave in a petition to the Justices in their own and brethrens' name, to be free of the yoke of prelacy, &c.; founding their petition on the King's gracious answer to their brethren at London. Besides, the Lord Massareene, their great and constant friend, being then at Court, had promise from the King that the Declaration about religion, emitted at that time, should have some favourable addition put to it for the Presbyterians in Ireland. Upon this they were called before the Council-table, and in discourse with the Chancellor, the praeses, they had opportunity to declare what had been their carriage, loyalty, and sufferings upon that account, in time of the usurper; and withal, their present principles of loyalty to his Majesty, and resolutions to give obedience to his laws, if not active, yet to endure the penalties, and that they resolved always to live as peaceable, loyal, and dutiful subjects. They were but unkindly entertained by the Council, divers bishops being then privy councillors,* besides other unfriends. They were reviled and mocked by the Episcopal party in Dublin, and the substance of their desires was not

---

* Heber states that, though Jeremy Taylor was "a nominal member of the Irish Privy Council, there is *no reason whatever* to suppose that he took a part in the measures of any administration."—*Life*, I. 50. The testimony here given by Adair suggests a very different conclusion; and the extraordinary eulogy which Taylor pronounced on Bramhall, when he preached his funeral sermon, attests that he approved of all the harsh measures of that arch-persecutor.

granted. From the answer of the Justices and Council may be seen what small encouragement the ministers had, and that no obstacle was put in the bishops' way to follow their designs. They indeed went on in their several dioceses against any minister of that sort, much according to the genius of the bishop himself—some more slowly and with greater commiseration and humanity—others with greater severity, especially where the throng of such ministers principally were, as in the dioceses of Down, Connor, and Derry.

The Bishop of Down coming to his diocese at the time when the brethren were in Dublin, had intelligence of them and their errand, and so had an envious eye upon them. However, he put off his first visitation till they returned; and finding they had obtained no encouragement, he immediately summoned them all to it. They could not then have a general meeting to consult. But Providence so ordered it, that a few days before the summons came, which they were expecting, most of them were called to the burial of an honourable and truly religious lady—the Lady Clotworthy—the mother of the now Lord Massareene. There they had occasion to advise together, and were not all of one mind as to their going to Lisnegarvey. However, most part met in Belfast a day before the visitation, and from thence went together to Lisnegarvey. The bishop being then at his house in Hillsborough, the brethren sent three of their number to him the day before the appointed visitation. Their errand was to tell him, that whereas they had received a summons to appear at his visitation, they could not appear in answer to that summons—neither as submitting themselves to episcopal jurisdiction, nor at all, in the public visitation. Yet they were willing to confer with him in private, that he might know they were men that walked by principle, and held not groundless opinions; and that though they were dissenters from the present church government and modes of worship, yet they were the King's true subjects. He desired they would give in on paper what they had to say. This they declined, on consideration that many of their brethren were not present. He told them he would receive nothing from them as a body, nor look on them in that light. They told him whatever they were, or whatever way he looked on them, they behoved to advise with one another in matters of that concernment—as their relation as ministers, their former correspondence in all such matters, and their Christian prudence, called for. Seeing they would give him no paper, he questioned them whether they held Presbyterian government to be "jure divino," and desired they would give a positive answer. They readily answered they did. To this the bishop replied, that there needed no farther discourse of the matter of accommodation if they held to that. They said it was a truth whereof they were persuaded in their consciences, and could not relinquish it, but must profess it as they were called; therefore, if answers of that nature would but irritate at the public visitation, they judged it better not to appear, but to confer with him freely in private. He answered, if they should make profession contrary to law in the visitation, they would smart for it. Therefore, seeing their foot in a snare, he desired them rather not to appear, and that as their friend. They thanked him, and withal said, that they conceived they might hold Presbyterial government to be "jure divino," and yet not transgress the law of the land, since they were not exercising that government; for, they knew that affirmative precepts bound not "ad semper." He answered, that was true, yet, that they were now subject to another government was contrary to law; and he said that though the King's late Declaration in matters of religion were extended to Ireland, it would do them no good. They returned, that there were many in England who held Presbyterial government to be "jure divino;" yet, at present, enjoyed the benefit of the King's Declaration. He replied, he saw not how that could consist. He then questioned them if they could take the oath of supremacy. They answered, they could not absolutely say what their brethren could do, since it was never yet put to them; but they judged, if that oath were moulded in the sense in which Bishop Ussher explained it, and wherein King James acquiesced, none of the brethren would refuse it. He said, that being informed by a good hand, before some of their number went to Dublin, that they intended to petition the Council for it with that explication (wherein the reader may know how groundless his information was), he did then inquire whether it was conformable to law to give it with that explication, and it was answered to him, it could not. Therefore, he would tender it to them in the grammatical sense, and said he knew none to take that oath but Jesuits and Presbyterians, who were the greatest enemies to monarchy, and most disobedient to kings—which he instanced in the case of the Assembly of Scotland, and in Calvin,* Knox, Buchanan, &c. He said, moreover, that where Presbyterians differed from Papists in some smaller things, they

* Taylor's antipathy to Calvinism breaks forth on all occasions. He was far more tolerant of Popery. Thus we find him saying to his clergy in a sermon preached at a visitation—"What good can come from that which fools begin, and wise men can never end but by silence? And that had been the best way at first, and would have stifled [discussions] in the cradle. What have your people to do whether Christ's body be in the Sacrament by con-substantiation or tran-substantiation ; whether Purgatory be in the centre of the earth or in the air, or anywhere or nowhere? and who but a madman would trouble their heads with the entangled links of the fantastic chain of predestination?"—*Works*, vol. VI. p. 523, edit. London, 1822. The man who dared to speak thus, and who ejected others for non-subscription, had himself subscribed the 17th, the 22nd, and the 28th Articles of the Church of England.

agreed in this great thing. However, neither this bishop nor any of the rest did urge this oath upon ministers, knowing the law did not allow them to urge it on any who bore not some office in church or commonwealth; and they did not look on these ministers as capable of ecclesiastical offices, not owning their ordination, much less to be in any office under the King. He said also, he perceived they were in a hard taking, for if they did conform contrary to their consciences, they would be but knaves, and if not, they could not be endured contrary to law: he wished them, therefore, "deponere conscientiam erroneam." The brethren, being somewhat troubled at that so odious comparison between them and Jesuits, and at his reflecting on the Assembly of Scotland and the worthy Reformers, shewed him his mistake in such a way as their circumstances could admit. On this they returned to their brethren at Lisnegarvey, where, after giving account of their discourse with the bishop, the brethren saw themselves in a hard taking, yet encouraged one another to fidelity and steadfastness.

The next day was the Bishop's visitation in Lisnegarvey, where he himself preached; but none of the brethren except two went to hear him. Thereafter, in his visitation all were called and none appeared; yet, he did nothing further that day. After dinner, two of the former four and another brother were sent to him to see if he would call the brethren altogether to his chamber to confer with him, which they apprehended he had proposed at Hillsborough; especially from his saying it was not fit for them to appear in public. When, accordingly, they went and proposed this to them, he wholly waived to answer their question, and fell angrily on reflections on Presbyterial government (having nothing to reflect on any particular brother, or on the particular actings of the Presbytery in this country, though fain he would if he could); and withal, proposing arguments for conformity, which engaged the brethren in some discourse of that nature. Notwithstanding, his own expressions the day before respecting them not appearing at the visitation, yet, he now alleged it was contempt that made the brethren not appear on that occasion. One said, it was the awe of God and conscience that made them not appear. He replied, a Jew or a Quaker would say so much for their opinions, and everybody would use that argument for the vindication of their erroneous courses. There were also some few of the brethren whom he called to him in private, to engage them to conformity, and gave them great offers of kindness and preferment; but he obtained not his purpose.*

The brethren repaired to their respective congregations, with expectation of the coming storm. For this bishop did, in one day in his visitation, declare thirty-six churches vacant. He did not make any process against the ministers, nor suspend or excommunicate; but he simply held them not to be ministers, they not being ordained by bishops. Therefore, he only declared the parishes vacant, which he was to supply (himself having immediately the charge of all the souls in his diocese, as he professed), and procured priests and curates for these parishes as he thought fit. The rest of the brethren in other dioceses were dealt with in the same manner in the end, though not with so great haste and violence. After this sentence, declaring the churches vacant, the ministers continued preaching for a while, till it became physically impossible for them to continue; curates being sent to some places and taking possession of the churches; others were violently

---

* It is not improbable that Adair himself was one of these brethren. Heber tells that, after this, the ministers entered into a new engagement among themselves "*to speak with no Bishop*, and to endure neither their government *nor their persons*."—l. 167. The falsehood of this story may appear from the succeeding narrative.

laid hands upon as they were going to their pulpits. Upon this they were all forced to desist from public preaching within two or three months after their places were declared vacant, except two—viz. Mr. Hamilton of Killead, and Mr. Cunningham of Antrim, who, through my Lord Massareene's intercession with the bishop, obtained about half-a-year's liberty after their brethren were silenced; only they must not lecture before preaching, according to their former practice.

At this time came a black cloud over this poor church. The old enemies became bitter and triumphed; and kept a searching and severe eye over the outed ministers that they might get some advantage of them. For, generally, they did reside in some places of their parishes, being excluded not only from their maintenance, but from their houses that the parishes had built for ministers—except those houses that were built by themselves, and were their own property. They did also, as the danger and difficulty of that time allowed, visit the people from house to house, and sometimes had small meetings of them by parcels in several places of the parish in the night-time, which were narrowly pried into and sometimes gotten knowledge of by these observers, and ministers called in question. Yet, Providence brought them off again. Besides, there were some who had been once of the brethren by profession, and ordained by them, who, now, turning with the times, became more dangerous than others. Yea, many who a few years before had persecuted them for adhering to their duty to lawful authority, now turning with the times, are their judges, and persecute them on another account.

CHAPTER XVI.

PROCEEDINGS OF THE IRISH PARLIAMENT—BURNING OF THE SO-
LEMN LEAGUE AND COVENANT—PERPLEXITY OF THE MINISTERS
—GREAT FIELD MEETINGS—MICHAEL BRUCE—DEFECTIONS FROM
THE GOOD CAUSE—THREE MINISTERS SENT TO DUBLIN—THEIR
PETITION TO THE DUKE OF ORMOND—CONDUCT OF THE MINISTERS.

IN the meantime, this year, in May, 1661, there was a Parliament called in Ireland. In the House of Lords there was not one man who favoured the Presbytery, save the Lord Massareene. They chose Archbishop Bramhall to be their chairman. There were some pains taken in the North to choose members for the House of Commons, who would be favourable; and some were so, together with divers from Munster who disrelished the bishops and ceremonies—who had been of Cromwell's party before, and were now to get their debentures established by Parliament.* This Parliament, though they declared against the rebellion in general, and more particularly against those who entered into the Confederacy, and carried on business against the Lord Lieutenant; yet, favour was showed to all the Irish (1) that came in upon the Cessation,† (2) who kept the terms of the peace, (3) who being abroad, did own the King in those places, and (4) who had not gone along with the Nuntio. These had pardon for all other things, as well as their former rebellion, and their estates given to them and their posterity. Yet there was no mercy to Presbyterians, but the law was ordered to be executed against them ; though, in the King's

---

* That is, who had lent money on public security during the late troublous times, and who were now anxious to obtain the additional security of an Act of Parliament.
† The Cessation was a treaty made by Ormonde with the confederate Romanists, in 1643.

absence, they had suffered for his interest, and for refusing the "Engagement." The Irish, indeed, thus favoured, were but few—about twenty knights and gentlemen.

Whatever were the principles and affections of some private men, the Parliament did immediately establish the former episcopal laws of Ireland, such as bishops, common prayer, &c. And they put forth a declaration or proclamation to this purpose, forbidding all to preach who would not conform; and ordered it to be sent through Ireland to every minister, to be read by him the next Sabbath after his receiving it. This proclamation came before many of the brethren had been otherwise forced to desist, and was on that account particularly sent to them, which strengthened the hands of their opposers. It was moved by some in Parliament to take severe courses with some of these ministers, in order to terrify the rest. Yet none were, nor could be found, guilty of anything deserving punishment, except Mr. James Ker, who had deserted the King's interest, as already related, but yet had returned again to his brethren long before this. He, knowing they might take advantage of this, withdrew with his wife to Scotland, where he died shortly after.

The Parliament of Ireland followed that of England not only in restoring the former way of government and worship, but in making an Act for burning the Solemn League and Covenant. This was accordingly done in all cities and towns through the kingdom, the magistrates in every place being directors and witnesses,* which, as it was pleasing to the episcopal party and the profane in the land, together with the Papists, so it was a sad mark of the times, and an

---

* On the 29th of July, 1661, Captain John Dalway, Mayor of Carrickfergus, was brought on his knees to the bar of the House of Lords, and fined £100, for not causing the covenant to be burned; but, on producing a certificate that he had duly complied with the order of Parliament, the fine was to be remitted, and he was discharged on payment of fees (*Reid* II. 259, *note*).

evil omen in the eyes of those who had conscientiously engaged in it, to see that sacred oath thus with contempt violated. It had been taken in the north of Ireland with great solemnity (as already related), and as long as it was stuck to by those who first engaged in it in Scotland and England, their undertakings were signally blessed. When it was broken and deserted, first by the sectarian party in England, confusion in Church and State had its rise from their proceedings.* Yet in the Usurper's time, those who were true Covenanters were the only persons who stuck to the King's interest, as well as to sound principles in religion—and that in all the three kingdoms. For those who had no liking to it, and were opposers of it, were the greatest compliers with the usurpers, and generally took the Engagement in support of the Commonwealth of England, as it was then established without King and House of Lords; whereas true Covenanters did refuse and suffer upon that account, not daring to violate the solemn oath. This appeared particularly in those parts of Ireland where the covenant had been before administered, and afterwards this Engagement pressed with much vigour. Yea, it may be said this oath was one special means of bringing the King to his throne, he being looked on then as a King in covenant, and who it was in charity supposed could not, in conscience and honour, but pursue the ends of it, which he had so solemnly undertaken both before and at his coronation. However, little opposition or testimony was given against these proceedings in Parliament; the minority otherwise minded partly seeing the current of de-

---

* This plain fact is too frequently forgotten. Oliver Cromwell, who had himself sworn to the Solemn League and Covenant, was one of the first to violate it; and, notwithstanding all that has been said of late in his favour, it cannot be denied that, in as far as he was personally concerned, he did nothing to advance the cause of constitutional freedom. He established a military despotism. The breach of the covenant was the first false step in his public career.

fection so strong, that they thought it was beyond their power to stop the course. The Parliaments of England and Scotland had already done the same, and it was accounted a crime to avow the covenant. Neither did that party so much as move for ease to tender consciences in the matter of conformity, although they had ground from the King's Declaration at Breda, and his Declaration after he came home; knowing that if they appeared in any kind against the course of the times, it might prejudice their worldly interest. The Parliament being then engaged in settling their newly-gotten estates, said that when once that were finished, they would then appear. But it was so ordered that they were disappointed in a great measure of their expectations. For the Parliament was dissolved, and these matters as yet left in uncertainty.

The ministers of the North in this juncture gave themselves especially to prayer, and did cry to God for help. They sometimes, also, privately met together for that end, in societies, to encourage one another, and take mutual advice how to carry themselves. They thought it their duty, though their hope was very small, to make an essay for some toleration, or immunity from the rigour of laws made over their consciences, by petitioning the Parliament. For this end they sent three of their number, Mr. John Hart, Mr. Thomas Hall, and Mr. William Richardson, to Dublin, with a commission subscribed by all the brethren of several societies—that, as they were advised by friends in Dublin, they might present a petition to the Parliament in their own and brethrens' names. Accordingly, they went thither, and drew up a petition, but could not get it presented; their best friends in Dublin advising them to return home after long attendance for an opportunity, and wait there on God for a better time. In this petition, the brethren owned their conscientious and peaceable subjection to the laws, either actively, wherein they found clearness—or passively, wherein they were of a different persuasion. They declared what had been their carriage in the Usurper's time in general; and they annexed to it a particular narrative of their actings and sufferings during that period—of their Address and Petition to the king on his return—of his Majesty's gracious answers to them, as well as his Declaration at Breda, and other grounds of hope that he had given to those who were of tender consciences, being otherwise good subjects. Notwithstanding these things, they complained of their present usage by the bishops, and petitioned for liberty to preach the Gospel without those impositions, to which they could not agree with peace to their consciences. This was the substance of that petition which could not have access to be read in the Parliament.

This essay failing, the ministers generally took themselves to the houses that they had either formerly of their own, or had lately built in their several parishes; and judged it their duty, as far as it was possible, to stay among their people, and to take such opportunities for their edification as the times could admit; partly conversing with them singly in private, and partly gathering them at convenient times in small companies and exhorting them from the Word. They resolved to go about their duty with as great prudence as they could—considering they had many adversaries and watchful eyes upon them, and not a few to represent them to the magistrates as disloyal and rebellious persons, if any ground had been given. They thought it more suitable to their case and more profitable to their flocks to do somewhat among them in a private way, without noise or alarming the magistrates, and thus continue among their people, than to appear publickly in preaching in the fields, which could have lasted

R

but a very short time, and would have deprived them of the opportunity of ordinarily residing among their people—which in the case of some who took another course, came to pass.

For, at this time there were two or three young men who had come from Scotland, and had been but lately ordained by the Presbytery here, and who, intending to return to Scotland and put themselves out of the bishops' reverence in this country, resolved to do some good before they went. They therefore called the people to solemn and great meetings, sometimes in the night and sometimes in the day, in solitary places, whither people in great abundance and with great alacrity and applause flocked to them. There they spoke much against the bishops and the times. This matter of preaching (as it was in itself commendable and faithful when rightly managed), did exceedingly please most people. These men were cried up as the only courageous, faithful, and zealous ministers by the common sort of people, and by those who had great zeal, but little judgment and experience; though not approved of by the more serious, prudent, and experienced Christians. The manner of it in daring the magistrate openly and calling great assemblies together in despite of authority, was, by that sort of people, thought great stoutness and gallantry.

The people, upon this, not only countenanced and cried them up, but liberally contributed for them; generally neglecting their own ministers who laboured more privately, and, in some sort, with greater difficulty among them. Thus they continued for a considerable time, going from one place and from one parish to another, as well as from one county to another, under disguise and oft in the night-time. Although the magistrates heard and took great notice of it, yet, they were not for a long time owned, in order to see if the rest would follow their steps—which many were longing for, that so they might have greater ground to accuse the whole Scotch Presbyterians of designs of rebellion, which many were oft suggesting to the Duke of Ormond, but could not get grounds to build their accusations upon. Only, they made use of this practice of these young men as much as they could, for a reflection upon the whole. And indeed, all the rest of the ministers at this time were in a very dangerous and sad case. They were beaten with rods on all hands; being put from the public ministry by the magistrate, they must walk prudently and peaceably, and yet for a time are counted fools, and frantic for the sakes of a few of their number—though they endeavoured with hazard and more than ordinary trouble, to be useful to their congregations as the times could bear. But yet, they are counted timorous cowards, and all they did was nothing, because they went not to the hills. They lived upon any small thing they had of their own, among the people, without maintenance from them, and yet must see others bountifully gratified. They must walk prudently; and yet keep up union and affection with an imprudent people. They were convinced of the imprudence of these men, and yet must not disapprove of them lest they lose their people. They saw themselves in little quietness and great hazard from the magistrates; and yet dared not in consequence, lay the blame on those who occasioned their hazard.

I am far from judging these young men, or questioning the integrity and good intentions of any of them. I am persuaded of one of them, Mr. Michael Bruce, who was most noticed, and indeed did most good at that time, that he was a person singularly gifted, truly zealous, and faithful, and also peaceable and orderly in his temper and conversation with his brethren, and in his whole way a very Nathaniel—of all which he hath given proof in the church of Christ for many years since that time.* This I judge a duty to say, lest any blot should remain on that truly godly and worthy brother. He was then but a youth, and so were the rest. They considered not what hazard their way brought on the whole brethren from the magistrate, in depriving them of the small opportunity they had to do good among their people; nor how it occasioned contempt and reflection from the more injudicious and uncharitable of the people, who usually are the greatest number; nor yet how it cut themselves short of occasion to do more good to their own congregations, if they had carried themselves more privately and prudently. For within a short time they were forced to flee the country, without the benefit of their presence and labouring among them as others did, to the great advantage of their flocks. Now, the people who had so much cried up the carriage and zeal of these youths before, and condemned the way of the rest of the ministers, soon saw the imprudence of the one, and the true prudence and courage of the other, in sticking to them under the difficulties and discouragements around them. They were convinced of this more and more, when that way the prudenter ministers took did, by degrees, and insensibly without much observation of the magistrate, make way for the more public exercise of their ministry, as afterwards it proved. And it is to be observed that the faithful ministers of Ireland, the first planters of the Gospel in these bounds, when they were put from the public exercise of their ministry by the bishops, did not use that way of gathering the people to

---

* Speaking of this minister, the late Rev. Dr. Bruce, of Belfast, says, "His grandson, also Michael, was my grandfather, whose younger brother was grandfather to the two baronets, Sir Hervey and Sir Stewart Bruce. My son (the Rev. W. Bruce), is in the seventh generation of Presbyterian ministers, in lineal succession from the Reformation in Scotland—a circumstance so uncommon, that I have thought it worth stating."—*Original Letters to Robert Bruce*, p. 28; Dublin, 1828.

the fields. But they dwelt privately in their houses, and received as many as came to them of their own parishes— though they had greater provocations to do so, because they got not the same liberty, but were shortly after chased out of the country by pursuivants from Dublin.

And let the reader know the end for which this passage has been observed : not to reflect on honest men, but to caution and tell ministers who are embodied with a society of godly ministers, and by their solemn engagements at their ordination obliged to walk in subordination to their brethren, that they take not singular courses of their own in such cases, though sometimes it may look like zeal; nor yet walk in a separate way, especially where they may have the advice of their brethren. For a society of godly ministers may expect more assistance and light than a single person. Besides, to my observation, and that of many others, it hath been found that brethren who have taken these singular courses of their own in this church—divers of whom might be instanced both in our own number and coming from Scotland in these times—have, within a very short time, been rendered useless in it; and some of them have deprived all the rest of a great measure of that extraordinary respect and applause which they had from the people— wherein the hand of God might have been seen. I only except that worthy brother, before mentioned, who did what he did in the singleness of his heart, and who, after long sufferings both in Scotland and in England, returned to this church, and was eminently useful in it.*

But to leave this subject. There was another thing added

---

* Some account of Michael Bruce has been already given in the Introduction. He has been described as a man of "great genius, and a liberal education—of extraordinary zeal for the glory of God and the good of souls—much given to meditation and secret prayer—a thundering, broken-hearted, and most affecting preacher." He died after the Revolution in Scotland, in 1693.

to the affliction of the brethren—viz. the falling off of several of their number, and their embracing the snare laid before them. These were Mr. Mungo Bennet, Mr. Caldwell, Mr. Wallace, Mr. Robert Rowan, Mr. Andrew Rowan,[*] Mr. Brown of Bellaghy, and afterwards Mr. James Fleming, who had stood out longer than the rest. All these had come from Scotland, with testimonials and recommendations from grave and godly ministers for their hopefulness and piety, besides other qualifications of learning, prudence, &c. They were ordained by the Presbytery here with solemn engagements at their ordination to adhere to Presbyterian government, the ends of the covenant, and subordination to their brethren. Notwithstanding in the hour of temptation, and embracing this present world, they renounced the covenant publickly, and their ordination by the Presbytery, and were re-ordained by the bishop. Thereafter, they turned other men than before—worldly, proud, severe on the people who discountenanced them, and haters of those faithful men who made them ministers. There were also one Dunlop, and Mr. Andrew Nesbitt, who went the same way, and proved no better than the rest. This Nesbitt, several years after, being sick and expecting death, as it fell out, sent for Mr. Adair, his nearest neighbouring minister, whom he had often before chided and reflected on for gathering the people of the parish by parcels where Nesbitt was then curate, and had threatened severity to him for so doing, besides oppressing the people on account of Nonconformity. Yet, finding himself going out of the world, with great expressions and

---

[*] Andrew Rowan was admitted Rector of Dunaghy or Clough, in Co. Antrim, September 13th, 1661; George Wallace was admitted Vicar of Holywood, in Down, on December 12th, 1661; and Mungo Bennet was admitted Rector of Coleraine, November 7th, 1665.—*Reid*, ii. 256, note.—Of nearly seventy Presbyterian ministers in Ulster, only those here named conformed.—*Reid*, ii. 255.

much seeming seriousness, he renounced the course he had been upon. He said he had sold his Master for a piece of bread—had joined with a set of men whom God was not among, a generation whom God would plague—and he doubted if there was mercy for him, with many words to that purpose. Mr. Adair told him he was glad that he was brought that length: he put him in mind of his former courses during these latter years, which had been very gross for oppression, pride, drunkenness, regardlessness of the Sabbath, and lying; yet, he added, that if he were sincere in what he expressed as to his repentance, and flying to Christ, there might be hope. But he was afraid if Mr. Nesbitt recovered that sickness, he would return again and forget his recantation. He replied, that, through God's strength, it should never be so. It is observable that those who turned to conformity from their brethren and the way of God, turned to be another kind of creatures than they had been generally. While they continued, they were sober, and some of them well gifted; when they conformed, they became loose, oppressive, proud, and divers of them profane. By this the authority and virtue of Christ's ordinances and government may be seen, and how Episcopal government is followed with, and gives place unto profaneness and wickedness of all sorts, not only in the people, but in the pretended ministers, as the universal experience of these times declared in all the three kingdoms, and as it has generally been observed not only by persons of piety and prudence, but by the most sober of the prelatical party themselves. It's but rare to find a minister among them moral and sober; and, as it is said, "from them profaneness goeth forth out through the land." And where profaneness doth not, hypocrisy doth; for the word in Jeremiah xxiii. 15 signifies both. This is a lamentation, and will be so till God arise to purge his church. O Lord, how long! When shall God arise!*

Throughout the year 1662, the poor, afflicted ministers in the country continued in performance of what duty they could to their people, as the times would permit, and in peaceableness and loyalty to the magistrate. Yet, they could not guard against the calumnies and misrepresentations of their observing adversaries to the Duke,† of clergymen, and others, who cast aspersions upon them, both as to their principles and practices. The Lord Massareene, their constant and great friend, dwelling then at Dublin, and being one of the Privy Council, and searching into all affairs, particularly what concerned the ministers of the North, wrote to some of the ministers of his acquaintance, showing it was convenient for them and their brethren to offer a vindication of themselves from the many informations that were given in against them to the Lord Lieutenant. He also sent a draft of that vindication to them to consider if they could subscribe it. The draft was fair, giving an account of their principles, particularly as to loyalty, with a narrative of their actings and sufferings for the King. Yet, the brethren, considering this particular way was not required by the Duke, but was only my Lord Massareene's overture, and, withal, that it was dangerous to draw up such a paper so as to please Court lords, without saying more than was right and suitable to their consciences, judged it more fit to forbear a particular vindication. Yet, they found themselves necessitated to do something; for my Lord Massareene, their great friend, hearing many speeches against them among the great ones in Dublin, told the Duke and some of the Council that he

---

* The account here given of the character of the Irish Episcopal clergy may be corroborated by many melancholy proofs. At the time of the Revolution, Queen Mary, the wife of William III., describes them as "the worst in Christendom."

† Of Ormond, then Lord Lieutenant.

expected some of the Scotch ministers to be shortly in
Dublin to vindicate themselves. The brethren, understanding this, sent three of their number—viz. Messrs. Patrick
Adair, Andrew Stewart, and William Semple—to Dublin.
They gave them instructions to consult with Massareene
about their case, and a commission to make their application
to the Duke for some token of his favour in their present
case, as they should find convenient, or should be advised
by Massareene and their friends there.

Accordingly, these brethren went about the beginning of
August, 1662, and continued there till the end of October.
At their first coming to Dublin, instead of a vindication,
they drew up a petition to be presented to the Duke, to the
same purpose as the petition mentioned before that was intended for the Parliament, owning their principles, and
begging immunity from bishops and ceremonies. They also
gave in another paper, showing the reasonable ground they
had for humbly expecting a favourable answer from his
Grace. The Duke was informed immediately of their
coming to town, and they continued there a fortnight before
they presented their petition, or made any application to
him. This was owing to my Lord Massareene's persuasion,
the ground whereof was this :—that noble lord being truly
concerned for the liberty and comfort of both ministers and
people in the North, as well as of the whole Nonconformists
of Ireland, did of himself devise some overtures, which, if
complied with, might be a favour to Nonconformists, and a
service to the King and kingdom. Of these he had discoursed to the Duke. He essayed to get them accepted in
favour of all Nonconformists, and he thought that these
being granted, would make the ministers' application easy.
But the Duke said he had not power to comply with them,
neither was he forward for any such motions in favour of

Nonconformists. These proposals therefore vanished. Meantime the Duke, knowing of the ministers being in town, became jealous and angry that they did not make application to him. He said to the Lord Mount Alexander, and to Sir Arthur Forbes, that since they came not, he would send for them. When the brethren heard this, the next day they presented the petition to himself, being introduced by Lord Massareene. After inquiring if they had any more to say—to which they answered, " Nothing "—he said he would do what was incumbent on him. The next day he said to the former noble persons (being familiar with them) that he was in a strait what to do with these ministers, for by their petition he perceived they had suffered *for the King*, and now they were like to suffer *under the King*.

After waiting several days, the ministers came to one of the Duke's secretaries, Sir George Lane, to remind him of their petition and its answer. He gave them some queries from the Duke to answer in writing—First, What those things were wherein they scrupled to act; Secondly, Who were the persons that wronged them, and wherein? Thirdly, Who of them were put from their houses? and Fourthly, Who they were for whom they petitioned? They answered to the first, that, having been ordained ministers of the Gospel by Presbyters, they were altogether unclear to receive another ordination; and withal they replied that, however they were clear for the doctrinal articles contained in the Thirty-nine Articles of the Church of England, as well as for the doctrine contained in the Articles of Ireland, concluded in the Convention of Dublin in 1615,* yet they were not clear to worship God according to the forms and cere-

---

* It is evident from this that all these ministers were very decided Calvinists, for there can be no controversy as to the theology of the Articles prepared for the use of the Church of Ireland in 1615. At this time the ministers dare not speak of the Westminster Confession of Faith.

monies prescribed in the Book of Common Prayer To the second they answered that, albeit they inclined not to complain of grievances (that not being their present aim, nor the aim of these other ministers), yet was it evident that for nonconforming, several of their ministers were in hazard of suffering by the civil law, and of excommunication by ecclesiastical courts—before which some of them were standing already processed—as well as of other sad consequences of that sentence, the names of these being particularly expressed by the brethren. To the third query they answered that divers particular persons might have grievances of this nature, yet they did studiously in their petition forbear to mention these things, lest they should be thought more sensible of inferior losses than the great loss of their ministry; and lest they should seem to doubt of the justice of those who were appointed to hear and redress such grievances. To the fourth and last query, they gave the Duke a list, being the same persons who subscribed the Address to the King about two years before.

After divers days' attendance, they got that paper given to the Duke. Thereafter, he caused their petition to be read in Council, and the other papers all subscribed by the ministers, as was by him required. Divers in the Council, and such bishops as were present, spake against the ministers and their papers with great animosity and indignation; and said they should be punished for contumacy and open professing against the laws; and that it was unfit they should have liberty to live among people to poison them.* There were also reflections upon them because they were Scotch Presbyterians, and some remembered the oppressions done by

---

* There is reason to believe that Jeremy Taylor was in Dublin about this time, and if so, we may infer that he was one of the bishops here mentioned. Adair, doubtless, derived his information from Lord Massareene.

the Scotch army while in Ulster. Others held their peace. My Lord Massareene pleaded with no less boldness and animosity for them. The Duke himself was moderate; he said they were unhappy who first suffered *for* the King, and then suffered *under* him; and he thought it just that what the King had promised them should be performed, and said that what these ministers had spoken in their petition, or answer to his queries, should not tend to their prejudice, since they spake their conscience, and since he himself had required them to subscribe it. He said he resolved to give no answer till he had examined the truth of their assertions anent the King's promises. My Lord Anglesey being present at that time was questioned in it; but he shifted any testimony that might seem to displease, and said he was no Presbyterian. My Lord Massareene openly told him that he sometimes professed the contrary; and that if he did not faithfully witness what he had heard from the King, God would make it meet with him another day. The brethren thereafter gave him a paper, putting him in remembrance of what the King had said when he was present—in which the King had spoken to the ministers, in their application to him, as a friend, and with a kind of familiarity. After this the brethren were informed that Lord Anglesey did own the paper they had given in as a narrative of the brethren's answer from the King. But, after much attendance and means used with all who seemed to be friends, and after intercession with the Duke, and after many fair promises, the result of all was, that they must live according to the law; that they might serve God in their own families without gathering multitudes together, they living peaceably, and to that purpose. This answer was left, in writing, the very hour the Duke was taking his horse for Kilkenny, and, with difficulty, a copy only, but not the original, was obtained by the ministers.

After these brethren had returned home, the young men, formerly mentioned, then remaining in the country, took the more liberty, and inconsiderate people took advantage, as if the Duke had granted the brethren some great thing. This being observed by the bishops, they sent a complaint to the Duke that he had given liberty to the Nonconformists. Upon which he sent a copy of the paper to them, but not to the brethren who had so long and with so great weariness waited on him. However, the brethren, this year, following their former courses, lived without great molestation performing what duty they could in their several parishes, and having their private societies one with another, in which they began to think of a way, not only of constant correspondence together, but of walking harmoniously in these times of trouble and difficulty. They had their meetings together for that purpose, and had correspondence from one meeting to another, as they could overtake.

CHAPTER XVII.

BLOOD'S PLOT — MINISTERS ORDERED TO BE APPREHENDED — TROUBLES OF MR. BOYD — HARDSHIPS OF THE IMPRISONED MINISTERS — DISARMING OF THE NORTHERN PRESBYTERIANS — EXECUTION OF LECKY — SOME INDULGENCE GRANTED — MESSRS. M'CORMICK AND CROOKSHANK — BISHOP LESLIE A PERSECUTOR — HIS DEATH.

BUT, in December following, 1662, there was a ground laid for trouble, not only to Nonconformists in other parts of Ireland, but to the ministers and people of the North. There was then in Ireland a considerable number of old Cromwellists, as they were called, who had a rooted antipathy to the King's Government, and some profession of religion, such as it was. These, in and about Dublin, finding themselves not in the condition they had been in before the King's Restoration, and finding oppression by bishops and by other ways growing upon them, began to contrive amongst themselves an overturning of the state of bishops, and rectifying the civil government, and restraining the Papists from that great liberty and countenance they had enjoyed, and, furthermore, securing a liberty of conscience to themselves such as they had enjoyed in Cromwell's time. About this they consulted much with one another in Dublin, in their meetings for that purpose, and agreed amongst themselves in their design. They had many considerable persons, both of the country and army, who were privy to it, and secret favourers, who would not yet appear. They sent to England to acquaint others there of their principles, and were approved, and promised assistance, if need required. One Thomas Blood was a principal actor in this contrivance. He had for some time been an officer in the King's army against the first Parliament, and was a true Cavalier. Thereafter, he had come to Ireland, where he had some interest in land near Dublin; and, falling into much acquaintance with one Mr. Lecky, his brother-in-law, a minister of the Presbyterian persuasion, and a man of good discourse and learning, he was drawn to own the Presbyterian principles. Thereafter, by the instigation of Lecky and others, he was persuaded to engage as the principal actor in this plot, being a person singularly fitted for such a design, in regard of courage, subtilty, strength of body, and great spirit, and who had experience in martial affairs. This man, with his associates, having had many consultations among themselves, thought it fit to try if they could draw in the Presbyterians of the North to join with them, they pretending the ends of the covenant with them. Accordingly, Blood and Lecky, by the advice and consent of the rest, came to the North to try the ministers and best of the people there. They first visited Mr. Greg, Mr. Stewart, and Captain James Moor, of Ballybregah,* calling them together to Mr. Greg's house, where they proposed their business to them, aggravating the iniquities of the times, the usurpation of the bishops, the tyranny of their courts, the increase of Popery, and misgovernment in every affair. As to what concerned the good of the people, they declared there were a number very considerable and well-wishers to a reformation desiring a redress of these things, yet without wronging the King's just authority, and were engaged in that design; and that, if the ministers and people of the North would concur, it might be an acceptable service and much promove the cause. They declared not the particular way how to get their design effected, but said if

---

* In Killinchy.

these three men would send to Dublin their thoughts of it, and any assurance of concurrence, they should then know the particular methods which were to be followed in the design. The three persons who were thus applied unto, being unacquainted with any such motions, were at first amazed at the folly or knavery, or both, of these so despicable persons who looked more like trepanners than anything else. They desired two things of them—first, that they would utter nothing prejudicial to lawful authority in their hearing; and, secondly, that being neither acquainted with the ends they aimed at, nor the means they thought of, they could say nothing; but, in general, that God's ends by lawful means, when proposed, could not be rejected by good men. But, withal, told them, that if they intended any secret evil, what a slander it should be to their profession, who were never seen to plot unlawfully for shunning what troubles God brought them unto. As for going to Dublin, they would know shortly whether they would do it or not; and so they parted.

Being thus discouraged by the three to whom they opened their business, they made no further attempt upon any in Down or Antrim; but went to Lagan and Armagh, where they met with the like discouragement, except from one or two ministers who afterwards were discovered to be of their mind—viz. Messrs. M'Cormick and Crookshanks (who afterwards were killed at Pentland.)* From that they went to the South and West of Ireland, where they drew their purpose to a great height; yet they never corresponded more with any in the North, or with the Scotch—who gave them nothing but discouragement. Notwithstanding—by their private consultations and meetings at Dublin, and correspondence with their confederates in other parts of Ireland, they carried

---

* In 1666.

on their business. But, there being one admitted to their secret contrivances in Dublin who secretly opened their whole designs and proceedings to the Duke, the Duke commanded him to continue in their society, and daily to inform him of their proceedings till the time they thought their business ripe. They were at length prevented and surprised on the 22nd of May, 1663. The plotters had appointed this morning to be the time wherein they would first surprise the castle of Dublin, and take the Duke's person into custody. For that end they had a considerable party in the town overnight—chief men of that party—with a number of men ready for their purpose. But their whole motion being known to the Duke, he that morning prevented them, and apprehended the principal persons, among whom was Mr. William Lecky; only Blood escaped—who may be called the head of the plot.* There was found among them their intended Declaration, wherein they pretended the ends of the covenant, showing the necessity of taking up arms because of the growth of popery, and the oppression of the bishops. But they were generally persons of Oliver's party who, before that, had forsaken the covenant; though it was alleged that a party of the standing army was engaged with them, but persons of no right or solid principles. There was also found an account of the names of those principally engaged; but

---

* In *Sylvester's Life of Baxter* (III. 88,) there is an extraordinary account of the subsequent career of Blood. When he escaped to England, he lived for some time at Rumford, where he followed the medical profession, under the assumed name of Dr. Clarke. He then attempted to take the Crown and Crown Jewels out of the Tower, and had all but succeeded when he was made prisoner. When brought into the royal presence, he told the King that he took the Crown not as a thief, but as an enemy, thinking that lawful which was done in war; and that if his life were taken away, it would be revenged. The King not only pardoned him, but subsequently often admitted him to his presence, some say "because his gallantry took much with the King, having been a soldier of his father's;" most say, "that he put the King in fear of his life, and came off upon condition that he would endeavour to keep the discontented party quiet."

S

no mention of the three in the North to whom Blood and Lecky had before applied—for these men had given Blood no encouragement or ground to expect any concurrence from them. Neither did these three reveal the matter to their brethren, lest the revealing of it should prove occasion of trouble to their brethren thereafter.

Notwithstanding, the Duke remembering that Messrs. Adair, Stewart, and Semple, had been a considerable time in Dublin, about half-a-year before this, and knowing the plotters had begun to meditate their business about that time, became jealous of these three, and immediately sent orders to apprehend them and send them up to Dublin by a guard. But, the Lord Mount-Alexander having special acquaintance with Mr. Stewart, and being persuaded of his loyalty, interceded with the Duke that he should not be sent for. Though my Lord Massareene was a Privy Councillor, yet he knew not at the first of sending for Mr. Adair. But upon knowledge of it, he went to the Duke, and spoke as much for Mr. Adair's loyalty as Lord Mount-Alexander had done for Mr. Stewart. He so far prevailed, that Mr. Adair should come of himself to Dublin, without a guard, and clear himself to the Duke. This letter he wrote to Mr. Adair, and sent it by post. But, before it came, Mr. Adair had been apprehended in his own house, by a party of the Earl of Donegall's troop, and secured close prisoner in the gaol of Carrickfergus, for three nights. Lord Massareene also wrote a letter to his lady's nephew, Sir Arthur Chichester, then Lieutenant of the troop, declaring the Duke's pleasure, and that if Mr. Adair were taken before that letter came, he should use him civilly. This he did accordingly, sending only one trooper along with Mr. Adair, in company with him and his servant; and also wrote a favourable letter to the Duke by that trooper, in Mr. Adair's behalf. When Mr. Adair came to Dublin, that noble Lord was pleased to intercede again with the Duke, that Mr. Adair should be committed to his custody, he becoming bail for his appearance, which the Duke, upon perusal of Sir Arthur's letter, easily granted. Thus Mr. Adair had a free confinement in Lord Massareene's house and the city for three months thereafter; and though he sent divers petitions to the Duke to call him and examine him of that plot, yet he was never called nor examined; but after three months was remanded to his own house, by a warrant under the Duke's hand, with only a certification that he would live peaceably.

Meantime Sir Arthur Forbes was in all haste sent to the Lagan, a place of which the Duke had great jealousy, to examine the ministers and suspected gentlemen there, which he did, and found no ground [for supposing] that any in their country were concerned in the plot; except that Mr. John Hart, having been in Dublin upon occasions the winter before, some of the plotters had applied to him as they had done to the two brethren in Down. But he had rejected the motion; only in his examination he spoke a word which brought Mr. Thomas Boyd,[*] a worthy man, into great trouble. For, in vindicating himself, not remembering what hazard it might bring to Mr. Boyd, he said to Sir Arthur he had abhorred that motion, as Mr. Boyd, in Dublin, knew. This examination being returned to Dublin, gave the Duke suspicion that Mr. Boyd was upon the plot; whereas it had only been proposed to him, and he had refused to be concerned in it. Upon which he was immediately apprehended, and kept long a close prisoner, and often sent for to the Duke, but would confess nothing that he

---

[*] Mr. Boyd was member for the Borough of Bangor, in Co. Down. For his supposed connexion with this plot he was expelled from the House of Commons.—*Reid*, ii. 277.

knew of the plot, not knowing what Mr. Hart had said. This did the more irritate the Duke against him, knowing Mr. Hart's deposition, that he had not been ignorant of it, till at last the Duke, in a fury, and with more threatening language, did show him the deposition. Whereupon, he finding no way of evasion, was forced to confess the way he knew of it—that Blood and Lecky, before their going to the North last winter, had proposed the business to him, but he would give no countenance to the design. The Duke enquired what they did there. He said they had spoken to Mr. Greg and Mr. Stewart, but heard no more of it, and supposed they had got no satisfying answer from these men. This brought these two brethren into much trouble thereafter, and himself hardly escaped the worst. But God's providence wrought for the innocent gentleman, though some hungry courtiers were gaping for his estate. Yet he had many friends by his wife, who were men of quality and interest with the Duke.

But to return to the ministers. Though Mr. Semple* was in the same order to be apprehended with Mr. Adair, yet, being at a great distance, and Sir Arthur Forbers upon examination finding no ground of accusation against him, or any of his brethren in the Lagan, except Mr. Hart, he took bail of them to appear when called, and they found no more trouble from this plot. But the noise of the plot becoming great, the Duke, and those about him, could not lay aside their jealousies of the Scotch. Therefore, within three weeks after its breaking up, the whole ministers of Down and Antrim, who could be found, were in one day apprehended, in the middle of June, 1663. The ministers of Antrim were brought to Carrickfergus, where they had liberty to be together in two private houses ; and though guards were upon

---

* Minister of Letterkenny.

them, yet they had the benefit of mutual society, where they remained for above two months. The ministers of Down were at first more hardly dealt with. They were sent to the King's castle at Carlingford, being seven in number—viz. Messrs. John Drysdale, John Greg, Andrew Stewart, Alex. Hutchinson, William Richardson, Gilbert Kennedy,* and James Gordon. They at first were put, or pounded, in a narrow room on the top of the house, far from friends or acquaintances, where they were in danger of starving, but that God stirred up the heart of a woman in the place, a stranger called Mrs. Clark, to supply them with necessaries. They were for a fortnight kept very close, till they were advised by Mr. Francis Hamilton, an officer of the company there, to write to my Lord Dungannon, who procured them the liberty of the town in the day-time; they returning to their narrow room at night, lying on the floor, four or five of them, as it were, in one bed. In the meantime, while the ministers who never heard of the plot, nor had even dreamt of any such thing, were thus upon groundless jealousies used, there came orders for disarming all the Scotch in the country—which was vigorously, closely, and suddenly executed. All men's arms were taken from them without respect of persons, by what standing forces and troops were in the country—though it never came to be known, and it is indeed utterly improbable that any one person in the country had ever known the least of it, except only Captain Moor, as before related, who a little after was sent for, and kept close prisoner in the castle of Dublin for a long time. However, the people carried peaceably; and their innocence in this matter, together with that of

---

* According to Dr. Reid, Gilbert Kennedy is probably a mistake for Gilbert Ramsay, minister at Bangor.—*Reid*, II. 279, note.

the ministers, did at last appear even to the Duke's conviction.

But the ministers' fears were, within a little, greatly alarmed, upon occasion of that passage, mentioned before, of Mr. Boyd's discovering the coming of Blood and Lecky to the North, and speaking to Mr. Greg and Mr. Stewart about the plot. When this was known, about the midst of July, 1663, orders were immediately sent to the Governor of Carlingford to send these men to Dublin with a guard, and that, in their coming thither, they should have no access to one another—which was accordingly done. For, after a month's imprisonment in Carlingford, where their mutual society much sweetened their hard lot, these two worthy brethren were taken from the rest, and separately, without any intimation of anything to them, were sent by two guards that same day to Dublin, and committed immediately to very close prisons, among those who were truly upon the plot, without, at first, any accommodation. They did not see one another by the way coming, nor in the prison till April following. After a few days, they were examined in the prison by the Earl of Mount-Alexander and the Lord Dungannon, as to what access they had to the plot. Mr. Stewart, having advice from my Lord Massareene conveyed secretly by Mr. Adair's means to him, to be ingenuous in his confession (my lord being confident that in his circumstances this would be safest for him), did freely acknowledge what had passed between them and Blood, as was before delivered. Whereupon, these lords told him, if there was no more between them, there was no hazard to him. But Mr. Greg, not having that same advice (it being impossible to get it conveyed to him) which Mr. Stewart had, did, upon his examination, stand resolutely to his denial that he knew anything of the proceedings of that plot—for, indeed, he did not hear of anything anent it after Blood's parting from him. But, after a day or two, the keepers telling him that Mr. Stewart had confessed all to these lords, he, not knowing Mr. Stewart's reasons for being so free, wrote a line or two in Latin to Mr. Stewart, challenging him for his confession to these noblemen, and telling him he had undone himself and them both. This paper he thought secretly to convey by the soldier who kept the door of the prison, and hid it within a paper of confections which he sent to Mr. Stewart in another part of the prison. But the soldier, suspecting there might be such correspondence, opened the paper, and, finding this line, carried it to the sergeant-at-arms, who kept the prison. He immediately carried it to the Duke, who was by it much irritated against Mr. Greg, and it occasioned his being deprived of much favour in prison, which Mr. Stewart had. Though this writing of that line was but an inconsiderate act in worthy Mr. Greg, and he had hard usage upon that account, yet God had endued him with an invincible spirit, so that he carried his hard usage with great and undaunted courage, being conscious to himself that what he had said to his examiners was true. Yea, the keepers of the prison, who were witnesses of his carriage and Christian magnanimity, confessed he was of a great spirit. Mr. Stewart, within five or six weeks after his imprisonment, had the liberty of the city, being under £1,000 bonds not to depart the city without leave. But Mr. Greg was kept close prisoner, and therein endured hard usage till April thereafter, in 1664.

Meantime, the plotters in Dublin were brought to their trial, and only three of them—to wit, a country gentleman and two officers—condemned to die as traitors, which sentence was executed upon them. As for Mr. Lecky, a chief contriver, together with Blood, his brother-in-law, and one of his parish, being kept much more severely than the rest in a low room in the Castle, in bolts, he fell distracted, and so continued for a while. He was sent from that to Newgate, as not being capable to be examined. Here, after a while, he recovered a little from his distraction, and, not being noticed by his keeper, got out one night in his wife's clothes, but was not in a capacity to dispose of himself so as to escape. He was therefore next morning apprehended, and thereafter condemned. Having been a Fellow of the College of Dublin, and in great respect for a smart scholar, and of a good temper, the College petitioned for his life, which was granted, if he would conform. But that he refused, and chose rather to die. Thereafter, he was tempted by some then about Court to accuse my Lord Massareene of the plot, they being jealous of my lord at that time, and thinking he knew it, being my lord's near kinsman; and, upon that, he should have his pardon. But he abhorred treachery of that nature, and therefore was executed, as the former were. These passages I had from a credible worthy man, who had them from his own mouth, a few days before he died. The rest after a while were let go, and some banished out of the kingdom. After the Duke had settled the business concerning the plot in Dublin, he, with the advice of the counsel, sent orders to the ministers of the North, now at Carlingford and Carrickfergus, that either they must depart the kingdom or go to prisons in other places of Ireland—and that within a fortnight after the order should come to their hands. The prisoners, having these orders sent them, immediately sent a petition to the Duke. But this petition, though presented to the Duke by the noble Massareene, their fixed old friend, had no return; but the former order must be observed. The brethren were, accordingly, in a great strait what to choose. However, all of them, save two, Mr. Keyes and one Mr. John Cowthard,* chose to depart the kingdom. Mr. Keyes was sent to the town of Galway, and Mr. Cowthard to Athlone, where they remained prisoners a considerable time. The rest generally went to Scotland, with a pass from some Justices of the Peace in the country, and yet not without bonds and surety given not to return without leave. Those of Antrim who went were, Mr. Hall, Mr. Crawford, Messrs. John and James Shaw; and of Down were, Mr. Drysdale, Mr. Ramsay, and Mr. Wilson; where God provided for them to live comfortably in a private station, and found there many friends beyond their expectation. There were divers brethren interceded for to the Duke, by persons of quality, to have liberty to stay in the country in a private capacity. Mr. Adair had the Duke's protection before. Mr. Robert Cunningham had a letter in his favour from my Lady Crawford Lindsay, sister to Duke Hamilton, and an acquaintance of the Duchess of Ormond. Mr. Gordon and Mr. Richardson had liberty of abiding in the country, through procuring of my Lady Ards, mother of the Earl Mount-Alexander, and the Countess of Clanbrasil: Mr. Hutchison by my Lord Dungannon's intercession: Mr. Hamilton of Killead, and Mr. James Cunninging of Antrim, were interceded for by my Lord Massareene and his lady. Some other ministers of these two counties of Down and Antrim had been out of the country, or out of the way when the rest were apprehended, and now absconded. The few who were of other meetings had not been at this time troubled. However, the generality of the ministers of the North were at this time either banished, imprisoned, or driven into corners upon occasion of a plot which they knew nothing of, and wherein upon the narrowest

---

* Or Cathcart, of Drumaul or Randalstown.

scrutiny nothing could be found againt them,* except what was mentioned before of the three brethren, Messrs. Hart, Greg, and Stewart, in which these brethren gave no grounds of disloyalty. The matter had been communicated to them in a private way, and they rejected it; they thus judged it had been crushed in the bud, and knew nothing of any further progress in it. And they thought it hard, and scarcely consistent with candour, to accuse the men, who had in a friendly confidence with them, represented the sad state of affairs, and desired to have them brought to a right channel without prejudice to the King's just authority.

Thus the few left in the country continued as formerly, endeavouring to converse among their people to their edification as the time would bear. And it is to be observed that after the Duke had narrowly searched into the carriage of the Scotch in this plot, and had found them unconcerned in it, he did, as some reward of their integrity, give the people in the North indulgence not to be troubled for six months with the official courts, in the matter of Nonconformity. And Providence ordered that during that time Bramhall the Primate died a sudden death,† and the Bishop of Dublin succeeded him—one Margetson—a man of a mild spirit, who, to ingratiate himself with the people of these parts, gave other six months' indulgence; and thereafter the Judges of Assize had not commission to trouble the people at the Assizes for Nonconformity. The bishops stormed at

---

* The account here given by Adair is fully corroborated by the following statement, "The most desperate of *the disbanded soldiers*—who projected the surprisal of the Castle of Dublin—escaped into England." "There has been lately discovered *a plot of the old English army in Ireland*," says Andrew Marvel, "to seize upon Dublin and the Lord Lieutenant, June 6th, 1663."—*Rawdon Papers*, p. 202, note. London, 1819.

† Bramhall died on the 25th of June, 1663. He was a native of Yorkshire, and was brought over to Ireland by Wentworth. He possessed great talent and considerable learning; but he was of a most domineering and intolerant spirit.

this begun favour for Nonconformists, and did process many to their courts upon account of Nonconformity. But most got off again for money as thereafter; there being wars between the King and the State of Holland, wherein he had considerable loss, and all sorts of people being much discontented, the edge of the bishop's fury was much blunted. Meantime, the few ministers took every opportunity, and made use of the small advantages they had, to creep up by degrees to the exercise of their ministry, in their own congregations especially. Mr. Stewart, in November, after his imprisonment, having been sick in prison, and having some special friend, got liberty to return to his house upon bonds given to live amenably to the law—*i.e.*, as was by lawyers interpreted to him—only to answer the law if he thought not fit to be conformable to everything in it. Mr. Greg and Captain Moore were released in March, 1664. Thereafter, the two brethren who had chosen imprisonment in Galway and Athlone were, upon bonds, released, and had liberty to return to their places. The brethren who were banished to Scotland returned by degrees, some a little sooner, some later; at first some few by intercession of friends; others came over thereafter upon their hazard, and so all were restored to their congregations, except Mr. Andrew M'Cormick and Mr. John Crookshanks, who had been upon the plot and fled to Scotland; and, not expecting or seeking for pardon in Ireland, joined thereafter with that party in Scotland which was broken at Pentland, and were there both killed. These were zealous men, but walked too much in a separate way from their brethren. They meddled in matters too high for them, and though they died in mercy to themselves, yet not without a remark of a fatherly chastisement for their folly— Job xxxvi. 12. For had they walked with their brethren, they might have been useful in their congregations, as now the rest of their brethren were, and they would not have brought any scandal of rebellion and disloyalty to the lawful magistrate upon their profession in Ireland. Yea, Mr. M'Cormick's guilt in the plot being immediately known after the breaking up of it, occasioned all that jealousy that was had of the rest, and much of that trouble they afterwards met with, though they were utterly strangers to the actings of, and combinations with, the plotting party. Besides, it is a just ground of observation that this man had not the education and learning fit for a minister; for he had been bred a tailor in a country place, and being then a great professor of religion, would (after he had wife and children) go to the University to be bred in order to the ministry. This he did, and stayed for a while, leaving his wife and children in great straits, but profited very little in learning, having then all before him, as the tongues, philosophy, divinity, &c. It was impossible his dull genius, with considerable age and little time, could attain to any competency of abilities. Yet he, in a short time, returned as ready to pass trials, which he did, but with little satisfaction to judicious brethren, save that they looked on him as an honest man, and thought he might be useful in some remote congregation. But, when settled in a congregation, he competed with the brethren; and, when times became confused, pretended a zeal above them all, not without reflecting on his brethren among the common people, as if they all had been but cowards. Thus he followed his own course, till he fell into the snare of this plot without acquainting any of them. This I have observed here, not in order to leave the stain upon the name of a man who in the main was honest, but to be a warning, and confirmation of the Apostle's command that every man abide in the calling wherein he was called, and that the profession of religion, though more eminent, should not puff men up to aim at things beyond their reach. God may make use of private men in some cases when the Church is destitute of pastors; but where there is not that necessity, and where there are no extraordinary abilities in nature, education, or grace, and no learning, the attainments of such persons are hardly, or very rarely, followed with usefulness in the Church of God.

The brethren about Lagan at this time had had more quiet than those of Down and Antrim upon the occasion before mentioned. Only Mr. Crookshanks, of whom before, resolving upon a single course of his own, first went to France a little time before the plot of Ireland; and in Rochelle, applying himself to the Protestant ministers there, to see if he could get employment, they told him it was rather his duty to return to his country and congregation, and adhere to his own people; and, if suffering came, it was his duty to suffer with the people for that truth which he had preached unto them. Upon this, he returned, and was engaged in the plot, and thereafter went to Scotland, as before stated. But Bishop Robert Leslie, son to the old bishop Leslie, who had deposed the worthy ministers before the rebellion of Ireland, envying that little ease and quiet of the ministers, summoned four of them to his Court—Messrs. John Hart, Thomas Drummond, William Semple, and Adam White. They, not answering his summons, he did at first pass the sentence of excommunication upon them; and before they could appear, he issued a writ, "de excommunicato capiendo," against them, and apprehended and imprisoned them without bail or main-prize. They were by the bishop appointed for the common gaol at Lifford; but, through the indulgence of the sheriff, they were permitted to dwell together in a house in the town, and all their friends had access to them. They were prisoners for six years, though they used all means possible, and their friends for them, for their releasement, and it was near the end of the year 1669 before they were released. Lord Roberts in his short time had dealt for them, and Sir Arthur Forbes had frequently interceded with Bishop Leslie, then his relation by marriage with his niece. But the bishop was inexorable, and upbraided the rest of the bishops for their slackness; whereas [he said] if they had taken the course he had done, the Presbyterians might easily have been crushed. The King, having information that they had been sufferers for him, and had suffered long imprisonment only for not appearing before the bishops' courts, which was contrary to their principles, and having this information from lawyers, wrote to the Lord Lieutenant and commanded their releasement; which was accordingly performed in October, 1670, after they had waited for above half-a-year for his answer, and had, in the meantime, been refused releasement by the Primate (who had been civil to the brethren of Down), except they took the oath of supremacy. They had taken various steps in order to be released—first, they petitioned the Earl of Ossory,* being then Deputy of Ireland, in his father's absence in England in the year 1664-5, and thereafter obtained an order for enlargement, but it was obstructed by the Bishop of Raphoe; secondly, they procured a "habeas corpus" to have their business tried before the Court of King's Bench, but there they had not relief; thirdly, they removed their business into the Court of Chancery, but there they met with nothing but revilings from the Chancellor who was Archbishop of Dublin, and their case made worse even, by their being put into the sheriff's custody and being sent to the gaol of Lifford, in which town they continued prisoners

---

* Son of the Duke of Ormond.

nearly four years. All justice thus failing them in Ireland, God stirred up a person of quality to represent their case to the King. Being informed of this, they sent over a petition to the King for their deliverance, which his Majesty taking into consideration, remitted their case to some of the lawyers —the favourable issue of which has just been narrated. But it is to be here observed, that this Bishop Leslie, as he did inherit his father's persecuting spirit, so in these times he became a mere epicure, giving himself excessively to eating and drinking. Whereupon, being of a robust body, he became so fat and heavy that he could not go alone, but as men supported his arms. He shortly after (1672) died suddenly, and with great horror of conscience.

CHAPTER XVIII.

PRESBYTERIANS BEGIN TO BUILD PREACHING HOUSES—OPPRESSIONS AND AVARICE OF THE EPISCOPAL CLERGY—LORD ROBERTS—MEETING OF MINISTERS—COLLECTION FOR DISTRESSED MINISTERS IN SCOTLAND—BISHOP LESLIE AND BISHOP BOYLE PERSECUTE—APPLICATION TO THE LORD LIEUTENANT—DEATHS OF MINISTERS—YOUNG MINISTERS ORDAINED—STRANGE CATASTROPHE IN A DUBLIN THEATRE.

MEANTIME, the brethren now returned, and, returning to their own homes, continued to be as useful as they could in their parishes, and had then private intercourse for mutual advice and strengthening one another's hands in these times. And thus, insensibly to the civil rulers, they took liberty to preach more publickly in barns, and such places in their parishes where the bulk of the people met, and did in the night administer the Sacrament to them;* and by degrees attained to such freedom that, in the year 1668, they began in divers places to build preaching houses, and there met publickly, and performed all ordinances in a public way. They had also their monthly meetings among themselves in convenient private houses in the country, where they began to revive discipline, examining the carriage of one another, and bringing scandalous persons to acknowledgment of their scandals, in some ordinary cases before the session in the congregation itself, and in greater scandal before the Presbytery.

---

* According to an Act passed in the Irish Parliament in 1665, every minister, except one episcopally ordained, who dared to administer the Lord's Supper, was liable to a penalty of One Hundred Pounds. Bishop Mant declares that such enactments "were demanded by the circumstances of the times, and were *essential to the well-being, not to say the being, of the Church!*"—*Hist. of the Church of Ireland*, I., 646-7.

In these things, they, not finding present opposition, and with some eye to God's protection, made an adventure; and it pleased the Lord to bless their first essay with success. It was no compliance with bishops, nor was it any application to the Court at this time, which tended to any liberty they had, but the observable providence of God who made divers things to concur in it. First, the edge of the magistrates' fury had been much blunted in their former causeless oppressing of the ministers, especially on occasion of that plot before mentioned. Secondly, they had found the ministers' loyalty when they had searched to the bottom. Thirdly, they now began to see that what the ministers did was from conscience, for God helped them to go about their work peaceably and painfully, under divers disadvantages. They had the jealous eye of the magistrate over them—the envious eye of the clergy, so called, watching for their halting—the people generally, for seven years together after their first ejectment, forsaking them as to maintenance, even when they were living among them, and doing what they could for them; only, it is not to be denied they had the people's affectionate respect, and some small accidental kindnesses from some particular persons, which, however, amounted to very little as to the support of their families. The people, too, were convinced of the ministers' constancy under variety of times, troubles, and sufferings. They were the same, and the Lord helped them to some liveliness in preaching, and the people to some hunger in hearing the Word, after this little beginning of a life from the dead. These things made the people adhere, so far as was possible, to their ministers, and attend the ordinances administered by them at the times and places that were appointed.

Again, the present legal churchmen became more and more distasteful to the people of all sorts. Men of estates

T

found their tenants oppressed, impoverished, and rendered unable to pay their rents, through the covetousness and draining of the superior clergy by their rents and tithes, but especially by the official courts, which were a heavy plague upon the people; and through their cruelty and unreasonable exactions for Nonconformity arbitrarily governing all— their lust, covetcousness, and power, being their only rule, especially where they knew anything was to be had. This disgusted the people, and made them cling more affectionately to the painful and laborious ministers of the Presbyterian persuasion, who had now attained to considerable countenance in the country. But there was like to be an interruption. For there was an information sent to the Lord Ossory, now Lord Deputy in his father's absence, from some unfriends in the North, that the ministers were setting up their Presbyteries as openly as ever, and that they were renewing the Solemn League and Covenant among the people : upon which he called Sir Arthur Forbes, and bid him try if these informations were true, not without threatenings if it proved so. Sir Arthur caused a Scotch gentleman, who had special acquaintance with some of the number, to write and signify to them that there were such informations given. This a brother immediately answered, shewing that these informations were false—which satisfied the Lord Ossory.

After a while, in September, 1669, Lord Robarts came over as Lord Lieutenant. He was represented as a person of great worth, for wisdom, learning, strictness in his commands, and severity against vice; no enemy to godly people, yet somewhat morose in his temper and carriage. This representation of him he answered in his practice during the short time of his government. He was a public discountenancer of all vice. The public players he stopped there, as well as other vicious persons. He was strict and peremptory upon the officers in the army, especially in two things—first, that they were forced to keep close to their quarters and garrisons where their soldiers were; and, secondly, that they were put to pay the poor soldiers exactly, whereas before they had used to recede where they pleased, and to spend much of the soldiers' pay upon their own extravagances. He had his reflections sometimes upon the bishops, and particularly him of Dublin, who was also Chancellor of Ireland, on account of the unmanageable charge he took upon him.*

As to the Nonconformists, though his own practice was always after the Episcopal forms of worship, yet he nothing disappointed their good hopes of him. For in his little time those in the North grew yet more confident and encouraged, and those in Dublin rather grew in the begun liberty they had under the Earl of Ossory. The Chancellor dealt with him to suppress the meeting there; but he told him if they were not Papists, and were peaceable and civil, he had no commission to meddle with them. The brethren in the North beginning to understand these passages, not only went on in their ministry without fear, but began to think of licensing young men to preach, and of recommending them to congregations where none of their number were. But the Lord Robarts' government was soon shortened. He came in September, and returned to England in the April following (1670). The occasion of this was the

---

* The reference here is to Michael Boyle, Archbishop of Dublin. He was nephew to Michael Boyle, Bishop of Waterford and Lismore, of whom it was wont to be said, according to Dr. Elrington, "that he would have done anything, or sold any man for sixpence profit." The Archbishop of Dublin, mentioned in the text, was as avaricious as his uncle. When Bishop of Cork, he appropriated to his own use all the livings that became vacant in his diocese, under the pretence that he could not find clergymen to accept them. Yet this man, who was now Lord Chancellor and Archbishop of Dublin, was afterwards made Primate of Armagh.—*Elrington's Life of Ussher*, p. 107-8, note.

temper of the soldiery, and because persons of quality in this time could not bear severity against vice. All degrees of that sort of people desired to be rid of the yoke, and from under such a severe governor. Many suggestions and complaints were sent over against him. He found he had many enemies in Ireland, and thought in his absence he might be clouded at Court. Whereupon he wrote to the King, desiring to demit his office, which the King, by persuasion of some about him, did immediately grant, and chose another one, Lord Berkely, in his room. Those who loved Lord Robarts' government blamed him for so suddenly giving it up, seeing there were no just grounds of accusation for his government, but that he could not comply with the debauched temper of the time and place he came to. Many things worthy of a noble judge appeared in him. The King had a good respect for him, as being one in England who during his Majesty's exile, did very largely and yearly send supply to him. However, the short time of his government in Ireland gave a dash to open profaneness, and some encouragement to the lovers of truth. There were brethren, and a little after this time, divers preachers came from Scotland, who called the people in the country to more public assembling together in the fields, and otherwise, than the ministers of the country judged then expedient.* The country ministers thought it more conducible to their work to be doing somewhat among the people in a more private way, as the times could bear, than expose themselves and the people both to present sufferings, and being deprived of their present liberty through more public appearances.

Amid other things they resolved to hold a general meeting

---

* One of these was the celebrated Alexander Peden. In 1682, he was again in Ireland, where he is said to have lodged in the house of William Steele, at Shoptown, Glenwherry.

of the brethren, a few to be deputed from each meeting, to consult as a committee for the welfare of the whole, and to recommend to the various meetings such steps as their present exigencies demanded. This meeting was in a time when ministers and people wanted not their grounds of fear that new troubles might arise; for the Parliament of England had made severe acts against the meetings of Nonconformists, and the Parliament of Scotland was no better disposed towards them. The Lord Berkely, new come from England to be Chief Governor in Ireland, was a man who had no repute for love to religion nor a good temper, bred a courtier, and little favour expected from him. However, the brethren, being met, went about what was incumbent on them—viz. only to relate the mind of their respective meetings as to such questions or cases as were stated before them, or had been given them in commission to answer; and, withal, to propose overtures to their several meetings, to be considered by them, and their answers to be communicated to the rest of their meetings from their first sederunt, if necessity required, or, at farthest, to the next committee, and by their brethren there to their meetings. First, there had been overtures agreed unto by the meetings of Down and Antrim for managing the work of ordination at that time in as prudential a way as the time would permit.* These were to be recommended to the consideration of the rest. Secondly, it was found to be the judgment of the meetings generally that baptism by private deceivers and

---

* By performing the act of ordination, the ministers exposed themselves to heavy penalties, and the bishops were especially watchful as to this point, hoping thus to cut off the supply of Presbyterian pastors. In 1673, Patrick Shaw, who had received a unanimous call from the congregation of Cairnmoney, was ordained privately at Larne. In 1672, John Haltridge, who had received a call to Islandmagee, was ordained at Ballycarry. In 1674, Robert Henry, who had received a call to Carrickfergus, was ordained at Mr. John Crawford's house, near Ballynure.

intruders without ordination should be declared no baptism, and that the children should be baptized by ministers of the Gospel. Yet, withal, it was thought fit that, before they were baptized, the brethren should have the joint advice of the gravest ministers in Scotland, and for that end that letters should be written to some of them to return their own and their brethrens' answer—which accordingly was done, and, their answer returned agreed with the judgment of the brethren in Ireland in that particular. Thirdly, a collection was proposed among their meetings and their congregations for supply of the ministers of Scotland banished for their non-compliance with some sinful injunctions of the Parliament of Scotland, and who were now sojourners in Holland. This was accordingly performed with great alacrity by the people, and a collection of £120 sterling transmitted to them, and their thanks returned to the brethren in Ireland. Fourthly, it was then overtured that the Synod's act anent reviewing the Presbytery's books should be put in practice; but most of these books were lost through the tossings and distemper of an honest, worthy brother, Mr. Thomas Peebles, Clerk to the Synod. Fifthly, that Mr. Greg should endeavour the composing a History of the beginning and progress of the Gospel in these parts, as the Synod had appointed him.* Sixthly, a public fast was proposed, partly because of the new Governor, Lord Berkely, from whom trouble to the church was feared, and partly for the unseasonableness of the weather. This was accordingly kept the third Tuesday of the month, and with such countenance from God and

---

* Dr. Reid says:—"Mr. Greg and his neighbour, Mr. Stewart, of Donaghadee, made some progress in this work. At the death of Mr. Greg and Mr. Stewart, Mr. Drysdale, of Portaferry, was next requested to carry on the work; and I find the meeting of Antrim in April, 1672, recommending Mr. Hall, of Larne, and Mr. Adair, of Cairncastle, to use diligence about the history of the Church of Ireland."—*Reid* II., 298.

presence in the congregations of the people, that even those who were but unfriends and coming to observe were convinced. And, besides, the Lord visibly answered prayer by a remarkable change of the season immediately after, so that the people where Presbyterians were least entertained, and where the people were otherwise principled, as in Lecale, found the benefit of seasonable rain after a dangerous and scorching drought which had come upon unseasonable and excessive rains before ; so that these people thanked God— since none would pray—that the Presbyterians prayed and fasted, and had obtained rain and a good season.

Immediately after these things, a storm threatened the ministers particularly, which began at the brethren of Down. The occasion whereof was specially the envy that the clergy had conceived at the begun liberty of the ministers and their public congregations and meetings among themselves. They had risen up from their graves twice, first being dead by the law as to their ministry, immediately after the bishops appeared in the country. They began a little after to creep out again, which, when they were beginning to do, shortly after, through occasion of the Plot, they were put in a worse case than before, being imprisoned, banished, and driven into corners. Now, they were up again under the bishops' eye, exercising their ministry, and the whole country flocking to them, and deserting the legal incumbents. The clergy fretted, but yet did not know how to help it. The ministers were not restrained by the magistrate ; they were loved and esteemed by the whole country, and had a respect, even from sober persons of the bishops' persuasion, beyond their own clergy. Though these things a little restrained their violence, yet they increased their envy and indignation. Besides, the people of the country generally neglected and slighted the curates in their burials, baptisms, &c.; and, when curates would officiously urge their service at burials, they were refused or resisted, which the Chancellor himself, who was also Archdeacon, had lately met with at a burial—who, when he would have read over the corpse of a person in burying, was resisted by a kinsman of his—a mean countryman—which did animate him, and he vowed revenge. Besides, the late fast, and the country's so generally owning that solemnity, and the visible fruit of it, did gall the prelatical clergy. They saw these things weakening their party, and strengthening the ministry of these poor men, and engaging the whole country to them. And yet they were ashamed palpably to condemn such things. But that which did more immediately occasion this threatened trouble was Bishop Robert Leslie, of Raphoe. He had by this time kept four worthy brethren nearly six years in prison, as before related. He, coming to these parts of the County of Down about his other occasions, did visit the Bishop of Down, one Boyle,* and did so stir him against the ministers and upbraid him for his negligence and want of zeal in not using the key of jurisdiction, that this bishop resolved to play the man in his dioceses, and even to a greater length than Leslie had done in Raphoe diocese. For, whereas, Leslie had persecuted but four, Boyle presently sent summonses to twelve brethren of Down to appear before his court, which he knew they would not do, and, therefore, resolved suddenly to go on to excommunication. Their names were—Masters John Drysdale, John Greg, Andrew Stewart, Gilbert Ramsay, Wm. Richardson, James Gordon, Henry Livingston,† Alexander Hutchin-

---

* In 1667, Roger Boyle succeeded Jeremy Taylor as Bishop of Down and Connor.

† This Henry Livingston, who was minister of Drumbo, near Lisburn, was nephew to the Rev. John Livingston, of Killinchy. Henry Livingston died April 7, 1697, aged 66 years. His son, who was also the Rev. Henry Livingston, was minister of Ballynahinch, where he was ordained in 1704. His nephew, Mr. William Livingston, of Lisburn, had a daughter, Anne, married to Mr. David White, of Ballymaglover.

son, Hugh Wilson, William Reid, Michael Bruce—who had but newly returned to his parish after great troubles and long imprisonment in Scotland and England—and Mr. Gilbert Kennedy, a Scotch minister, who had settled for a time in a country parish. The first summons none of these ministers received, yet they were thereupon called at the next court and noted contumacious. The second summons was sent and left at their houses, and, contrary to the usual custom of meeting only monthly, the next court was appointed within a fortnight, that so he might sooner win to the sentence of excommunication against them, and thereafter proceed to the ministers of the next county—the other Diocese of Connor.

The brethren of Down, after meeting and consultation in this case, resolved to send one of their number with a supplication to the Lord Lieutenant, and made use of what friends in Dublin they could. But they judged it fit, in the first place, to sound the bishop if any abatement of such severity might be expected from him; the rather that he had, since his coming into the country, carried quietly, they thought they might enquire the ground of this sudden alteration. Accordingly, June 30th, 1670, Mr. Drysdale and Mr. Hutchinson were sent to the bishop, but with this further instruction, that if they found not good ground of hope from the bishop, Mr. Drysdale should immediately repair from him to Dublin. They came to Hillsborough, where the bishop had his house at that time. Having sent to him, showing they were waiting to speak with him,* he, in a great fury and disdain, returned answer he would not speak with them, but

---

Their daughter, Rebecca White, was married to John Barnett, of Ballyagherty, near Saintfield, father of the late John Barnett, Esq., of Belfast, and grandfather of the Rev. John Barnett, D.D., of Moneymore.

* We have here and afterwards clear proof of the falsehood of the story told by Heber, that the ministers had entered into an engagement "to speak with no bishop."

in open court to-morrow. Yet, thereafter, upon the Archdeacon Pringdooles suggesting to him it would be evil looked on, not to hear what the ministers had to say to him; the brethren were again sent for, and being come to him, they found nothing but railing language—calling them all rebels from the beginning, and that they had seduced the people. He said, though he had little hope to do good to the seduced people, yet, he resolved to execute the law against them. Thus, after some discourse by these brethren unto him, defending their carriage with truth and soberness, they left him; and Mr. Drysdale, according to appointment, went forward to Dublin, to make application to the Lord Lieutenant. But before this, a letter having been written to Sir Arthur Forbes, informing him of the case, he went to the Lord Lieutenant, and was by him recommended to the Primate Margetson, to relate the case to him. Sir Arthur—knowing the loyalty and sufferings of the ministers of the North from the beginning upon the King's account; and being not only of unquestionable loyalty himself, and a great actor and sufferer for the King before, but also in high favour with his Majesty, and a Privy Councillor and Chief Commander in the army—did prevail with the Archbishop and the Chancellor Boyle, then Archbishop of Dublin, that a letter should be written to the Bishop of Down, to forbear any further prosecuting that business against these ministers till the 10th of August following, at which time the Primate himself would be in the North, being the year of his triennial visitation. This letter being written, did force the Bishop of Down to desist against his will. For that being the Archbishop's year of visitation, inferior bishops were not to meddle with jurisdiction but by his appointment. This letter came before Mr. Drysdale reached Dublin. However, being there, he went to the Primate and informed him of the case, who only inquired whether the ministers had exercised the power of jurisdiction and ordination—the two things proper to the bishop. Mr. Drysdale told him there had been nothing of that hitherto (as indeed the brethren were but upon a way to it). The bishop said if he came to the North, he would do as he saw cause. Thus were the brethren and people of their charge left in suspense as to any determination of their cause; their adversaries looking to the bishop and his authority for restraining their liberty, and themselves looking to God for a merciful event.

Meantime, before the 10th of August, 1670, two worthy brethren were removed out of this life. Mr. John Greg was buried, July 22nd, and Mr. Richardson having been at his burial, took immediately a fever, and was buried that day week, July 29th. They were two of the ablest and most useful men among the whole number. Mr. James Cunningham of Antrim had died a while before—a prudent godly man; and Mr. Thomas Crawford a while before him again —an able and sincere minister of Christ. Mr. James Shaw, a zealous worthy preacher, was laid by, through sickness, this strange afflicting trouble coming on his family after the death of his wife. There had been great ground of jealousy that she, in her childbed, had been wronged by sorcery of some witches in the parish. After her death, a considerable time, some spirit or spirits troubled the house by casting stones down at the chimney, appearing to the servants, and especially having got one of them, a young man, to keep appointed times and places, wherein it appeared in divers shapes and spake audibly to him. The people of the parish watched the house while Mr. Shaw at this time lay sick in his bed; and, indeed, he did not wholly recover, but within a while died, it was thought, not without the art of sorcery; though otherwise he was not only valetudinary, but broken with melancholy.* Mr. Gilbert Ramsay, too, having taken a palsy within a short time thereafter, and the little remainder of his strength and spirits decaying, he died. He was a true Nathaniel, of good abilities, sent over to Bangor by famous Mr. Blair, and deceived not his expectations. And shortly after died, also, Mr. Thomas Peebles, a man learned and faithful, eminent in the languages and history.

These were sad troubles to the poor afflicted ministers, to have some of the choicest of their brethren taken from them, by death, and their enemies raging against them. But they were not forsaken by their great Master. He supported their spirits, and followed them with remarkable and seasonable providences. On the day of Mr. Richardson's burial, there was a meeting appointed at Mr. Stewart's house, who had been also unwell and unable to travel, and there they began to enter on trial three young men—viz. Mr. John Cunningham, in reference to the parish of Donaclony, Mr. William Legat, and Mr. George Montgomery, in order to license them to preach. They appointed a private fast, to deal with God for the continuance of their liberty, and preventing the fury of the bishops, to be held on the 16th of August, 1670. The Lord was pleased to hear their prayer. For first the Lord Lieutenant had advised the Primate to moderation toward ministers; secondly, the Primate himself was not of a persecuting temper, but rather inclinable to engage the country and to increase his estate; thirdly, his letter to the Bishop of Down was not well enough relished by him; he saying that the Primate had wronged him in taking upon him to hinder the exercise of his authority in his own

---

* This belief in witchcraft was prevalent in the seventeenth century. It was greatly promoted by King James' *Dæmonology*, published in 1597. Jeremy Taylor is said to have believed in apparitions, and, when holding a visitation at Dromore, to have examined a person named Taverner respecting a ghost which had been giving him trouble. (See his *Life*, by Heber, ii. 250.)

diocese; and comparing himself in learning and fitness to govern with the Primate. Whereupon a sharp contention fell out between them. But the Primate, understanding his own superiority, did rather own it in this matter, being engaged in it, and alleging the Bishop of Down had brought him to needless trouble without his own advice. When the brethren sent to him to know what they might expect as to their process, he returned answer that these gentlemen (for so he called them) needed not fear a surprisal in that matter in haste; and thus the process ended as to the brethren of Down, and the bishop, with his clergy there, found that his intentions against the ministers of Antrim were prevented.

This mercy came seasonably to this poor church in divers respects. It proved a continuation of the ministers' liberty, and a confirmation of it—a dash, too, to those of the prelates who were more violent, and that by their own Primate of Ireland. It was some evidence and fruit of the King's clemency and favour to the Presbyterian ministers of the North of Ireland; and also an evidence of the moderation of the Lord Lieutenant Berkley, and that he was no enemy to these ministers. And further, it fell in mercifully, being after and about the time of the deaths of divers useful and worthy brethren, which otherwise in itself was a bad presage to this church. Yet the gracious God made up that loss divers ways; partly by providing young men, whom, by degrees, the brethren ordained and planted in congregations, and partly by sending divers able and worthy ministers from Scotland, who settled in this church for a time. And all this was the more remarkable, that it was in the time when Nonconformity, both in England and Scotland, was much discountenanced, not only by severe Acts of Parliament—whereby in England five persons might not meet together for worship, otherwise than the law prescribed, and in Scotland not so much as family worship must be performed, if there was but one person more than the family itself present—but, both in England and Scotland, meetings of Nonconformists, called conventicles, were most strictly pursued and suppressed. Many, both ministers and godly people, were put to great sufferings both then and divers years after, only because they could not comply with the prelates, their curates, or their courses, but would worship God with their own minister, or with other godly ministers of their own sentiments. And though they did all in a private way, and shunned as much as possible to give offence to the magistrate, yet their privacy did not save them from violence, especially in Scotland, where the great work which engaged the King's council there, and the forces they had in the country for many years, was to find out these meetings, to apprehend the ministers and other persons, and then to pass sentence of banishment, fining, and imprisonment, upon them; whereupon many sad consequences followed, which it is not pertinent here to relate, only to observe God's dealing with his poor church in the North of Ireland, the most unlikely to obtain any favour of this kind. They were not only opposite in their principles and practices to the prelatic way, as others of their persuasion in the other two kingdoms; but they were in a manner strangers in another country, being of the Scotch extraction, and on these accounts being hated and despised by those of the English who were prelatical. They generally were of the meanest extraction and sort of people, yet Providence ordered them liberty and quiet, when others more deserving, and who had greater ground of expectation, were deprived of it. Thus the ministers with the people having, by the wonderful Providence of God, an open door given them, continued in the exercise of their ministry, and their assemblies daily grew, so that within a while every congregation erected a house for their meeting together, and began to celebrate the sacrament in their public assemblies.

Meantime, there fell out a passage in Dublin, at Christmas, 1670, which, though not properly belonging to the History of the North of Ireland, yet, as relating to Presbyterians, is not unworthy to be recorded. There had been, a while before, builded at Dublin, a large stately house with three stories of galleries, for acting the stage-plays,* at the cost and free-will offering of noblemen and other persons of quality, unto which the bishops contributed largely; though at the time they refused to give countenance or assistance for building a church at Dame Street, where there was great need, through the multiplying of inhabitants in that city; much above what could be contained in the churches formerly built, especially in that place of the city. To this house came a great number of noblemen and ladies, besides other persons, and clergymen, the first day of Christmas, being Monday (26th December). The play acted was one called by them "The Nonconformist." And there, among other parts of the play, the poor shadow of a Nonconformist minister is mocked and upbraided; and at last is brought to the stocks, prepared for this purpose, that his legs may be fastened. Those of the greatest quality sat lowest; those next in quality sat the next above; and the common people in the upmost gallery. But behold, when this shadow is brought to the stocks, as an affront upon Presbyterian ministers, and to teach great persons to deal with like severity toward them, down came the upper gallery on the middle one, where gentlemen and others sat, and that gallery broke too, and much of it fell down on the lords and ladies. Divers were killed, and

---

* This theatre was in Smock Alley, and was built in 1662.—*Reid*, II. 308, note.

many hurt. Among those that were hurt was one of the Lord Lieutenant's sons, and the Lady Clanbrasil, who, the year before, had caused to be pulled down the preaching-house at Bangor. Such providences, so circumstantial in divers respects, will not pass without observation of impartial and prudent persons, for surely they have a language if men would hear.

HISTORY

OF THE

CHURCH OF IRELAND,

AFTER THE SCOTS WERE NATURALIZED.

BY THE

REV. ANDREW STEWART,

MINISTER OF DONAGHADEE.

STEWART'S
History of the Church of Ireland.

PREFATORY NOTICE.

THE Rev. Andrew Stewart, or Stuart, was minister of Donaghadee from 1645 to 1671. His father, who was also the Rev. Andrew Stewart, was a man of eminent piety. He was minister of Donegore, near Antrim, from 1627 to 1634. The following account of one of the last scenes of his earthly career has been preserved. "Being called to the burial of that excellent man of God, Mr. Josiah Welsh [of Templepatrick], who was his neighbour minister, Mr. Stewart stood some time at the grave, as a sad observer of such a thing, and to some who were by said, 'Who knows who will be next?' but none answering, he said to them, 'I know,' and then turned away, and went home to Donegore on foot, and entering into the church, did bolt the doors, where he tarried some two hours ; and, after going to his house, he fell asleep on his bed with an excess of grief, whence he never in health rose again, but was buried that day month [July, 1634]. When his wife returned, whom he had left with Mr. Welsh's widow, she inquired what he had been doing; to whom he said, 'I have been taking my leave of the church of Donegore, and I was there taking timber and stones to witness, that in my short time I had laboured to be faithful; and that, according to my light, I have revealed the whole counsel of God to the people.' How great a testimony of the conscience was this !"*

The author of the following short portion of the History of the Church of Ireland, was only ten years of age at the time of his father's death. The family were left in straitened circumstances; but the wants of the widow and her children were graciously supplied. When little more than twenty-one years of age, young Andrew was ordained to the pastoral charge of Donaghadee, where he laboured a quarter of a century. Fleming, in his *Fulfilling of the Scriptures*—the first part of which was published in 1674—speaks of him as a worthy clerical brother, with whom he corresponded. "Mr. Andrew Stewart, minister of Donaghadee," says he, "was a great observer of confirmations of the truth, whom I cannot mention without sorrow at the remembrance of the late removal of so eminent and useful a minister of Jesus Christ."†

In the early part of 1670, Mr. Greg of Newtownards was requested by his brethren "to endeavour the composing a History of the Beginning and Progress of the Gospel" in the North of Ireland;‡ but he died in the July of the same year, and the task seems to have then devolved on Mr. Stewart. Kirkpatrick, in his *Presbyterian Loyalty*, speaks of both these gentlemen in terms of high commendation. "Mr. John Greg, Presbyterian minister in Newton, and Mr. Andrew Stewart, Presbyterian minister in Donaghadee, were," says he, "men of great sagacity, judgment, and

---

* Fleming's *Fulfilling of the Scriptures*, i. 393.
† *Fulfilling of the Scriptures*, i. 392.
‡ Adair's *Narrative*, chap. xviii. p. 294.

veracity, as many yet alive can testify."* Mr. Stewart's work is divided into three chapters, and is entitled "A Short Account of the Church of Christ as it was (1.) Among the Irish at first; (2.) Among and After the English entered; (3.) After the Entry of the Scots." The author, as is plain from various intimations, intended the third chapter to be the principal portion of his work; but his death, in the beginning of the year 1671, prevented the completion of his design. The first and second chapters, though constituting by far the greater portion of the manuscript, are of little historical importance, and some of the materials are gathered from very doubtful authorities. All the lights of modern investigation have failed to illustrate satisfactorily the dark period to which they relate. The fragment of the third chapter, which is here published in full, supplies very valuable information. It ends abruptly; but those who delight to study the ways of the God of grace, will peruse it with no ordinary interest.

The copy from which the following fragment has been taken by my nephew, Mr. George Wilson, is deposited among the Wodrow MSS. in the Advocate's Library, Edinburgh. The subjoined letter, from the Rev. Andrew Crawford, minister of Carnmoney, will explain how the Historian of the sufferings of the Church of Scotland happened to obtain the transcript. It may be proper to add that Mr. Livingston, mentioned in this communication, was the minister of Templepatrick, and the correspondent of Wodrow.

---

* *Presbyterian Loyalty*, p. 166. The reader will recollect how much Mr. Stewart wrongfully suffered in consequence of his supposed connection with Blood's plot.—See Adair's *Narrative*, p. 278.

CARNMONEY, NIGH BELFAST,
September 7th, 1724.

REV. AND DEAR SIR,

The Papers which come along with this are a copy of some papers which were left by my uncle, the Rev. Andrew Stuart, minister of Donahadee, in the County of Down, and North of Ireland. The original was written with his own hand. I could have no greater assurance that it is his writing, except I had seen him write it, having carefully compared the writing with many other manuscripts of his, from the great respect I did justly bear to him, and found it a valuable performance. I took an exact copy some years ago for my own use; but the original itself being not now in my custody, I have transcribed this from my own copy with the greatest care and with my own hand, which, though it is not so fair as I could wish—as multitude of business would not allow me the necessary time a fair draught would require— yet, I nothing doubt you will find it legible.

My near relation to the deceased author renders it improper for me to give you an ample character of him; but, if you desire any further information concerning him, some care shall be taken to obtain it from more proper hands. His father was minister in Dunagor, in the County of Antrim, before the rebellion of the Irish in the year 1641, and among the first Presbyterian ministers who laboured in these parts after the Reformation; and my uncle, being then a young man, had the opportunity of being an eye witness to some of the most remarkable passages which he has inserted in these papers; which, if they give you any satisfaction in the reading, or can serve you in any of the good purposes you have in view, it will be my great satisfaction. However that be, you may depend on the exactness of the copy which I now send you by the influence and at the earnest desire of my dear brother, the Rev. William Livingston, who appears very solicitous to serve you, and joins with me in desiring the favour that you would allow it a place among your valuable Collection which you have made, and are still making, for the service of the church.

I hope you will proceed in your exemplary industry; and that the Lord may assist and give you success in all your labours, is the fervent prayer of, rev. and dear sir, your most affectionate brother and humble servant,

AND. CRAFORD.

For Rev. Mr. Wodrow.

STEWART'S HISTORY.

[WODROW MSS., LXXV. 40. (Rob. III. 4, 17.)]

THE THIRD AND CHIEFLY INTENDED PART OF THE HISTORY OF THE CHURCH OF IRELAND AS THE GOSPEL BEGAN, WAS CONTINUED AND SPREAD IN THIS ISLAND UNDER OUR LORD JESUS CHRIST, AFTER THE SCOTS WERE NATURALIZED.*

HAVE given some account before, how the entry of the Scots was into this Island, and upon what political grounds it was established. I am now to show what course and prosperity the word of God had amongst them; but, before I come to this, I must show a little further what was done in the entry of King Charles I. Yet, let it still be remembered, that from the days of King James, and from the aforesaid Act made in his time, the North of Ireland began to be planted with Scots inhabitants, but they were so few at first and so inconsiderable, that they were not much noticed nor heard of almost, till after King James died and King Charles succeeded; in whose days the Scots began to be noticed, and yet they were not at first noticed by Charles himself, till the days of his deputy, or Lieutenant Wentworth — commonly called the Earl of Strafford.

---

* The Scots were encouraged to settle by an Act of the Irish Parliament, in 1614. About 20 years afterwards another Act for "naturalizing of all the Scottish nation," was passed. It is to the first Act that Stewart refers.

King Charles, therefore, appointed him to be Lord Lieutenant of Ireland—a man of mighty state, but exceeding perverse against all godliness and the professors thereof. Under him the King held a Parliament in Ireland (commonly called decimo Caroli), in which some things concerning the church were enacted — yet such as need not be much stuck upon—in regard, the most remarkable thing was the clergy giving to the King eight entire subsidies, which fell to be about the year 1634, at which time Ussher was Primate of all Ireland; yet, they did not this for nothing, for afterwards they obtained a large Act to enable restitution of impropriations, and tythes, and other rights ecclesiastical to the clergy, with a restraint of alienating the same, and this is to be seen at large in the 10 and 11 Caroli. But, leaving these things, I intend with a straight course to carry on the History of propagating the Gospel among the new plantation of Scots, and to declare how it began, and by what instruments the Lord did it.

Whereas I said before, King James had prepared a place and liberty in Ireland for them, and having given some lands to some men whom he had nobilitated, these men sought tenants for their lands; and from Scotland came many, and from England not a few, yet all of them generally the scum of both nations, who, for debt, or breaking and fleeing from justice, or seeking shelter, came hither, hoping to be without fear of man's justice in a land where there was nothing, or but little, as yet, of the fear of God. And in few years there flocked such a multitude of people from Scotland that these northern counties of Down, Antrim, Londonderry, &c., were in a good measure planted, which had been waste before; yet most of the people, as I said before, made up a body (and, it's strange, of different names, nations, dialects, tempers, breeding, and, in a word, all void of godliness), who seemed rather to flee from God in this enterprise than to follow their own mercy. Yet God followed them when they fled from him—albeit, at first it must be remembered that they cared little for any church. So God seemed to care as little for them, for the strangers were no better entertained than with the relics of Popery served upon a ceremonial service of God under a sort of anti-Christian hierarchy, and committed to the care of a number of careless men whom the law calls priests, who were only zealous to call for their gain from their quarter—men who said, " Come, ye, I will bring wine ; let us drink, for the morrow shall be as this day, and much more abundant ;" and thus it fared with the people at first towards the end of King James' and beginning of King Charles' reign, for, in very deed, it was such people, such priests.

In those days, because the plantation was of Scots, the King appointed Scotsmen to be bishops where they dwelt, so Echlin* was made Bishop of Down, and after him Leslie; Knox, Bishop of Raphoe, and after him John Leslie ; and other bishops were made from among the Scots—as Maxwell, Adair, and afterwards Baily. But, these seeking to ingratiate themselves with the King, and to be sure that they, being strangers, should come behind in nothing, ran beyond all in violent carrying forward the breeding of their countrymen to kindly conforming to the English order of doctrine, discipline, worship, and government. Only the Scots who had estates and lands given them appeared forward ; the rest, as I said, cared little what profession was uppermost, and yet thought it a scorn to be hurled against their will into

---

* One of Echlin's daughters was married to Henry Maxwell, Esq., of Finnebrogue, County Down ; and another to Dr. Maxwell, Bishop of Kilmore, the founder of the Farnham family in County Cavan. The Rev. J. R. Echlin, Ardquin, County Down, is lineally descended from him.

a sudden change of what they had been bred to ; and, therefore, though they had not the feeling of things from any principle of grace in their hearts, yet the very pride of their heart and a sort of nationality biassed them to scorn conforming, though they joined with it, because it was the King's will and the law of the land.

Thus, on all hands Atheism increased, and disregard of God — iniquity abounded, contention, fighting, murder, thieving, adultery, &c.—as among people who, as they had nothing within them to overawe them, so their ministers' example was worse than nothing, for, from the Prophets of Israel, profaneness went forth to the whole land. And verily at this time the whole body of this people seemed ripe, and soon ripe for the manifestation, in a greater degree, of God's judgments or mercy than had been seen for a long time ; for their carriage made them to be abhorred at home in their native land, insomuch that going for Ireland was looked on as a miserable mark of a deplorable person—yea, it was turned to a proverb, and one of the expressions of disdain that could be invented to tell a man that Ireland would be his hinder end. While thus it was, and when any man would have expected nothing but God's judgment to have followed the crew of sinners, behold the Lord visited them in admirable mercy, the like whereof had not been seen anywhere for many generations. For, among them who had been permitted to preach by the bishops, there was one Mr. Glendinning, a man who never would have been chosen by a wise assembly of ministers, nor sent to begin a reformation in this land, for he was little better than distracted—yea, afterward did actually distract—yet this was the Lord's choice to begin the admirable work of God, which I mention on purpose, that all men may see how the glory is only the Lord's in making a holy nation in this profane land, and that it was not by might nor by power, nor by man's wisdom, but by my Spirit, says the Lord. This Mr. Glendinning had been bred at St. Leonard's College, in St. Andrew's, and, finding little place in Scotland when things were so carried as to satisfy laudable order in the church, he runs to Ireland with the rest, and, having been ordained a minister, is placed in a parish near to Antrim, called Oldstone.

Mr. Robert Blair was come to Bangor, and began to found a blessed work there before Mr. Glendinning went to Oldstone, or anything of that nature did appear in his ministry; for he, coming first to Carrickfergus, and there beginning to preach, Mr. Blair came over from Bangor upon some business, and occasionally hearing Mr. Glendinning to preach, perceived some sparkles of good inclinations in him, yet found him not solid, but weak, and not fit for a public place, and among the English; on which Mr. Blair did call him, and, using freedom with him, advised him to go to some place in the country among his countrymen—whereupon he went to Oldstone, and was there placed, where God made use of him to awaken the consciences of a lewd and secure people thereabout, his preachings being threatenings; and being of a forward zealous temper according to his light (this passage I had from Mr. Blair among divers other things relating to that time), this man, seeing the great lewdness and ungodly sinfulness of the people, preached to them nothing but law, wrath, and the terrors of God for sin; and in very deed for this only was he fitted, for hardly could he preach any other thing; but behold the success! for his hearers, finding themselves condemned by the mouth of God speaking in his Word, fell into such anxiety and terror of conscience, that they looked on themselves as altogether lost and damned, as those of old who said, " Men and brethren, what shall we do to be saved ;" and this work appeared not in one single person only, or two, but multitudes were brought to understand their way, and to cry out, " What shall we do ?"

I have seen them myself stricken,* and swoon with the Word—yea, a dozen in one day carried out of doors as dead, so marvellous was the power of God smiting their hearts for sin, condemning and killing ; and some of those were none of the weaker sex or spirit, but indeed some of the boldest spirits, who formerly feared not with their sword to put a whole market town in a fray ; yea, in defence of their stubbornness, cared not to lie in prison and in the stocks, and, being incorrigible, were as ready to do the like the next day. Yea, I have heard one of them, then a mighty strong man (now a mighty Christian), say that his end in coming to church was to consult with his companions how to work some mischief, and yet at one of those sermons was he so catched, that he was fully subdued. But why do I speak of him ? we knew, and yet know, multitudes of such men who had no power to resist the word of God ; but the heart, being pricked and smitten with the power of God, the stubborn, who sinned and gloried in it, because they feared not man, are now patterns of sobriety, fearing to sin because they fear God ; and this spread through the country to admiration, so that, in a manner, as many as came to hear the word of God, went away slain with the words of his mouth, especially at that river (commonly called the Six-Mile Water), —for there this work began at first—thereafter at Larne by Mr. Dunbar. For a short time this work lasted as a sort of disease for which there was no cure, the poor people lying under the spirit of bondage ; and the poor man who was the instrument of it, not being sent, it seems, to preach Gospel

---

* If Mr. Stewart died at the age of forty-six, he could not have been more than eight or nine at the time to which he here refers.

so much as law, they lay for a time in a most deplorable condition, slain for their sin, and knew of no remedy. The Word they could not want, and yet the more they heard it, the more they could not abide it, as Paul says.

But the Lord, who said to Israel after they had been two years at Mount Sinai, " Ye have dwelt long enough about this mount," did so to those afflicted consciences; for the report of this harvest flying abroad, brought over several zealous godly men, who most of them were young men who could not be admitted in Scotland unless they would conform, and they, hoping that God would accept their labours in Ireland, where an effectual door seemed to be opened,* came to this land, and in a short time came those memorable persons to the County Antrim—

1. Mr. Josias Welsh, son to the famous Mr. John Welsh ; he pitched at Templepatrick as chaplain to Captain Norton, so he was next neighbour to the Oldstone.

2. Mr. George Dunbar, who had been once minister in Ayr, in Scotland, but, being outed by the bishops, came to Ireland, and laboured with great effect. After he was put from Ayr, he was for a time prisoner at Blackness, and in Ireland first preached at Carrickfergus, but having no entertainment there, stayed a while at Ballymena, then came to Larne, or Inver, by whose means all that country heard the Word, and were first gathered unto the Lord.

3. Mr. Robert Cunningham, at Holywood, in the County of Down, had been one of them who, before the coming of the rest, were like to have conformed, but proved a most excellent minister in the Lord's work.

4. Mr. James Hamilton, that worthy man who died

---

* It is evident from this that these ministers were admitted into the church without being required to conform.

minister at Edinburgh. After he had been famous there, he was at this time minister at Ballywalter, in the Ards, County of Down.

5. Mr. John Livingston, son to the very worthy Mr. William Livingston, who had been minister at Lanark in Scotland. He was minister of Killinchy, in the County of Down.

6. Mr. Robert Blair, who was a star of the first magnitude, and appeared eminent in the Lord's work before the rest came, was, from being Professor of Philosophy in Glasgow, invited hither by Sir James Hamilton, and embraced the charge of Bangor—by whose means, also, not only was his neighbour, Mr. Robert Cunningham, like another Apostle, instructed in the way of God more perfectly, but his spiritual wisdom and learning was a great ornament and help to the beginnings of this church.

At this time of people gathering to Christ, it pleased the Lord to visit mercifully the honourable family in Antrim, so that Sir John Clotworthy and the lady his mother, and his own precious lady, did shine in an eminent manner in receiving the Gospel, and offering themselves a first-fruits of their honourable families to the Lord, and did worthily in cherishing these beginnings—whose example instantly other gentlemen followed, such as Captain Norton, and others of whom the Gospel made a clear and cleanly conquest; and by their means some more godly ministers were added, as we shall hear afterward.

Now, remember what fever the whole country was in, and hear how it was allayed; for, God sending Mr. Welsh upon that water side, the first of the work began, God gave him the Spirit to preach the Gospel, and to bring the Word to heal them, whom the other by his ministry had wounded, so that the slain were breathed upon, and life came into them; and they stood up as men now freed from the spirit of bondage; then did love enter instead of fear; the oil of joy for the spirit of heaviness; and, withal, strong desire of knowledge, peace of deeply exercised consciences, a full walking, and a great desire in many to walk in the ways of God. Indeed, the joy and spirit of that time in this place can't by words be well expressed.

Then, those that feared the Lord spake often one to another, and the Lord hearkened and heard, and put them (as it were soon) among His jewels, if He have any jewels in any part of the earth. This is much to be observed when you consider what stuff he had to make them of, and when you think again that, without law or liberty sought or obtained of the rulers, Christ entered upon that work at his own hand, and strengthened his kingdom in Ireland by putting it in the hearts of a people who had been rebels all their lives long.

When, therefore, the multitude of wounded consciences were healed, they began to draw into holy communion, and met together privately for edification (a thing which in a lifeless generation is both neglected and reproved); but now the new life forced it upon the people who desired to know what God was doing with the souls of their neighbours who (they perceived) were wrought on in spirit, as they had been.

There was a man in the parish of Oldstone, called Hugh Campbell, who had fled from Scotland, for he had killed a man there. Him God caught in Ireland, and made him an eminent and exemplary Christian until this day. He was a gentleman of the house of Duket Hall. After this man was healed of the wound given to his soul by the Almighty, he became very refreshful to others who had less learning and judgment than himself; and, therefore, invited some of his honest neighbours who fought the same fight of faith to meet him at his house on the last Friday of the month, where, and when beginning with a few, they spent their time in prayer, mutual edification and conference of what they found within them, nothing like the superficial and superfluous worship of some cold and old idle-hearted professors who afterwards made this work a snare to many; but these new beginners were more filled with heart exercise than with head notions, and with fervent prayer rather than conceity gifts to fill the ear—yea, the Lord sent down the fire of love, real affection, and fervency among them, to declare that He accepted their sacrifice as a sweet savour to the Lord.

This meeting, as I said, began with very few; but still, as they truly increased, so did this meeting for private edification increase, and still at Hugh Campbell's house on the last Friday of the month—at last they grew so numerous that the ministers who had begotten them again to Christ thought fit that some of them should be still with them to prevent what hurt might follow.

INDEX.

Aberdour—58.
Adair, Rev. Patrick—25, 124, 149, 154, 182, 188-90, 194, 197, 216, 217, 234, 241, 263, 265, 274, 275, 281, 294.
Adair MS.—1, 43, 234; Bishop—314; MS. Introduction, x., xi.
Adair, Rev. William, sen.—102, 116, 117, 119; jun., Introd., ix., x., xiii., xxx.
Adair, Sir Robert—151, 152, 155, 201; Introduction xxx.
Advocates' Library—309.
Aird, Rev. John—92.
Albemarle, Duke of—242.
Alexander, Lord Mount—266, 274, 278, 281.
Alexander, William, Earl of Stirling—34, 35.
Allen—195.
America—46.
Anabaptism—149; Anabaptists—195, 215, 216, 222, 224, 231, 235.
Ancrum—58.
Anglesea, Earl of—128.
Anglesey, Lord—243, 268.
Antrim—9, 16, 20, 27, 28, 41, 60, 90, 96, 105, 122, 177; Meetings at—41, 185; Castle—29; Earl of—68.
Ards, Lady—30, 281; Lord of—59, 86, 90, 94, 117, 132, 155, 160, 162, 164, 167, 168, 169, 170, 172.
Argyle, Lord—117, 118, 175; his Regiment—93.
Armagh—71, 214.
Army, Scotch—88.
Articles, Irish—91, 266; Thirty-Nine—266.
Ashe, Rev. Mr.—242.
Assembly at Glasgow—50; of Scotland—96, 101, 121; at St. Andrews, 97.
Aston, Sir Arthur—174.
Athlone—283.
Ayr—21, 53.
Ayrshire, Carrick in—53.

Baillie, Rev. Robert—54.
Baily, Bishop—314.
Baird, Rev. Mr.—92, 93, 100; John—136.
Ballintoy—135.
Ballycarry—155, 182, 203.

Ballykelly—107, 117.
Ballymacarrett—47.
Ballymena—96, 105, 122, 167 ; Synod of—224, 241, 243, 318.
Ballymoney—124, 135.
Ballynure—293.
Ballywalter—12, 96, 98, 117, 123, 319.
Band, Black—51, 68.
Bangor—6, 7, 38, 96, 103, 124, 207, 304 ; Act of—210, 211, 213.
Bann, River—167.
Barnett, Rev. John, D.D.—297.
Barrow, Colonel—180, 207, 208.
Barry, Sir James—234.
Basnage, Monsieur—4.
Baty, Rev. James—94, 98, 121.
Baxter's Life—25 ; his opinion of Cromwell—227.
Baxter, Rev. James—140.
Beal, Colonel—128.
Belfast—42, 90, 96, 100, 103, 104, 128, 161, 168, 169, 179, 191.
Bell, Mr.—48, 119.
Bellaghy—262.
Benburb—132.
Bennet, Rev. Mungo—262.
Berkely, Lord—293, 294, 301.
Bernard, Rev. Dr.—66 ; Introduction, xxiii., xxvi.
Bewly—36.
Billy—106, 124, 135.
Bishops—240.
Black, Rev. Mr.—100.
Blackness—313.
Blackwater, The—132.
Blair, Rev. Robert—1-15, 21-25, 27, 29-31, 32-37, 42, 44, 46, 47, 50, 52, 53, 95, 98, 316, 319 ; his Life—7; his Death—58 ; dealings with Glendinning—17-19 ; his opinion of Cromwell ; his character ; Introduction, xvi., xviii., xxi., xxiii., xxviii.
Blood's Plot—270-272 ; his career—273, 276, 309 ; Introduction, xx., xxi.
Bohemia—94.
Bolton, Sir Richard—24, note.
Boyd, of Trochrigge—5 ; Thomas, M.P.—275.
Boyle, Archbishop—291, 293 ; Bishop—296.
Boyse, Rev. Joseph—178.
Bramhall, Bishop—39, 62, 244, 246, 253 ; death of—282.
Breda—174, 232, 237, 256, 257.
Brice, Rev. Edward—1, 20.
Broadisland—103, 182.
Broghill, Lord—236, 242, 244.
Brown, Rev Mr.—262 ; Andrew—42.
Bruce, Rev. Robert—2 ; Introduction, xxxi. ; Rev. Michael—259, 260, 261, 297 ; Introduction, xxx. ; Rev. Dr.—260 ; Rev. W.—260 ; Introduction, xi.
Buchanan—249.
Buckworth, Bishop—22.

INDEX.

Burleigh—88.
Bury, Sir William—236.
Bute, Isle of—44.
Buttle, Rev. David—122, 124, 129, 131.

Cairncastle—96, 207; Introduction, xiii.
Calamy, Rev. Mr.—242; his Life and Times—178.
Calvin—249; Calvinists—266.
Calwell, Rev. Mr.—262.
Cameron, Mr.—5.
Campbell, Archibald—42; Hugh, of Duke's Hall—61, 320; Campbell's regiment, 92.
Canterburian's Self-conviction—54.
Carlingford—277, 278, 280.
Carlow—71.
Carlyle, Thomas, quoted—227.
Carnmony—293, 310.
Caronis—134.
Carrickfergus—6, 9, 10, 16, 26, 52, 60, 68, 88, 90, 96, 102, 117, 128, 130, 136, 150, 179 202, 276, 280, 318.
Cartwright, Mr.—10.
Cassander, Anglicanus, and Scoticanus—25.
Castlereagh—48.
Caulfield, Lord—82.
Cavan, County of—115, 214.
Censures, Privy—133.
Cessation, The—253.
Chaplains, Scotch—92.
Characteristics of Livingston, quoted—42.
Charlemont—82.
Charles, Prince—26; Charles I.—145, 312; Charles II.—162, 243.
Chichester, Colonel—100; Sir Arthur—274, 275.
Clanbrasil, Countess of—281, 304.
Claneboy, Lord—6, 10, 12, 27, 59, 86, 90, 94, 95, 155, 173.
Clarke, Mr.—277.
Clogher, Bishop of—62.
Clotworthy, Sir Hugh—17, 84; Major, 167; Lady, 191, 206, 247; Sir John—176, 191; 216-220, note, 232, 242, 319.
Clough—167.
Cochrane, Captain Brice—150.
Cockburn, Rev. William—120.
Cole, Sir William—87, 115, 116, 117.
Coleraine—70, 72, 90, 105, 172, 175.
Colleges—233.
Colville, Rev. Dr.—130, 131.
Colwort, Rev. Henry—20, 52, 58.
Comber—96, 103, 124, 192, 207.
Commission Court, High—21, 67.
Confession of Faith—135.
Conclave at Rome—76, 79.

Conformists—99, 122.
Connor—176.
Connaught—79, 175.
Convocation—91.
Convention, The—230-33, 235-6, 239-40.
Conway, Lord—167.
Coote, Sir Charles—139, 148-9, 156-7, 162-3, 175, 180, 230, 236, 244.
Cornwall, Thomas—98, 99; Rev. Gabriel—225.
Covenant, National—68; Solemn League and—103, 106, 108, 115, 143, 144, 213, 230; Burning of—254.
Cowthard, or Cathcart, Rev. John—281.
Cox, Rev. Samuel—231, 233.
Crawford, Rev. Thomas—281, 293, 299; Rev. Andrew—309, 311.
Crookshanks, Rev. John—272, 283, 285.
Cromwell, Henry—223, 224, 225, 231; Richard—227, 236; Oliver, 145, 146, 153, 174, 200, 202, 215, 219, 220, 222; death of—226; character—227, 255.
Cullenan, of Raphoe—63.
Cunningham, Rev. John—300; James—252, 281, 299; Rev. Robert, of Holywood—9, 16, 318; death and epitaph—49; of Taboin—129, 137; Rev. Hugh—92, 119, 121, 130, 209, 210.
Cunningham, Lieutenant-Colonel—158, 163, 224.
Cunningham, Sir John—112.

Dæmonology—300.
Dalway, Robert—43; Captain John—254.
Dalzell, Major—102, 170, 177.
Davidson, Rev. John—5.
Deacons—12.
Debentures—253.
Declaration—156, 160, 161, 163, 171, 175, 241, 249, 257.
Delirium Tremens—13.
Derry—70, 107, 108, 113, 163, 167, 170.
Dick, Rev. John—148.
Dickson, Rev. David—2, 48, 53, 193.
Directory for worship—136.
Donaclony—300.
Donaghadee—96, 124, 191, 308, 310
Donegal, Earl of—100, 274.
Donegore—26, 307, 308, 310.
Douglas, Rev. Robert—175.
Down—28, 60.
Drogheda—174.
Drummond, Rev. Thomas—130, 285.
Drysdale, Rev. John—94, 98, 122, 210, 277, 281, 294, 296, 298.
Dublin—26, 37, 48, 70, 72, 73, 80, 170, 233, 240, 246, 303; Castle of—82, 83, 176.
Dumfries—58, 118.
Dunadry—176.
Dunbar, Rev. George—21, 33, 317, 318; Battle of—158, 227.
Dundalk—153, 173, 179.

Dundonald—120, 124.
Dungannon, Lord—277, 278, 281.
Dunlop, Rev. Mr.—262.
Duntreath, Lady—20.
Dunluce—106.

Eagle's Wing—42.
Eccles, Captain—149.
Echlin, Bishop—10, 21, 22, 33, 39, 314.
Edinburgh—50, 55, 58, 118.
Edmondstone, Mr.—155.
Elders—12; elderships erected—96.
Eglinton's regiment—92, 93.
Elizabeth, Queen—8, 91.
Ellis, Fulk—60; Major—156, 167, 169.
Elrington, Rev. Dr.—291; Introduction, xxi., xxvi.
Engagement, Scotch—141, 170; Cromwell's—192, 193, 198, 200; the Engagers—148.
England, New—40, 43, 44.
Enniskillen—87, 114, 115.
Episcopal party—215; clergy—264.
Eustace, Sir Maurice—244.

Fairfax—145.
Fast appointed—99, 101.
Fenton, Mr. William—120, 121.
Ferguson Rev. Archibald—122, 124, 129, 132, 136, 139, 149, 194, 206, 216.
Ferguson, Dr. Victor—234; J. F., Esq.—234.
Fermanagh—214.
Flanders—76.
Fleetwood, Lord General—194, 195, 207, 215, 217, 218, 222, 227.
Fleming, Rev. James—262; "Fulfilling of the Scriptures"—308.
Forbes, Sir Arthur—232, 266, 275, 276, 286, 290, 298.
France—75, 76.
Freeman, Mr.—28-31.
Friars, Irish—27.
Fullarton, Rev. William—121, 128.

Galbraith, Mr. Humphry—107, 110; Major James—113.
Galgorm—130.
Galloway—53, 191.
Galway—224.
Gamble, Rev. David—130.
Geddes, Janet—56, Introduction, xiii.
Germany—94.
Gibson, Dean—1, 7.
Girwin, David—42.
Glasgow, Rev. Archibald—140.
Glasgow College—1, 2, 5.
Glenarm—6.

Glencairn's Regiment—92, 93, 150, 167.
Glendinning, Rev. James—16-19, 315, 316.
Gordon, Rev. James—124, 182, 277, 281, 296.
Gowan, Rev. Thomas—Introduction, xxxi.
Graham, Rev. James—121.
Greenham, Rev. Mr.—3.
Greenwich—35.
Grey, Rev. John—124, 148, 210, 224, 225-6, 271, 276-9, 282, 294, 296 ; death of, 299, 308.
Grevinchovius—30.
Greyabbey—175.
Groomsport—40.

Hall, Rev. Thomas—124, 166, 256, 281, 294.
Haltridge, Rev. John—293.
Hamill, Rev. James—121.
Hamilton, Rev. James—12, 16, 42-3 ; death—58, 95, 98, 117, 118, 318.
Hamilton, Sir Frederic—87, 107-8 ; Captain—129, 177 ; Mr. Francis—277.
Hamilton, Rev. Robert—136, 252, 281 ; Rev. George—140.
Hamilton, Duke of—143, 281 ; Colonel John, 176.
Hart, Rev. John—225, 256, 275-6, 281, 285.
Heber, Bishop—246, 297 ; Introduction, xxvi., xxxii.
Henderson, Rev. Alexander—36 ; Rev. Hugh—102, 136.
Henry, Rev. Robert—293, 300.
Hepburn, Captain—110.
Heylin, Rev. Dr. Peter—Introduction, xv., xvi.
Hill, Frank—48 ; Colonel—196.
Hillsborough—247, 297.
History of the Rebellion—74.
Holland—97, 283, 294.
Holywood—96, 104, 117.
Howe, Rev. John—227.
Hubbard, Rev. Mr.—10, 20.
Hume, William—105 ; Hume's Regiment—80, 93.
Huston, Colonel—195.
Hutchinson, Rev. George—101, 132, 136 ; Alexander, 277, 281, 296.

Inchiquin, Lord—171.
Independency—149
Infanta of Spain—26.
Intrigues of Rome—76.
Ireton—175.
Irvine—48, 53.
Islandmagee—103, 136, 171.
Italy—75.
James I.—91.
" Jet Black Prelatic Calumny"—84.
Jones, Bishop Henry—193, 196, note.
Jones, Colonel—134, 161, 173.
Justices, Lord—83, 84, 86.

INDEX.

Kennah, William—62.
Kennedy, Rev. Antony—124, 153, 182, 184; Gilbert, 277, 297.
Kennedy, Captain—127, 129; William Trail, Esq.—Introduction, xi.
Ker, Rev. James—124, 135, 165-6, 194, 199.
Kern—9.
Keyes, Rev. William—241, 281.
Kildare—80.
Killead—281.
Killileagh—96, 123, 136, 171, 241.
Killinchy—26, 123, 271, 319.
King, Sir Robert—128.
Kircudbright—58.
Kirkpatrick—Rev. Dr. James—308; Introduction, x., xiv.
Kneeling at the Lord's Supper—2, 39.
Knox, John—249; Major, 150; Bishop—26, 314.

Lagan—87, 129, 137, 148, 149, 276.
Lambert—229.
Lanark, Lord—143.
Langford, Captain—217.
Larne—96, 124; Lough—32.
Laud, Archbishop—54, 95; Introduction, xvi., xxvii.
Lauder, Rev. Andrew—148.
Lawyers—81.
Law, Archbishop—3, 4, 5, note.
Lawson, Captain—107, 117.
Lecale—295.
Leckie, Laird of—61.
Lecky, Rev. Mr.—271, 273, 279, 280.
Legat, Rev. William—300.
Lees—120.
Leinster—79.
Leland, Rev. Dr.—Introduction, xv.
Leslie, Bishop of Raphoe—62, 314; Rev. Charles, 62.
Leslie, General—88, 105, 141.
Leslie, Rev. Henry—33; Bishop, 62, 245, 285-7, 296, 314.
Leslie, Rev. Mr.—112.
Letterkenny—112, 130;
Lifford—286.
Lindsay, Lady Crawford—281.
Lingard, Rev. Dr.—74.
Lisnegarvey—90, 128, 152, 156, 159, 177, 247.
Lithgow, Rev. John—121.
Livingston, Rev. Alexander—148; Rev. Henry, 296; Rev. William, 309, 311.
Livingston, Rev. John—5, 26, 33, 40-2, 45-7, 50, 52, 123, 132, 136, 319; Death, 58, Introduction, xvi., xvii., xxi., xxviii.

London—40.
Londonderry—72, 90, 214, 313.
Lord's Day—91, 227, 238.

Lord's Supper—28, 116, 288.
Loudon, Earl of—146.
Lough Fergus (Carrickfergus)—44.
Lough Ryan—44.
Louth—80,
Luther—75.

Maguire, Lord—79, 83.
Maine, Rev. Henry—170.
Major, Judge—24; Rev. Mr—140.
Malignants—124, 238.
Manchester, Lord—242.
Manifestations, strange—32.
Mant, Bishop—288, Introduction, xvi., xxi.
Manton, Rev. Dr.—242.
Margetson, Primate—282.
Mary, Queen—264.
Massareene, Lord—17, 220, 246-7, 252-3, 264-7, 274, 278, 280-1.
Matthews—120.
Maxwell, Rev. John—33; Bishop, 62, 314.
Maxwell, Dr.—39; Captain, 163; of Finnebrogue, 314.
Maybole—205, 206.
M'Bride, Rev. Mr.—84.
M'Cabbin, Fergus—53.
M'Cart, Owen—132, 173.
M'Clelland, Rev. Mr.—42, 47, 52, 58-9, 62, 117, 119.
M'Cormick, Rev. Mr.—272, 283, 284.
M'Kail, Rev. Matthew—101.
M'Kail, Rev. Hugh—120.
M'Mahon, Colonel—83.
M'Neill, Donald—120, 121, 128, 135.
Meath—80.
Mein, John—50.
Mervyn, Colonel—107, 110, 113, 116.
Miller, Archibald—47.
Milton, John—153, note.
Monaghan—214.
Monck—90, 134, 138-9, 148-51, 153, 156-7, 159-61, 228-9, 236-7.
Montgomery, Mr. Hugh—171; Sir James—175.
Montgomery, Rev. George—300.
Monroe, Colonel George—133, 149, 167, 169-70, 172, 176-7.
Monroe, Major-General Robert—88, 109, 117, 125, 128, 132, 139, 150-1.
Montrose—90, 122, 127, 170.
Moore, Roger—79; Captain, 217, 271, 277, 283.
Moore, Mr.—163.
Morgan, Major—196.
Mount-Alexander, Lord—266.
Mountcashel, Earl of—131.
Mountjoy, Viscount—158.

Mountrath, Earl of—244.
Muff—107.
Naturalizing of the Scots—312.
Nesbitt, Rev. Andrew—262.
Nevin, Mr.—95.
Newgate—280.
Newtonards—96, 103, 117, 123, 136, 224, 308.
Newtonlimavady—107, 117.
Nick—14 ; Nihil Damus, 14.
Nonconformist, The—303.
Norris, Tobias—192.
Norton, Captain—318, 319.

Oath, Black—51, 59, 60, 64, 77, 95, 103, 111.
O'Connolly, Owen—83, 86, 176.
Oldstone—16, 20, 318, 320.
O'Neill, Sir Phelim—82, 132, 133.
O'Neill, Owen Roe—132.
O'Quin, Rev. Jeremiah—124, 135, 165, 166, 184, 187, 194.
Ossory, Earl of—286, 290.
Oswell, or Oswald, Rev. Mr.—2.
Orange, Prince of—178.
Ordination—293 ; Introduction.
Ormond, Marquis of—156, 162, 165, 167, 170-72, 259, 265 ; Duchess of—281.
Orrery, Lord—230, 232, 244.

Paisley—58.
Pale—63, 79, 80.
Papists—26, 65, 66, 105, 115, 123.
Parliament—77, 81 ; Long—219, 236.
Parsons, Sir William—83.
Peden, Rev. Alexander—292 ; Introduction, xxix.
Peebles, Rev. Thomas—92-3, 124, 182, 294 ; death of—300 ; Introduction, xxxi.
Pentland—155, 272.
Perth Assembly, Articles of—2.
Philips, Mr.—107.
Pont, Mrs.—61.
Portaferry—96, 98, 208.
Portumna—224.
Prayer, private, in church—55.
Prayer, Common—100, 238, 267 ; Introduction, xxii., xxv.
Preachers, Field—258, 260.
Prediction, Ussher's—66.
Presbyterian Loyalty—308, 309 ; Introduction, x., xiv.
Presbytery, First—93.
Preston, Battle of—148, 149, 153.
Price, Rev. Mr.—120.
Protestors—204, 209.
Puritans—63, 67, 77.
Pursuivants—40.

Queries of the Duke of Ormond—266, 267.

Ramelton—113, 130.
Ramsay, Rev. Gilbert—124, 182, 277, 281, 296; death of, 300.
Raphoe—112, 113; Bishop of, 62, 63.
Rawdon, Colonel—192; Sir George, 245.
Ray—112, 130, 137.
Rebellion of 1641—51, 70-80.
Redferne, James—72.
Reid's History of Presbyterian Church—24, 39, 43, 60, 61, 95, 106, 107, 120, 155, 158, 183, 245, 254, 262, 275, 277, 294, 303; Introduction, xii., xx.
Reid, Rev. William—297.
Renwick, Rev. James—Introduction, xxix.
Representation, The—153, 154, 155, 165.
Resolutioners—204.
Restoration, The—228, 239, 240.
Revenue, Commissioners of—184, 191, 206.
Richardson, Rev. William—171, 241, 256, 277, 281, 296: death of, 299, 300.
Ridge, Rev. John—9, 16, 20, 53.
Roberts, Rev. Francis—223.
Robarts, Lord—243, 286, 290, 291, 292.
Rochelle—4.
Roman Antichrist—75.
Rotterdam—58, 168.
Route—105, 214.
Rowan, Rev. Robert—262; Rev. Andrew, 262.
Rowley, Mr.—29, 30, 117.
Rule, Principal—178.
Rump Parliament—200, 202, 215, 219, 236.
Rupert, Prince—141.
Rutherford, Rev. Samuel—58.

Salamanca, University of—27.
Saunderson, Lieutenant-Colonel—112, 158.
Scott, Rev. John—92.
Seaborn—46.
Semple, John—61; Rev. William—130, 209, 210, 265, 285; Rev. Henry, 148, 276.
Separatists—27.
Service Book—48, 54, 55.
Shaw, Rev. Antony—149, 169, 225; Rev. James, 149, 201, 281, 299; John, 281; Patrick—293.
Simpson, Rev. James—92.
Sinclair's regiment—89, 92.
Six-mile Water—28, 317.
Skeffington, Sir John—220.
Sorcery—299.
Spain—75, 76.
Spotswood, or Spottiswood, Archbishop—5, 50.
Sprint, Mr.—25.

INDEX.

St. Andrews—57, 316.
Stephenson, Dr.—Introduction, xi.
Stewart, Rev. Andrew, sen., 26, 307; jun., 124, 191, 193, 206, 210, 217, 265, 271, 274, 277-9, 282-3, 294, 296, 308, 309, 310, 317.
Stewart, Sir Andrew—37, 38; John, Provost of Ayr, 42.
Stewart, Major—61, 62; Mr., 135.
Stewart, Sir William—63, 86, 90, 112-3, 115; Sir Robert, 86, 90, 107, 110, 113, 115, 117, 165.
Stewart, Captain Alexander—127; Sir Alexander, 158, 163-4, 170, 173.
Strabane—62, 116.
Strafford—37, 59, 67, 73.
Stranraer—50, 51, 58, 117.
Stroan, or Strandtown—47.
Sylvester's Life of Baxter—25, 273.

Taboin, or Taughboyne—112.
Taverner—300.
Taylor, Rev. Timothy—183-90, 192.
Taylor, Bishop Jeremy—244-6, 248-9, 267, 296; Introduction, xxvi., xxx.-xxxiii.
Temple, Sir John—72, 74.
Templepatrick—96, 124, 182, 207, 318.
Tender, The, or Engagement—193, 200.
Theatre—303.
Thornton, Mr.—107.
Tipperary scheme—201.
Tithes—241.
Torphichen—26.
Trail, Lieutenant-Colonel—156.
Trueman, Mr.—68.
Tuam, Archbishop of—106.
Tyrone—214.
Ulster and its early state—8, 9.
Union, Army Bond of—127.
Upton, Mr.—135.
Urney—130.
Ussher, Primate—21, 24-5, 33-4, 66, 91, 123, 245, 249; Introduction, xv., xxi., xxvi.

Venables, Colonel—174-5, 177-9, 180, 182, 184, 192, 194, 196, 202, 206.
Vernet—98.
Vesey, Rev. Thomas—106, 121, 128; Hugh, 184, 194, 234, 244.
Visitation, Taylor's—248, 250.

Wallace, William—40.
Wallace, Captain—122; Colonel, 149, 155, 168.
Wallace, Rev. James—130; Rev. George, 225, 262.
War, Council of—156, 157, 161, 163.
Watson, Rev. Mr.—112, 113; Rev. Dr.—121, 128.
Weeks, Rev. Mr.—185, 186, 187-8, 190.
Weir, Rev. John—102, 117; death of, 118.

Welsh, Rev. John—20, 318; Introduction, xxii.
Welsh, Rev. Josias—20, 27, 33, 38, 318; his death, 40, 41; Introduction, xxii.
Wentworth—60, 95, 218.
Wexford—71, 174.
White, Rev. Adam—285; Rebecca, 297.
Whitehall—238, 239.
Wicklow—71.
Wight, Isle of—145, 146, 219.
Wilson, Rev. Hugh—281, 297; Mr. George, 309.
Witches—299, 300.
Wodrow, The Historian—309, 310, 311.
Wood, Rev. James—58, 193.
Worcester, Battle of—227.

Young, Andrew—48.
Young, John, Esq.—130.
Young, Rev. Robert—140.

Zanchy, Colonel—195.

Marcus Ward & Co., Printers, Belfast and Dublin.

www.ingramcontent.com/pod-product-compliance
Lightning Source LLC
Chambersburg PA
CBHW020219240426

43672CB00006B/363